823.912 L782s 2004
Lodbell. Jared

novels o

HA
WE   COLLEGE

D1457462

The Scientifiction Novels of C. S. Lewis

ALSO BY JARED LOBDELL

The Detective Fiction Reviews
of Charles Williams, 1930–1935
(McFarland, 2003)

The Scientifiction Novels of C. S. Lewis

Space and Time in the Ransom Stories

Jared Lobdell

McFarland & Company, Inc., Publishers
Jefferson, North Carolina, and London

LIBRARY OF CONGRESS CATALOGUING-IN-PUBLICATION DATA

Lobdell, Jared, 1937–
    The scientifiction novels of C. S. Lewis : space and time in the
Ransom stories / Jared Lobdell.
        p.   cm.
    Includes bibliographical references and index.

    ISBN 0-7864-1824-9 (softcover : 50# alkaline paper)

    1. Lewis, C.S. (Clive Staples), 1898–1963 — Fictional works.
2. Science fiction, English — History and criticism.   3. Ransom,
Elwin (Fictitious character)   4. Life on other planets in literature.   5. College teachers in literature.   6. Space and time in literature.   I. Title.
PR6023.E926Z785   2004
823'.912 — dc22   2004006356

British Library cataloguing data are available

©2004 Jared Lobdell. All rights reserved

*No part of this book may be reproduced or transmitted in any form
or by any means, electronic or mechanical, including photocopying
or recording, or by any information storage and retrieval system,
without permission in writing from the publisher.*

Cover art ©2004 RO-MA Stock

Manufactured in the United States of America

McFarland & Company, Inc., Publishers
  Box 611, Jefferson, North Carolina 28640

For my father and mother,
Charles and Jane Hopkins Lobdell,
and for my wife, Jane Starke Lobdell

Acknowledgments

I am indebted to my friends Walter Hooper and the late Owen Barfield for their assistance with various questions over the past three decades and more. Thanks to them also in their capacity as Professor Lewis's executors, and to Professor Lewis's publishers, for original permission to use various quotations from his works, unpublished and published. I want to express my thanks also to Kathryn Lindskoog and Douglas Gresham for their assistance, especially in Chapter III.

But my principal debts are in my family. To my wife, Jane Starke Lobdell, I owe much for her encouragement, and her putting up with a writer-in-progress on a work-in-slow-progress. This book is dedicated to her. Finally, I am particularly indebted to my parents, whose copy of *Out of the Silent Planet* I first read one magic day in Ho-Ho-Kus, New Jersey, in the summer of 1951: This book is dedicated to them also.

Table of Contents

Let Paul rejoice with the Scale,
who is pleasant and faithful,
like God's Good Englishman
— Christopher Smart, *Jubilate Agno*

Preface

We are used to calling it science fiction, but Lewis himself used an older term, "scientifiction." My revival of that term is not purely antiquarian; when it was used it encompassed not only what we call science fiction, but also that indeterminate field of the 1940s and 1950s sometimes called science fantasy (which leads up to Ray Bradbury), and also a portion of that great realm that has come, since the advent of *The Lord of the Rings*, to be called fantasy. Rather as an eighteenth-century novel may predate the divide between novel and romance, so Lewis's "interplanetary" novels may be considered to predate the modern divide between fantasy and science fiction, if by a hair's breadth. I am not trying to set up my escape route from critical condemnation for going beyond my appointed bounds, but *praemonitus praemunitus* and my readers have been warned that my net here is cast wide and deep. At the same time, I do not want it thought that I believe that all forms of popular or formula fiction are pretty much the same thing. Indeed, this is one of several very different books I have published or republished over the last two years based on a view of the work of each of three authors, Charles Williams, J. R. R. Tolkien, and C. S. Lewis, that runs counter to the idea that they wrote the same kind of fiction.

Briefly, in the view taken in these several books, Charles Williams wrote theological novels (not entirely unlike mystery stories) descending from the shilling shocker. Tolkien created modern fantasy while writing an adventure story in the Edwardian mode — an adventure story partaking of both pastoral and pilgrimage. And Lewis was writing satirical pageant, whose roots may lie in the medieval morality play, in Sidney and in Spenser (and thus in the obscure literary form of pastoral), and whose nearer ancestors may be found in the eighteenth century. But I would claim, and this book suggests, that this satirical pageant and pastoral is the broad area of literature — call it the genre if you will — of which science-fiction is the modern subgenre. The Ransom stories are inspired by "scientifiction," and may be considered as science fiction, but in my view should also be considered as part of this genre, this broad area, of which science fiction is largely a current subgenre.

The point is worth some attention. We are many of us aware of the problems of definition for both fantasy and science fiction. Science fiction stories have been described by a number of their writers as stories that would not have happened if there had not been science-induced change from present circumstances. These stories by C. S. Lewis have something to do with that, but if they are to be treated as science fiction, we might rather use James Blish's definition, Blish being a science fiction writer much influenced by Lewis. He suggests (James Blish [William Atheling, Jr.], "Probapossible Prolegomena to Ideareal History" in *The Best of James Blish*, 1979, pp. 349–358) that while science fiction is indeed social satire, it is more precisely the form taken by religious syncretism in the present age (present *Spenglerian* age) of the West (p. 355) — by syncretism meaning the wrenching out of context of religious forms from other cultures. As satire, it is the literature, the *mythos* (in Northrop Frye's sense), of the winter, and of the megalopolis. Because it is syncretistic, it becomes a kind of "show-and-tell" tour of the author's world, and because the syncretism is religious, it is a tour of the author's religious world — not for nothing is one of Blish's best-known essays on science fiction called "Cathedrals in Space." Within this context, the Ransom stories are indeed a kind of science fiction.

That they are space- and time-travel stories is, of course, not to be denied. There have been, indeed, other forms of syncretism. One, from our Renaissance but bearing a considerable resemblance to this twentieth-century form, is provided by Sir Philip Sidney in what we may call Arcadian epic. This too can be satirical pageant, as we are reminded in reading Sidney's *The Countess of Pembroke's Arcadia*. Briefly, it is my contention that Lewis wrote what I will call "Arcadian" science fiction, as Tolkien wrote fantasy, and Williams wrote thrillers. Just as my recent examination of Williams's detective-fiction reviews (*The Detective Fiction Reviews of Charles Williams*, 2003) provides a kind of key to both

Williams and detective fiction, and my examination of the rise of Tolkienian fantasy (*The Rise of Tolkienian Fantasy*) provides a kind of key to both
Tolkien and the nature of fantasy, this book is designed to provide a kind
of key to Lewis, the nature of science fiction, and his (and its) place in
English literary history, though concentrating on one particular type.

That type is what I have called *Arcadian*. It may be asked, Why?
Why that adjective? We most of us know — we think — what Arcady is.
I am not sure we do. Yes, it has something to do with the shepherd's scene,
the rural world, and especially (in Lewis's case) the rural English or Irish
world, the preference for the time-honored countryside over the dark
satanic mills. It is, moreover, a classical world (for Lewis at least), as
Arcadia was a Greek province in classical times. But this, however rural,
is not a rustic world — though the introduction to it (as in Sidney) may
be. The point is that in this classical Arcadian world, things are simple.
In Lewis's Arcadian world — which is, by his pattern, the prologue to his
other worlds (which also participate in Arcady) — things are likewise either
simple, or rural, or at least familiar, even if conventional as Arcadia is
conventional. But it is, like much of the classical, a stylized world. It is
also, in this, much like other science-fictional worlds, as well as the worlds
of the fairy tale or *Märchen*. We will see how this works as we go on.

Of Lewis's books, we are dealing only with those in which Elwin
Ransom is a character, the three usually called Lewis's "space trilogy" —
Out of the Silent Planet, *Perelandra*, and *That Hideous Strength* — and the
time-fragment to which Walter Hooper gave the title *The Dark Tower*,
and to which I have given (for its hypothetically completed version) the
putative title, *An Exchange in Time* (even, perhaps, *An Exchange with
Time*). In Chapter III, I have ventured to suggest what might have happened with the time-fragment had Lewis finished it: I believe the ven-
turing has improved my understanding both of the fragment and of the
other books as well, by making it possible to take the same kind of look
at each of the four. (The essay appeared in slightly different form as "Prolegomena to a Study of C. S. Lewis's Arcadian Science Fiction: How
Would *The Dark Tower* Have Come Out?" in *Extrapolation*, 41, no. 2
[2000], pp. 175–196.)

I have in the past suggested that — even though spoken of as the
space trilogy — these Ransom novels were not a trilogy in the sense that

they play a single theme or center on a single concept, after the manner of the Greek *trilogia* ("The Ransom Novels and Their Eighteenth-Century Ancestry" in Charles Huttar and Peter Schakel, eds, *Word and Story in C. S. Lewis*, 1991, pp. 213–231). Now I have come to change my opinion: I am now suggesting that they do — in a way; in a way involving the moral imagination — which is part of the reason for my introducing the whole matter of the moral imagination in Chapter I. The fragment of the fourth Ransom novel, the "scientifictional" time-travel novel published by Walter Hooper as *The Dark Tower*, we are considering as intended, first, to be part of such a *trilogia* in the Greek sense (with *Out of the Silent Planet* and *That Hideous Strength*), then as part of an intended *tetralogia* (including *Perelandra*).

As Williams is to be seen as the writer of "theological thrillers" descending in the right line from the shilling shocker (and like Golden Age detective fiction serving as redemptive comedy), and Tolkien as heir to the traditions of pastoral and pilgrimage brought together in the Edwardian adventure story (and thus creating modern fantasy), so Lewis is to be viewed as a novelist working the vein implied by the development of character into pageant through satire — which is part of the mainstream history of the British novel, as of the development of science fiction. (Though he is nonetheless writing a kind of pastoral.) Because the novel as we know it is essentially an invention of the eighteenth century, much of the search for Lewis's antecessors lies there. Because he was a Victorian medievalist, part lies in Victorian and in medieval times — and the Renaissance times he did not separate from the medieval. Because he was an avid reader of "scientifiction" some lies there also. In Chapter I, I have tried to place the four books in a context of England's literary history, not so much as with *The Lord of the Rings* in *The Rise of Tolkienian Fantasy*, but more than is generally done.

Chapter II is given the title "Malacandra, or Space Travel *Out of the Silent Planet*," and covers *Out of the Silent Planet* as the first book in either the trilogy that was written, or the one I believe he planned, or in the tetralogy. Chapter III, "*The Dark Tower* or An Exchange in Time," covers this as the second book in a planned trilogy or as a second book of four, to be chronologically (in Ransom's life) between *Out of the Silent Planet* and *Perelandra*. The chapter following is called "*Perelandra*, or

Paradise Retained," covering that book as the second in the existing trilogy (or perhaps third in the tetralogy). Chapter V is "Thulcandra, or Our Time under *That Hideous Strength*"— it covers *That Hideous Strength* as the final book in each or either trilogy, or the tetralogy.

In the sixth chapter, I discuss Lewis's Arcadian science fiction, as a type if not a genre, and I make some suggestions on how the stories in this particular realm of what we call myth may be linked with mythmaking — mythopoeisis — generally. Finally, there is the seventh chapter, on "C. S. Lewis and the Myth in Mythopoeia" (published originally in *Extrapolation*), suggesting what, in the end, Lewis made of his experiment in Arcadian science fiction. I suggest in Chapter VI that the Ransom stories are both pageant and pastoral as — in sum — Arcadian science fiction. And I suggest that the fairy-tale mode informing both the Arcadian pattern of pageant and the Arcadian epic tracing its roots to Sannazaro and Heliodorus makes this Arcadian science fiction a somewhat more complex thing than Blish's (or Frye's) ironic and hivernal literature of religious syncretism. In Chapter VII I suggest that Lewis's scientifiction has become myth and look at what this implies.

Partly because these books (except perhaps *Perelandra*) are in both the pastoral and the fairy-tale mode — of which more later — each of chapters II through V looks (1) at the opening of the book being considered, an opening rooted in the pageant of daily life; (2) at a transitional academic nexus in the course of the book (such as Ransom as philologist in *Out of the Silent Planet* or the economics of Distributism in *That Hideous Strength*); a nexus between the opening rooted in daily life and the perilous realms of the spirit to which the book progresses (these perilous realms here being understood as, in some sense, Arcadian); (3) at the perilous realms and the contribution the book makes to our understanding and exploring the dichotomy between the ordinary and the extraordinary (one of Lewis's chief concerns); and (4) at the return to habitual self at the end. This last is a little difficult in *An Exchange in Time*, where Lewis did not write the return, but I have suggested lines along which it might have occurred, with Walter Hooper's somewhat hesitant blessing.

Why is this book appearing now? Partly, of course, because I have finally finished writing it, after more than thirty years. Partly because the

Preface

Ransom stories are very much the creations of one particular place and time, and there was another and increasingly popular creation of those years, Tolkien's *The Lord of the Rings*—and once again in these days, as in 1965–66, attention has turned to Tolkien's creation. And thus a certain amount of new attention has been focused on the Inklings, that group (mostly of scholars) who gathered around C. S. Lewis in Oxford in the later 1930s and the 1940s. The war years were the great years of the Inklings, and the Ransom stories are, above all others (certainly above *The Lord of the Rings*), an Inklings creation.

Moreover, the Inklings — Oxford-connected men meeting in Lewis's rooms and at the Eagle and Child ("Bird and Baby") — were essentially Lewis's creation, a point generally recognized by the Inklings themselves, among others, and he, as author of these stories at least, was theirs. This last is of particular importance in considering the relationship between the time-fragment (*The Dark Tower*) and Tolkien's *The Notion Club Papers* (now published in Christopher Tolkien, ed., *The History of Middle-Earth*, Vol. IX, 1992, pp. 145–330). With his voracious and retentive memory (Tolkien's phrase), and most especially with his tendency to pick up things from his friends, Lewis was as much subject to influences as Tolkien was not. The Ransom stories, thus rooted in the Inklings in particular and in Lewis's university experience in general, are novels of intellect. And that very eighteenth-century quality, inhering in British novels before the great divide into novel and romance, lies behind and beneath their "scientifictional" nature — before the great divide into fantasy and science fiction, as the eighteenth century came before the great divide into romance and novel.

When I began writing this book, academic titles with the colon were popular and becoming more so. Thus my original title of this was *God's Good Englishman: Elwin Ransom in Space and Time*. Fashions change and it bears a more prosaic and less colonized title, but I could not forbear to keep the original epigraph, because it links that eighteenth-century man, Clive Staples Lewis, with the very eighteenth-century strangeness of Kit Smart's *Jubilate Agno*, and that is fitting, proper, and — I believe — illustrative.

Jared Lobdell
Elizabethtown, Pennsylvania
June 2004

I

The Ransom Stories in Their English Literary Context

Perhaps it would be well to begin with some ways in which Lewis's work is linked with the eighteenth century, before looking at those before and after, I am no expert in eighteenth-century English literature — certainly not so much an expert as Professor Lewis was, and, of course, the eighteenth century was not the principal subject of his scholarship. That he was an eighteenth-century man is quite a different point — a highly valid point, and a point made in reviews and lectures with considerable skill and knowledge by my friend, Professor Claude Rawson. As that eighteenth-century man, he might be expected to write in something like an eighteenth-century mode, and in some ways he did. But to speak of "writing in an eighteenth-century mode" is about as useful, without further definition, as speaking, without further definition, of "writing in a twentieth-century mode." The first includes Pope's *Essay on Man* and *The Rape of the Lock*; it also includes *Gulliver's Travels*, *Tom Jones*, *Rasselas*, *Otranto*, *Udolpho*, and *Vathek*; as well as Ossian, Percy's *Reliques*, and the *Lyrical Ballads*. Similarly, the second includes Masefield, Saki, and Rupert Brooke, Robert Bridges, Eliot and Pound, Auden and Spender, Buchan and Kipling, James Joyce, Samuel Beckett, Stephen Vincent Benét and Thornton Wilder, Thomas Pynchon, C. S. Lewis and Ronald Tolkien, Sinclair Lewis and Upton Sinclair, Ernest Hemingway, Sylvia Plath and Virginia Woolf, G. K. Chesterton — the point is sufficiently made, I fancy. So which of the eighteenth-century works, and which of the authors, is particularly relevant to C. S. Lewis?

Obviously, *Gulliver* (and indeed much of Swift), and Defoe, at least in *Robinson Crusoe*—and, as we will see, Johnson in *Rasselas* (and indeed much of Johnson). On the other side, the Romanticism of Walpole and Ann Radcliffe and of Ossian and Percy. The *Lyrical Ballads*? If not they and Wordsworth and Coleridge together, certainly Coleridge and Wordsworth separately. The key is that Lewis had a strong and wonderful capacity for visualizing from books as well as learning from books. Moreover, the books that were the greatest aid in the visualizing they aroused would tend to be those he most enjoyed — in both the common and the Alexandrine sense. (That is, in the special sense of "enjoy" in Samuel Alexander's *Space, Time, and Deity*.) Remember that for Lewis, his books "all began with a picture" and he is a highly pictorial writer. Remember that one of the failures (for him) of *The Three Musketeers* was the lack of weather. Lest the introduction of Dumas at this point should lead us astray, we should remember that when we speak of the eighteenth century, at least for the younger C. S. Lewis, we are fundamentally speaking of the eighteenth century in England — or at least in Great Britain. It is true that, so far as we know, the last new book Lewis read was *Les Liaisons Dangereuses*—but that was much later, after the marriage to Joy and after W. H. Lewis became a scholar of seventeenth- and eighteenth-century France.

The business of building up a picture by details of description, like Hogarth in *Gin Lane*, is part of eighteenth-century England. The combination of Latinity and plain English likewise. And the wit — not the least thing — and meaning not only the wit of Swift, whom Lewis so much enjoyed, but also "And thou! Great Anna! whom three realms obey / Doth sometimes counsel take, and sometimes *tea*." Or "Oats: A grain which in England is generally given to horses, but in Scotland, supports the people." Or "Let Paul rejoice with the scale, who is pleasant and faithful, like God's good Englishman" (and think of Eddi and Padda in Kipling's "The Conversion of St. Wilfrid"). Or Johnson refuting Berkeley (which is witty but not entirely perceptive) — and especially Boswell reporting Johnson. It will be recalled that the refutation of Berkeley is from Boswell's reporting, which indeed is the source of most of what we know of Johnson's wit — as, for example (Boswell's *Life*, iii, p. 167) "When a man knows he is to be hanged in a fortnight, it concentrates his mind wonderfully"—or (ii, p. 307) "The Irish are a fair people;—they never speak well of one another"—or the pun in the following exchange (iv, p. 99): "'The woman had a bottom of good sense.' The word *bottom* thus introduced was so ludicrous ... that most of us could not forbear tittering. 'Where's the merriment? ... I say the woman was *fundamentally* sensible.'" There is an echo of this last in Lewis's comment that to call a Portuguese gastronome who essayed a haggis a gastronomic Columbus was wayward, for he might better be called a vascular da Gama.

Of course, eighteenth-century men were not confined to the eighteenth century. They did not read only eighteenth-century literature. They also (Dr. Johnson being the indication) read Shakespeare and Sidney and Spenser—and (Bishop Percy being the indication) they began what we think of as the Celtic revival and the medieval revival. And I know that in the eighteenth century, novel and romance were still united. The age of Johnson (and Percy) incorporated knowledge of earlier ages and earlier writers. These earlier ways are part of the furniture of Lewis's mind, as much as later science fiction. This book deals more with them than with science fiction, which is, after all, a late-comer—barring Niels Klim and one or two others. In fact, these "eighteenth-century examples" of science fiction are not to our point, for in them, as in Cyrano de Bergerac's *Comicall Historie of the States and Empires of the Sunne and the Moone*, we have at best an accidental precursor, like Leonardo's flying machine. The true history of the genre at which we are looking goes by somewhat slower and more scenic routes.

It is not my immediate purpose to set out those routes here, but to look at four characteristics of Lewis's "science-fiction novels"—indeed, of Lewis's work—whose examination may serve to illuminate both work and achievement. But before that examination, we should pause to consider three common genres or subgenres of literature coming out of the Middle Ages: these are pageant, pastoral, and pilgrimage, and all may be said to take the scenic route. They seem to be related, but what can we say—in our context here—about the relation?

The figures in a pageant are usually stock figures—attitudes in fancy clothing, so to speak—as in *Alice in Wonderland* (which is also a pastoral) or the medieval morality plays (which at the very least lie behind the pastoral of *The Beggar's Opera*). As Lewis noted in his discussion of

Alice, "who sees strange sights should not himself be strange." One might almost say that the individual characters who see the strange sights — or have the strange adventures — should not be individualized. That would be a distraction. In a pageant, that is obvious, and it sets up no tensions: as we all know, the fineness of the pageant is in the costumes, in the gilding, which is part of this artistic Englishness. It is not in the individual delineation of character.

It is likely that the necessary association of pastoral with countryside acted in the English creative genius to amalgamate pastoral with redemptive comedy or eucatastrophic romance, to produce the English phenomenon of pastoral-with-judgment — long before Northrop Frye developed his taxonomy or Nikolaus Pevsner defined the Englishness of English art, or Tolkien first wrote about *eucatastrophe* in "On Fairy Stories" (his Andrew Lang lecture in 1938).

Pastoral can be remarkably varied. There are, besides the usual examples (Sidney and Spenser), *Alice* or *The Beggar's Opera*, the opening of Kipling's *Stalky & Co.*, the flood in *Sir Gibbie*, the Henty books, the wonderful storm in Surtees's *Handley Cross*, some of the scene-setting in E. Nesbit's Psammead books, the Virginian landscape in Buchan's *Salute to Adventurers*, the passage in Scott's *Ivanhoe* where the horizon is enlarged to include the greenwood, the landscapes of Crockett's *Kit Kennedy, Country Boy* and his *Black Douglas*, the Great War landscapes of *Greenmantle*, Robin Hood and the *selva oscura*, and — of course — our present subject of study.

Now it may be said that surely any story takes place in some surroundings, and if the surroundings are those of the countryside, is that all we need to have a pastoral? Even a pilgrimage must take generally place somewhere — at least in imagined soulscapes. But a pastoral takes place in a countryside. Nevil Shute (1899–1960) wrote a short novel called *Pastoral* (1944), a story of flying in the opening days of World War II, which is also a story of a secret countryside of the heart, and a story with a strong sense of the English countryside. It even ends with judgment. That it could also be called a romantic comedy is not irrelevant here. Nor is it irrelevant that a story of flying is necessarily a story of the interaction of man and nature. That too is part of pastoral. And that is part of the way this all comes together. The flood in *Sir Gibbie*, "up Daurside," the great storm (hurricane) in *Handley Cross*, the malevolence of the willows in Blackwood's story of that name, or of the snow in Blackwood's "The Glamour of the Snow" and their derivatives even to Tolkien's *The Lord of the Rings*, are all part of this interaction of man and nature. It is a very different kind of interaction from man's asserting control over nature. Almost it is nature asserting control over man. But there is an order in it, a pattern, a *mythos*, that the ancients expressed with their naiads and dryads and their shepherds of Arcady. Arcady is ordered, and when the order is broken, judgment ensues.

Pilgrimage as a form, a genre or subgenre, is necessarily post-classical: it is a creation of Christianity and essentially a medieval creation. To be sure, pastoral is a Renaissance re-creation of an ancient form, and the creation or re-creation of a time when cities were distinct from their countryside. As a re-creation, it is at least to some degree artificial. If we look at this distinction between artificial pastoral and natural pilgrimage through the countryside, we might conclude that they did not and could not mix. This would be untrue: they mix, perforce, when there are cities to contrast with the countryside, and still pilgrimages, as in the times of the Celtic revival and medieval revival. But, as the distinction reminds us, we may conclude that *Piers Plowman* and *Pilgrim's Progress*, for all that they take part in pastoral settings, are not pastoral. In that conclusion we would be correct. The road is not the field. And the caveat on distraction holds true for pilgrimage as for pageant. Just as Everyman in the medieval play must be every man, so Christian in the *Pilgrim's Progress* must be every Christian. On the other hand, it is universalization by the particular that is the hallmark of pilgrimage as it is of the modern novel. Recall Glotonye in *Piers Plowman*. Here is certainly a major point of distinction.

It may be suggested that artistic "Englishness" — so well adapted to pageant (as in Lewis's science fiction) — will be adapted to pilgrimage only when there is judgment, which is when types are raised to archetypes. Here it may be worthwhile to look briefly at Pevsner on the English light touch, the English consciousness of landscape, the English view of painting as psychological interpretation, in his *Englishness of English Art* chapter on Blake ("Blake and the Flaming Line," pp. 117–146). Here he is speaking of Gainsborough (p. 123): "What raises his portraits to the height of the best painted anywhere in Europe in the eighteenth century is three qualities, all equally English: their psychological understanding, their feathery lightness of touch, and their sympathetic setting in landscape." The setting *in* landscape is the point. The road, I repeat, is not the field.

This should be enough to suggest, if not delineate, what we are about here. The four characteristics we will be examining are (1) Englishness of technique, (2) Englishness and moral imagination, (3) moral imagination and quality of mind and book, (4) the fairy-tale mode (which says something about both quality of mind and of book). Before we go further, we might perhaps pause to consider a question. Why are these the matters we are discussing here, if our purpose is to set out something of the genre in which Lewis was writing, to which, if you like (remembering his words in the *Preface to Paradise Lost*) he was contributing? Well, you might say, we will be looking at pageant, at pastoral, perhaps even at pilgrimage. All of these are English forms (though not only English), and all, in our context, are English in Pevsner's sense as well as the common sense. So we will begin by looking a little more at this matter of Englishness.

A Kind of Englishness

We tend to think of pageants as plays — the medieval mystery or miracle play, for example, or the pageant plays of Shakespeare, and pre-eminently *King Henry IV*. The characters are not fully drawn, or if they are, they are drawn as caricatures or types, whether good or evil. But there is a gorgeousness to true pageant: I would suggest that the miracle plays have perhaps the same relation to true pageant that a traveling Punch-and-Judy show has to real theater. And this brings us to the gilding — the gorgeousness — of the English art that Sir Nikolaus Pevsner studied (in *The Englishness of English Art*, 1956). To be sure, the characters are to some extent abstractions, just as Squire Western and Squire Allworthy are abstractions (from their originals) in *Tom Jones*. And as abstractions, also archetypes. Pevsner's Englishness involves both moral intent and the belief that the detailed observation of daily life points the moral.

The pageant of detailed daily life goes on in the foreground, while the background is gilding and illumination and the sheer joy of description. But the detailed observation is of the surface of daily life, and of character only as reflected on that surface. Hence we feel that the characters are abstractions, or even, as with *Piers Plowman*, allegory.

The pageant has a moral lesson. Medieval literary examples might be Langland (with his fair field full of folk) or Chaucer (with his Retraction). But the "Englishness" is far from being purely medieval. Also, it may be recognized that this definition of Englishness bears a resemblance to the English humorist Stephen Potter's definition of humor (Stephen Potter, *Sense of Humour*, 1954, pp. 16–29) — the detailed (but pointed) observation of daily life. That is (getting ahead of myself for the moment) the humor of Boswell's Johnson: it is an English humor.

This repetition of the word "English" suggests a problem I had best deal with immediately. How can I speak of the "Englishness" of C. S. Lewis when Lewis was in fact an Ulsterman, and did not think of himself — so Mr. Barfield told me — as English (and I have lately written on Lewis's "Irishness"). It may well be asked, how can I use as epigraph for this book that passage from Kit Smart about *God's Good Englishman*? The answer to this is partly that God's Good Englishman is Elwin Ransom, not C. S. Lewis. But it is also partly that artistic "Englishness" is not a matter of birth. Swift had it too, in full measure, and Swift was Irish. Gavin Douglas had it (Lewis's own example in *English Literature in the Sixteenth Century*), and Douglas was Scots. It is a matter of the didactic purpose of art and the fulfillment of that purpose by the detailed description of daily life — moral pageant in the foreground, detailed observation behind, as in a book of hours. On these characteristics hangs the Englishness of C. S. Lewis.

I confess that, until Mr. Barfield set me straight, I had wanted the phrase to refer to both Ransom and Lewis in full measure — but the reference will do as is. Lewis was Irish, though his art is English, like Swift's. Elwin Ransom is English, not least in his names — a point deserving close attention, as we learn from the *Notion Club Papers*, if we had not already learned it from the passage in *Perelandra* (p. 147) on the origin of the name *Ransom*. In fact, Tolkien suggested, in *The Notion Club Papers*, that the English tongue (in its earliest form) had a connection to the language spoken by Elven-kind, and it is certain that in his mythology for England, England was landfall for those who escaped the drowning of Atlantis. In that context, the Englishness of Elwin Ransom is important — and, who knows, in that context even the Irish Lewis might be taken as English. It is, after all, the Celtic *imram* that lies at the roots of Tolkien's Numénor and Eressëa, and when Tolkien sought a mythology for England he sought also the fair elusive beauty that some call Celtic.

The whole matter of Lewis and Irishness I am taking up in my introduction and notes to an edition of a brief account of his father's language patterns — one might say, his father's *dicta*— that Lewis and his brother, W. H. Lewis, compiled in 1922 under the title *Pudaita Pie*, as well as having recently published an essay on "An Irish Friendship in English Lit" on Lewis and Nevill Coghill. It is my belief that Lewis's use of words is not essentially or especially Irish — less so than his father's (which is part of the misunderstandings revealed in *Pudaita Pie*). And it occurs to me that one of the principal differences between Irish English and what I guess we would call English English is that in Irish English the words build up the pictures rather than simply presenting them. Yeats's line on the "bee-loud glade" may be taken as wonderfully describing our world — the antithesis of plainly describing other worlds. And Lewis, as we know, began his works with pictures.

In his Narnian books, he quickly converted those pictures into moral instruction, Christian moral instruction, thus getting past the watchful dragons (as Walter Hooper has reminded us in his little book by that title). But he would claim such quick conversion was an exception, and for the Ransom books, perhaps the claim would be just. The *harandra* and *handramit* do presumably have an origin in the highland and lowland viewed from his boyhood home. The bubble-trees of Perelandra almost certainly come from the interplay of a child's mispronunciation of laboratory as bubble-tree, with the trees bubbling with fragrant exhalations in the Third Heaven of *The Book of the Secrets of Enoch* (letter CSL to the author, 22 October 1963). The origin of the time-fragment (*The Dark Tower*) lies in Tolkien's time-telescope focused on one spot. None of these is fundamentally either didactic or Christian.

But it is worth noting that he was sufficiently concerned about the criticism that his stories were didactic in origin to deny it — and that the criticism was sufficiently widespread for him to be concerned. And, of course, if his imagination was schooled in the moral imagination (Burke's sense) — and it was — his books would *volens-nolens* point a moral. Thus, for all his denial, here I am in this book, claiming knowledge of Lewis and in some sense adding my voice to the chorus of those who find his art didactic: I am suggesting that his art is English in the particular way in which Pevsner uses that word — his art exists to preach and the mode of the preaching is the detailed observation of the minutiae of daily life. Let me give some examples of the kind of thing I am talking about here, choosing from Lewis the critic of medieval literature.

He praises the poet Layamon's description of Arthur, turning alternately red and white when he learns that he is the king. He praises the description of Mordred bleeding "both over the upper sheet and the nether sheet," and observes, "Best of all, we are told how much it cost (£20,000) to send the expedition in search of Sir Lancelot." Similarly, he rejoices in Gavin Douglas's prologues in the Middle Scots *XIII Bukes of Eneados*, with (for example) Douglas, on a frosty morning, leaving the window "a lytill on char" and crawling back under the "claythis thrinfauld." (This example is from *English Literature in the Sixteenth Century, Excluding Drama*, p. 88.) Not only did he recognize the trait; he obviously welcomed it. But that is only the second part of "Englishness" — can we also claim that the purpose of Lewis's art is to preach, when he himself denies that this was his intent in creating the art?

I believe Lewis was indeed so much a man of the Old Western civilization, and especially of England before the Industrial Revolution (thus eighteenth-century England), that he did perforce what he did not intend (or believe he intended) to do. He was, of course, during the war years, a preacher in the popular sense of the word, and indeed a popular preacher of the Word, and his books would have been the weaker — if indeed they would have been possible — had he taken them out of the moral imagination, or the moral imagination out of them. Of those sermons that have been published, one ("The Inner Ring") precisely embodies the point made about Mark Studdock in *That Hideous Strength*. Moreover, Lewis himself pointed out the identity of concern between *The Abolition of Man*, which is clearly didactic, and *That Hideous Strength*, which is supposed not to be. In short, it would appear that, during the period in which he wrote the Ransom stories, Lewis was preaching and intending to preach. What becomes of his denial of didactic purpose?

If we look closely at two points, it seems to me that the denial makes sense. First, in making it he was describing the process of creation, its efficient rather than its final cause. Second, much more important, he was denying he wrote in order to preach the Christian gospel, except, of course, when he was avowedly doing so (as in Narnia): his novels are not intended as apologetics. Yes, he preaches a moral code. No, he did not design the novels to prove the case for Christianity, or define Christian behavior. They may do so, but they were not written to do so. Or, at least, he did not believe they were meant to do so — except, it may be, *Till We Have Faces*, his favorite, not mine. But he wrote the kind of books he liked to read, and he liked to read George MacDonald.

Englishness, Moral Imagination, and Coleridge

As I say, it has only recently occurred to me that the trilogy — either trilogy — may be a *trilogia* in the Greek sense. Indeed it has only been since I began re-writing this book, particularly the part on *That Hideous Strength*. And it is here I believe I must make additional appeal to the eighteenth century, specifically to Burke's moral imagination, and then to the Coleridgean view of the imagination, a view certainly rooted in the eighteenth century. This may be somewhat round-about, inasmuch as Lewis's mentor here is neither Burke nor Coleridge — rather Owen Barfield. But I am looking at original, not proximate origins, the common experience of the English mind, not Mr. Barfield's leaping mind.

Dr. Johnson once observed that all reasonable beings naturally love justice, and a play is the better for a triumph of persecuted virtue (on this in connection with Charles Williams, see my edition of *The Detective-Fiction Reviews of Charles Williams 1930–35*). In Coleridgean terms, the highest triumph of the secondary imagination, or of imaginative synthesis, is thus a triumph of the moral imagination. But, of course, the full triumph of the moral imagination requires the triumph of imaginative synthesis. Mere "Englishness" will not be enough, though it is the first step.

This moral imagination, as Burke told us, embraces tradition, looks to theology and history and humane letters for evidences of human nature and of the permanent things: "The moral order is perceived to be something larger than the circumstances of one's time or one's private experience; one becomes aware of membership in a community of souls" (summary in Russell Kirk, *Eliot and His Age*, p. 47). By moral imagination, Burke meant "that power of ethical perception which strides beyond the barriers of private experience and events of the moment — 'especially,' as the dictionary has it, 'the higher form of this power exercised in poetry and art.' The moral imagination aspires to the apprehending of right order in the soul and right order in the commonwealth...." Thus, "in Burke's rhetoric, the civilized being is distinguished from the savage by his possession of the moral imagination — by our 'superadded ideas, furnished from the wardrobe of a moral imagination, which the heart owns, and the understanding ratifies, as necessary to cover the defects of our naked shivering nature, and to raise it to dignity in our estimation.'

"Drawn from centuries of human experience, these ideas ... are expressed afresh from age to age" (Kirk, pp. 47ff)— and we should remember both that "naked shivering nature" and the wardrobe. What we are looking at here is an artistic apprehension of right order which makes it possible for the artist to see the pattern of his own experience or his own invented world as part of the pattern of being, *sub specie aeternitatis*. It is something like the *Tao* of Lewis's *The Abolition of Man*, though that is framework, while *That Hideous Strength* is the invented story and invented world built on that framework. Lewis himself observed that this novel was a tall story about deviltry, making the same serious points that he made in *The Abolition of Man*, and that in the novel the outer rim of the deviltry needed to be shown touching some profession with which the author was familiar — and thus the academic profession (*That Hideous Strength*, Preface). Given his experiences in academe, his may be disingenuous, as we shall see from his diary, but it shows that he recognized his appeal to this moral imagination.

Englishness (Pevsner's sense) strikes me as a particular form of the moral imagination. In what follows I am calling, as I have noted, on both Burke and Coleridge. This may seem rather heavy going, and perhaps going astray, given that C. S. Lewis was neither Coleridgean nor Burkean, but (as we know from his diary and from *Surprised by Joy*), an advocate of the philosophy of Samuel Alexander's *Space, Time, and Deity*. But I am something of a Burkean, and of a Coleridgean, and I believe with Mr. Barfield that the common consciousness of mankind has some inter-identification with the moral order of the ages — which is connected with Lewis's view of the *Tao*—and that this moral imagination is indeed embodied in the acts of the secondary imagination. I believe that dissolving and reconstituting perceptual unity is what happens in a work of art, and the greatness of the art is tied to the relative balance of passivity (primary imagination) and activity (secondary imagination), if the moral imagination is active throughout.

Moreover, though Lewis was not a Coleridgean, Barfield was, and Lewis and Coleridge (as Robert Penn Warren has noted) share a particular view of allegory and symbol, though they may well differ on the *value* of allegory (Warren, *New and Selected Essays*, pp. 353–54). Specifically, in Coleridge's view (but in Warren's words), the "symbol is distinguished by being focal, massive, and not arbitrary"— while allegory (in the special sense used by Coleridge) "is not focal or massive and is arbitrary." In Coleridge, the symbol participates in the unity it represents. It thus goes beyond form to partake of underlying reality: the service of Holy Communion is not merely commemorative but sacramental. In support, Warren quotes Lewis (in *The Allegory of Love*): "On the one hand you can start with an immaterial fact, such as the passions which you actually experience, and can then invent *visibilia* to express them. [This is allegory.] But there is another way of using the equivalence which is almost the opposite ... which I would call sacramentalism or symbolism. If our passions, being immaterial, can be copied by material inventions, then it is possible that our material world in its turn is the copy of an invisible world. ... The attempt to read that something else through its sensible imitations, to see the archetype in the copy, is what I mean by symbolism or sacramentalism." This passage should guide us in determining what is the "reality" of "real life" and in seeing why Lewis preferred the dogs he knows to the hounds of heaven, kennels to labyrinths, and why he is concerned with "realising" the (apparently) unreal.

The scenes and themes I have considered in *Out of the Silent Planet* are (1) the "down-to-earth" quality of Ransom's fantastic voyage from the beginning, (2) Ransom as philologist as the transition to the realms of the spirit, (3) the threat of madness, and (4) the scene with the Oyarsa at the end. We might keep in mind, as we consider the third of these, Lewis's own concern with madness, and what he wrote about his ravenous lust for interplanetary spaces. The connection of all this to prologue (as in Shakespeare's *Henry V*) will be taken up later. We can say here that the sections that might be called prologue are, as in the *Arcadia*, pastoral as well.

The scenes and themes I have considered (and extrapolated) in *An Exchange in Time* are (1) the academic beginning and particularly the "chronoscope" sections, (2) the discussion of the nature of time, as the transition, (3) Scudamour's visit to the place of the Stationary Smokehorses, as an excursion in the realms of the spirit, and (4) the return to our time. Of course, these latter two are extrapolations. Perforce, I am looking at the visit to the place of the Stationary Smokehorses in part for the light it sheds on the difference between the real and the unreal, and I am making use of Ransom's discussion of the *eldila* in *Out of the Silent Planet* in this connection.

The scenes and themes I have considered in *Perelandra* are (1) the framework, including the beginning, (2) the pageant of what I call the Great Conversation, much of it Miltonic in inspiration, and thus the closest thing to a link between our world and the perilous realms (but *Perelandra* is not fully in the fairy-tale mode), (3) the travel through the realms of Perelandra (the planet), which are spiritual realms, and particularly the floating islands and the caves on the fixed land, and (4) the Great Dance at the end. Here again we deal with the demarcation between the real and the unreal, but there is less of the "real" as we generally understand that word.

Finally, the scenes and themes I have concentrated on in *That Hideous Strength* are (1) the beginning, including the satiric portrait of intellectual or academic bureaucracy and infighting, focusing on the college meeting, (2) Lewis's Distributism as a transitional nexus, (3) what I have called the Last Dinner, the climactic scene at Belbury, and (4) Curry and the matter of his temporal salvation, as the bridge for our return to the realms we know. Here an underlying theme is ordinariness and all four parts have (mostly) a quotidian academic nature, though rich and strange are the clothes in the wardrobe in which they are garbed. But rich and strange though the clothes may be (that clothe our naked shivering nature), Lewis's moral imagination is still concerned with the humble and commonplace, even with the vulgar. Almost, one might say, with the rustic. Like Father Brown (who describes himself both as vulgar and as rustic), he does not believe any "frantic astronomy would make the smallest difference to the reason and justice of conduct. On plains of opal, under cliffs cut out of pearl, you would still find a notice-board, 'Thou shalt not steal'" (Chesterton, *The Father Brown Omnibus*, p. 13).

Here we come to the question of imagination *per se* and thus, finally, to Coleridge. His discussions of the imagination in the *Biographia Literaria* (1817, I, pp. 60ff) will be recalled. Here is the key passage: "The Imagination then I consider as either primary or secondary. The primary Imagination I hold to be the living power and prime agent of all human perception, and as a repetition of the finite mind of the eternal act of creation in the infinite I Am. The secondary Imagination I consider as an echo of the former, coexisting with the conscious will, yet still as identical with the primary in the kind of its agency, and differing only in degree and the mode of its operation. It dissolves, diffuses, dissipates in order to recreate: or where this process is rendered impossible, yet still at all events it struggles to idealize and to unify."

For Coleridge, then, the primary imagination is the ordinary agent of perception and consciousness; the secondary imagination — the knowing of knowing — is the direct or self-conscious knowledge of the operations of the primary imagination: it is the "organ" of philosophy, the "vison and the faculty divine" that "suddenly shines upon us" (*Biographia Literaria*, ed. Shawcross, 1907, I, pp. 173, 166, 167). (The associative power, it will be remembered, is fancy.) Imaginative synthesis consists in part in passive primary imagination in perception and in active secondary imagination as it dissolves and reconstitutes perceptual unity and common consciousness. One might expect to find the primary imagination in the prologue, the secondary in the *dissolve* into the full story — and that the act of dissolving and reconstituting perceptual unity and common consciousness (breaking and remaking reality) will, in an author like Lewis, be part of the fundamental argument of the book.

Mr. Barfield has convincingly argued (*What Coleridge Thought*, 1971, ch. 1 and 2) that Coleridge was essentially concerned with morals. He has also convincingly argued the metaphysical logical priority of inward-directed imaginative power (*What Coleridge Thought*, pp. 64–67), so that the centrifugal force of sensibility is simply a particular perspective on the centripetal inward-directed imagination, a kind of "separative projection." That is, sensibility — directed outward — is a way of seeing imagination, directed inward, as projecting oneself on the outward world. We may tell the well-known story of Mrs. Barbauld as Coleridge told it, so to speak, on himself (see Warren, pp. 335–336): "Mrs. Barbauld once told me that she admired *The Ancient Mariner* very much, but that there were two faults in it — it was improbable and had no moral. As for the probability, I owned that might admit some question, but as to want of a moral, I told her that in my own judgment the poem had too much; and that the only, or chief, fault, if I might say so, was the obtrusion of the moral sentiment so openly on the reader as a principle or cause of action in a work of such pure imagination."

Coleridge goes on to say that a work of pure imagination should perhaps have no more moral than a story out of the *Thousand Nights and a Night*, "of the merchant's sitting down to eat dates by the side of a well, and throwing the shells aside, and lo! a genie starts up, and says he *must* kill the aforesaid merchant, *because* one of the date shells, it seems, put out the eye of the genie's son." But one suspects Coleridge of jesting here, one might even say of putting poor Mrs. Barbauld on. In fact, a poem of pure imagination — and this is Warren's point — must necessarily have a moral point, however the author (or the Muse) may choose to point the moral. Moreover, if the world is a copy, sacramentalism is precisely the right way to look at the world of appearances, of shadows or shades, and symbols do precisely participate in the unity they represent. As Lewis reminded us in "The Weight of Glory," we have never met a mere mortal.

More on Lewis and Eighteenth Century Qualities

Further justification may be required (despite my Burkean and Coleridgean arguments) for the concentration here on the eighteenth-century qualities of Lewis's work. After all, the literary antecedents of these Ransom stories are few of them eighteenth century — H. G. Wells and David Lindsay (of *A Voyage to Arcturus*) come to mind as perhaps the chief inspiration for and even sources of a great portion of *Out of the Silent Planet* and of the existing fragment (*The Dark Tower*). Milton comes to mind — however problematically — for *Perelandra*, but a very medieval Milton as interpreted by a late Victorian. And while it would be a brave man who would try to track down all the sources, analogues, or influences for *That Hideous Strength*, the tracking down would surely be done in other centuries.

It is not, in fact, in sources and analogues but in quality of mind and the kind of book being written that the appeal to the age of Johnson (or of Swift) is made in the pages following. Moreover, it was in the eighteenth century that the first critical work was begun that enables us now to recognize the "fairy-tale mode" to which Lewis referred at the beginning of *That Hideous Strength* and in which, indeed, all four novels are written, though in a rationalized faerie — but "rationalizing" of faerie is itself an eighteenth-century thing. Moreover, the eighteenth century is the time of Poussin (in France), the ironic pastoral, the mixing of shepherd and Shepherd, pastor and Pastor — which we will take up further on, but which we should keep in mind all along.

Another relevant eighteenth-century characteristic of the novels as a group is the sense, not that the world is mad (that belongs to the twentieth century), but that madness, drunkenness, death and destruction, Bedlam and Tyburn, are all part of the ordinary nature of things. Lord Chesterfield writes his intensely wearisome letters to a presumably wearisome son, and Richardson recounts the triumphs of virtuous Pamela in what is to some the apotheosis of literary boredom — but grotesquerie and Gin Lane, "drunk for a penny and dead drunk for tuppence," Macheath and Peachum, Cowper in his madhouse and Kit Smart in his praying fits, Boswell's *Life* imitating art, and the interminable (but pleasant and faithful) anecdotes of John Nichols, are what to me mark England's eighteenth century. And Swift, of course. And Dr. Johnson himself.

The epigraph to this book is taken from lines by poor Kit, and it may be worthwhile here to recall the Johnsonian anecdote. When the doctor was informed of the nature of Smart's madness — personal uncleanliness and praying fits in public — he responded that he was no great lover of clean linen himself, and that he would as lief pray with Kit Smart as with any man. The story may seem far from the Oxford of C. S. Lewis. But Lewis was not only (like Johnson) a "clubbable" man (and a "pubbable" one as well), he also shared the massive surface unconcern for what people were thinking, and particularly, as in this anecdote, an ability to distinguish moral goodness from manners — to be passionately concerned about the one (while remaining unsurprised by whatever the world could bring), and passionately unconcerned about the other. The tramp in *That Hideous Strength* is an example of this eighteenth-century (and specifically Johnsonian) set of traits in Lewis, but the traits do not come through only in *That Hideous Strength*. There is a good example distinguishing moral goodness from manners in the character of Cyril Knellie in the time fragment and would be a better example in the finished novel I call *An Exchange in Time* (or perhaps better, *An Exchange with Time*, to recall *An Experiment with Time*).

It may require some justification to be taking a critical look not only at the finished novels, but at the unfinished fragment. And I have already heard the suggestion that my taking it on myself to change Walter Hooper's title and to suggest what Lewis would have written are exercises in hubris, or perhaps chutzpah. Even so, and be all that as it may, Ransom does appear in this book, and it, no less than the others, is a novel of ideas: moreover, it requires some kind of putative finishing-off fully to see the ideas and the function of Ransom. I know that Walter Hooper hesitated long and thought hard before he published it. I know that MacPhee in *The Dark Tower* differs (not for the better) from MacPhee in *That Hideous Strength*, and that Lewis used bits and pieces of the unfinished work in the finished (or even of the finished in the unfinished?), so that we may be double-counting some of our evidence. That, of course, we can check after the counting starts. It may require justification to look at the book for another reason, because it apparently worked itself into a dead end and there Lewis left it.

It may also require justification because Kathryn Lindskoog and others believe the book to have been written by someone other than Lewis. But the character of Ransom in the fragment, the ideas about time, the inspiration from Spenser's *Faerie Queene* and the "scientifictional" working out of the realm of Faerie, the flash of invention from Tolkien's "time-telescope focussed on one place" (1938)—all these—so accurately reflect the Lewis of 1938 that I do not believe a later emulator or imitator could be responsible for them. That being the case, I take *The Dark Tower* to be of some importance within the body of the Ransom stories. I believe Walter Hooper's view of the book's lifelessness is overstated—so much so that I have ventured to try to find a further life and suggest how Lewis might have hoped to work it out. Two indications of my conjectural reconstruction (perhaps a better word is "extrapolation") are included in the chapter on *An Exchange in Time*, my name for my suggested completed version.

I have looked throughout at the eighteenth-century characteristics of the Ransom novels, and I have suggested that the most relevant eighteenth-century characteristics are that the novels are both satirical pageants and novels of ideas—which, of course, is what science fiction is. The operative difference between the eighteenth-century novelists and, say, Dickens, is that in Dickens the characters take over, while in the eighteenth-century novelists—however well the characters may be realized—the ideas and the intellect remain pre-eminent. Robinson Crusoe is not a character study, unless it is a character study of Everyman. (The intellect would, I think, be separatively projected in sensibility.) Now the ideas and the intellect are of greatest importance in Lewis—but one of the ideas is the importance of "ordinariness" and the "quiddity" of things. (It will be remembered that the appreciation of the "quiddity" of things was a gift given Lewis by his friend A. K. Hamilton Jenkin. See *Surprised by Joy*, p. 199.) But if these are stories revolving around ideas and intellect, how can we look at them as character studies?

I should make it clear that they are not character studies in a post–Dickensian or even a Dickensian sense, and certainly not in the sense that the great Russian novels are. Even so, they are perhaps significantly closer to character studies than *The Lord of the Rings*, than most science fiction, even than Lewis's own Narnia stories. The reason that I am emphasizing the eighteenth century here, and building on its foundations later, is twofold. One is to find out what Lewis was really doing, in which we will be aided by looking at his antecessors in any century. The other is that the interaction of pageant and satire that produced the English novel is to be seen most purely in the eighteenth century — and in Dickens — before (in current critical parlance) novel and romance separated. And it is this same interaction that produces science fiction, so our study here may illuminate that genre or subgenre. Also, as we suggested earlier, the phenomenon of the pictorial pastoral in the eighteenth century likewise illustrates this interaction of pageant and satire, and there is something of the twentieth-century irony Blish finds in science fiction to be found in the paintings that usher in the so-called age of reason.

The uncertainty as to what Lewis was doing is, unfortunately, one more effect of the myth of the Inklings (or "Oxford Christians") as a unified group designedly providing a radical and reactionary alternative to the evils of modernity — a myth to which some attention is paid in the chapters that follow. But not much attention, because, in his own study of the Inklings, Humphrey Carpenter has largely taken care of any need to skewer that particular misinterpretation. (In fact, the most radical posture taken by a group to which Lewis belonged seems to have been in English criticism, and the group was not the Inklings but that earlier Lewis-Coghill-Tolkien-Dyson nexus referred to as the Cave — and this was to some extent the radicalism of Brooks and Warren, and the *explication du texte.*)

One further point. It might be objected that the character of Elwin Ransom is not sufficiently developed — nor, indeed, is Ransom so important in *That Hideous Strength* (whatever may be the case in the other novels) — that his character can reasonably be made the centerpiece of a book, even one as short as this. I disagree. Ransom is indeed the unifying element. Even the eldila are present through him. The "realization" of the Malacandrian world in *Out of the Silent Planet* is tied to Ransom's absorption into and acceptance of Malacandrian life, including the underpinnings of that life. The same process holds in the Perelandrian sphere — once again, for Ransom. It holds in the othertime of *An Exchange in Time* — partly for Ransom, and would hold for him more if the book were finished. And it holds on the Tellus of *That Hideous Strength*, through him in his new identity as Fisher King of Logres. True, there is a unifying theme to the books, but theme alone is not enough to tie them together without Ransom. It is Ransom that is the sufficient unifying element for the "trilogies" or the tetralogy. Certainly those who read *Out of the Silent Planet*, *Perelandra*, and *That Hideous Strength* as well as those who have published them have perceived them at least as a set. We can do no less, though by including the fragment, we may be doing somewhat more. And we have one more point to consider before viewing the novels seriatim.

The Fairy-Tale Mode

The fairy tale as we know it comes to us from the eighteenth century. To be sure, *Les Contes de ma Mère l'Oye* may come from the very end of the seventeenth, and the Brothers Grimm did not publish their collection until the very early nineteenth, but it was in the eighteenth century that *Les Contes* was first Englished, and in the eighteenth that we become aware of both fairy tale and folk tale as a genre — in fact, it was in the eighteenth that we came to care whether they existed at all, and that the Grimms began their collecting. Which is what enables us to talk about a "fairy-tale mode" of writing. Those who want to know more about fairy tales and what they portend may of course consult Professor Tolkien's classic lecture: the point here is that Lewis is making use of a discovery based in the eighteenth century.

All four Ransom stories are in the fairy-tale mode (some may question *Perelandra*, at least in part), but *That Hideous Strength* most certainly so. Of that book, Lewis asks, "why — intending to write about magicians, devils, pantomime animals, and planetary angels" he nonetheless begins with "hum-drum scenes and persons"? (p. 7) And he answers that this is the mode of the fairy tale, though we "do not always notice its method, because the cottages, castles, woodcutters, and petty kings with which a fairytale opens have become for us as remote as the witches and ogres to which it proceeds."

Even so, many of us believe — or act as though we believe — that our earth is generally a prosaic workaday sort of planet, unsuitable to being a realm of the spirit, or of witches and ogres, or of incarnate evil. We do not believe in the applicability of the fairy-tale mode. In one sense, of course, we know that the "future" envisioned in *That Hideous Strength* never came to pass, any more than the future envisioned in *Brave New*

World or *1984* came to pass (though, admittedly, we cannot write off all the specific details of the Orwellian vision, much less its central core). The no. 41 bus going by and the newsboy crying his paper are "real life" — while the world of the spirit is not, even it is written with utmost realism — shall we say, journalistic realism?

And yet, if the question of realism were raised in connection with *Out of the Silent Planet* and *Perelandra*, we must surely say that the *canali* on Mars not only are not canals but do not exist, and that, far from being a garden of the Hesperides, Venus is a hot, rocky, unliveable ball enveloped in methane gases. This point was raised by Tolkien in his *critique* of the stories (*The Notion Club Papers*, pp. 164ff), in which he distinguishes between scientific and literary credibility. If those facts are not important to our reading of *Out of the Silent Planet* or *Perelandra*, why should the divergence between the Tellus of *That Hideous Strength* and our own everyday earth detract from our reading of that novel? To this question there are two possible answers (with various further permutations possible).

First, the "machinery" may not work — the willing suspension of disbelief may need too much willing — and this not because Lewis has not done a good job with the machinery but because a "science-fiction" story set on Earth should be further in the future than merely vaguely "after the War." (Neither Huxley nor Orwell believed they were writing "science fiction.") Second, Lewis may simply not have done a good enough job in subcreating his world (using Tolkien's term). If he is going to make the rare and beautiful blue moon to shine or put fire in the belly of the cold worm, he should make sure that the moon or the worm is plausible, if no more. And some would claim he failed to do so in *That Hideous Strength*. It is an untidy grab-bag of a novel, and the untidiness is not conducive to the full suspension of disbelief.

On the second point, I would argue that the humdrum scenes and persons in *That Hideous Strength* in particular are quite well done: I have had my own experiences with academic politics. And I am willing to believe that the rest of the quotidian descriptions are equally well done, as with the inn at Cure Hardy, for example, or the train to St. Anne's. The fault, if any, does not lie here. That it does not lie in the "Englishness" of the descriptions in the latter part of the book I hope to show in due time. I would like to suggest here that the difficulty lies more in the machinery than in Lewis's ability to manage it, and lies specifically in the matter I referred to before — our inability to think of our earth, our plain old everyday earth, as a realm of the spirit. Tolkien complained of the "Williams-ish-ness" of *That Hideous Strength* (my word, not his). But it is hard not to believe that something even more Williams-ish was needed to display Earth as a spiritual realm. Or perhaps something Shandean.

Quite possibly, it would be easier for readers of the trilogy to accept *That Hideous Strength* as pageant, with all the gilding and heraldry and Pevsner's Englishness that the word implies, if the second volume were *An Exchange in Time* rather than *Perelandra*. As I have noted elsewhere (in *Word and Story*), the sensuousness of the descriptions in *Perelandra*, the realization of the mystical experience in the Great Dance, the "feel" and flavor of Perelandra and (I think) the beauty of holiness, all make it hard to come back to earth. They make it especially hard to come back to the Earth of Bracton College and the N.I.C.E. And they certainly do not make it easy to recognize the heraldry, the pageantry, the gilding, the "Englishness" of that earth which are in fact present in *That Hideous Strength*, and which are among the things that make it appealing to me.

It is, Lewis says, a fairy tale: that is, it begins in humdrum surroundings and at a time only vaguely designated, and goes from there to the "witches and ogres" — or "pantomime animals" and "planetary angels" — of Faerie. But not, in the case of the animals and angels, entirely of Faerie. Lewis may have come to inhabit that realm in the Narnian books, and may have exchanged our time for Faerie in the book we have been discussing, but there is little or none of Faerie in *That Hideous Strength*, and none at all in *Out of the Silent Planet* and *Perelandra*. The special sense in which it is not only present but guides *An Exchange in Time* we have already mentioned. This absence in the finished books is not surprising. For the roads in Lewis's fiction (beginning with *The Pilgrim's Regress*) lead to heaven or hell, but the road to Faerie has been the road between, and it is doubtful Lewis would have taken it without Tolkien. It was Tolkien (in the person of Ramer, his "Ransom") who suggested that one could time-travel into Faerie (*The Notion Club Papers*, p. 172). It was Tolkien who succeeded in combining Faerie with traditional Christian doctrine, though only in a pre–Christian world very far from the world of Elwin Ransom.

But the "fairy tale" called *That Hideous Strength* is a very different mixing, not Faerie with Christian doctrine, but a mixing of myths, each of them derived from a contemporary writer, indeed from a friend of C. S. Lewis. The two sets of myth — Williams's Arthuriad and Tolkien's "mythology for England" — are not perhaps mixed entirely successfully. But even if there is a certain oil-and-water quality to the mixing, we should not on this account overlook the considerable strengths of the book. Nor should we overlook the fact that a mixing of myths is characteristic of science fiction as defined by James Blish. For after all, one of the things we are looking for in this study is a way of looking critically at the genre or subgenre of science fiction.

After some thought, I have appended to the volume, as Chapter VII, my paper on "C. S. Lewis and the Myth in Mythopoeia" given at the Mythopoeic Society Conference in 1994 and published in *Extrapolation* (as "An Irritation of Oysters: C. S. Lewis and the Myth in Mythopoeia," vol. 39, no. 1 [Spring 1998], pp. 68–84). My work on Lewis has shifted to his "Irishness" and his friendships, and it seemed worthwhile to put this between the same covers as this study of the Ransom stories, to which it is related, albeit tangentially. On the other hand, to include my essay on "The Ransom Stories and Their Eighteenth Century Ancestry" (published in Peter Schakel and Charles Huttar, *Word and Story in C. S. Lewis*, 1991, pp. 213–231) would be an exercise in largely needless repetition.

I

Malacandra, or Space Travel
Out of the Silent Planet

This chapter, like the next three, looks at certain themes or scenes that seem to me to be especially revealing — not of Lewis, nor even necessarily of Ransom, but of what, in any useful sense, the particular book under consideration is "about," and what kind of book it is. All four books have a characteristic organization or pattern, a characteristic "fairy-tale" motion (as defined in the preface to *That Hideous Strength*); all have a moral imagination so characteristically English as to define or constitute "Englishness" (Pevsner's sense), and a characteristic attitude toward the intermingling of ordinary and extraordinary — characteristic, *inter alia*, of science fiction.

To give a little more detail than in the introduction, the scenes and themes we will particularly examine in *Out of the Silent Planet* are (1) the "down-to-earth-ness" (quotidianity?) of the fantastic voyage from its beginning on an earthly walking tour all through its tour of Mars, (2) Ransom as philologist, as words as the nexus between the quotidian and the spiritual, with appeal to Tolkien's views as expressed in *The Notion Club Papers*, (3) the threat of madness, with an appeal to Lewis's own personal history, and (4) the climactic pageant scene with the Oyarsa of Malacandra at the end as the beginning of the homeward journey. We should keep in mind, as we consider the third of these, that madness is one way of setting bounds, definitions, between the ordinary and the extraordinary, and this is one of our overall concerns here.

Let me repeat here that the bounds and links of the ordinary and the extraordinary are a chief focus of all of Lewis's work, though this becomes most obvious when he is most under the influence of Charles

Williams. In discussing *Out of the Silent Planet* I have focused specifically on the possibility of madness in this connection, but the same matter lies couching in the scene with the Oyarsa at the end of the book. In discussing *An Exchange in Time*, I have focused on Scudamour's (extrapolated) visit to the place of the Stationary Smokehorses; in discussing *Perelandra* I have focused on the descriptive passages generally; and in discussing *That Hideous Strength* I have focused on the subwarden of Bracton College, Curry. All these are firmly down-to-earth, and all of them are nonetheless extraordinary.

It is worth asking, before we get into this set of topics, what exactly I have in mind for a goal. Specifically, I hope to show a pattern in each of the four books, and for this chapter specifically in *Out of the Silent Planet*, that will help to show each book as pastoral as well as pageant — and thus the whole as *Arcadian* science fiction. Why? Because I believe that the concentration on the *science* in science fiction has to some degree hidden from us the underlying genre, which, being a kind of pastoral, is indeed Arcadian. Let us reflect briefly here on a few things we know of Lewis. He was a medievalist. He liked country walking (which some call hiking, but it's not quite the same thing). He wrote books for children, and was particularly fond of Kenneth Grahame's *The Wind in the Willows*. None of this seems to have much to do with science fiction. And yet *Out of the Silent Planet* is unquestionably science fiction. But — I would argue — of a particular kind. And maybe — as I think I will also argue — this particular kind is a kind of clue to what science fiction can be about.

Lewis was a medievalist (and born a Victorian): the reason medieval visions are pastorals is in part, I suspect, that the Middle Ages were pastoral ages. I think the Victorian age cherished that pastoral time, and — the life of the person recapitulating the life of the people — looked to childhood as pastoral, as the golden age for the person lost to the people as a whole. Kenneth Grahame noted the loss of Arcady in adulthood (*The Penguin Kenneth Grahame*, 1983, p. 5): "Well! The Olympians are passed and gone. Somehow the sun does not shine so brightly as it used; the trackless meadows of old time have shrunk and dwindled away to a few poor acres. A saddening doubt, a dull suspicion, creeps over me. *Et in Arcadia ego* — I certainly did once inhabit Arcady. Can it be that I also have become an Olympian?"

One other point to be made here. There are wolves in the pastoral (else why do we need the pastor?) just as there are dangers in Grahame's Wild Wood, and dangers in all of Lewis's landscapes. Both material and spiritual. In this version of pastoral, the progress is, more or less, from the fields we know — the home fields, as it were, the daily life — through some kind of nexus where the physical and the spiritual touch; then the sense (perhaps the experience) of powers abroad in the land, spiritual powers as well as physical; and then, finally, climax and judgment. That is the progress, as I read it, of English pastoral, and Arcady is where pastoral takes place. Now, in the matter of pastoral, it is important to note that the other half of the Englishness of English art — the belief that art exists to preach, that detail points to a moral as well as adorning a tale — comes up hard against the amorality of pastoral. The fifth book of the *Arcadia* performs the comedic function of sorting out the cross-identities and misadventures in the semblance of a trial and judgment, even though the judgment may be amoral, as with Pirocles and Musidorus.

Here is William Empson: "The essential trick of the old pastoral, which was felt to imply a beautiful relation between rich and poor," (Mr. Empson has written) "was to make simple persons express strong feelings (felt on the most universal subject, something fundamentally true about everybody) in learned and fashionable language (so that you wrote about the best subject in the best way)" (Empson, *Some Versions of Pastoral*, p. 11). In his study, Empson sought to "show, roughly in historical order, the ways in which the pastoral process of putting the complex into the simple (in itself a great help to the concentration needed for poetry) and the resulting social ideas have been used in English literature" (p. 23).

Empson speaks (p. 242) of "the obscure tradition of pastoral." And he speaks of "the writer of the primary sort of pastoral [identifying himself] with his magnified version of the swain" (p. 242). We sometimes overlook the fact that the last book of *Arcadia* is indeed a legal trial — though the picture of Macedonia in Arcadia's seat, judging Pirocles and Musidorus, strains against our normal understanding of the phrase *legal trial*. In any case, the judgment is in some sense the appropriate response to the amorality or highly mixed morality of the pastoral in progress. (But that mixed morality or amorality is of the earth, earthly — of the Silent

Planet — and voyaging in the heavens should clear that matter up.) We will have more to say on this in the rest of the book, and most particularly in Chapter VI.

Malacandra Down-to-Earth

We will begin at the beginning of *Out of the Silent Planet*. We are introduced to Elwin Ransom, philologist and fellow of a Cambridge college, as "the pedestrian" on a walking tour somewhere in the Midlands. Lewis was, of course, a walker, given to just such tours (with his brother, with Owen Barfield, Tolkien once, Dom Bede Griffiths once, A. K. Hamilton Jenkin in the pre–Inkling days). On this tour, Ransom (unlike Lewis on his) is alone, tramping, as we find him, from Much Nadderby (where he has been refused a bed at an obviously empty inn) to Sterk. The emotions recounted could well be Lewis's own, derived from a similar incident on one of his tours. Be that as it may, when an old woman mistakes him for her half-idiot son coming home from The Rise, the farmhouse where he works, Ransom promises (half in hope of a bed at The Rise) to look in and make sure her son gets on his way. Whether such an incident was part of Lewis's own history I cannot tell, but the detailed look at Ransom's feelings in the situation he has placed himself in suggest that it might have been. In any case, the passage is highly characteristic of Lewis and his Englishness: he speaks of what he knows, and we receive his testimony.

Ransom assents to the woman's request with mixed motives: she is obviously upset and in need of help (the pure motive), but he needs a place to spend the night (the impure motive). Her son does (presumably) make it home eventually. And Ransom does find a place to spend the night, though not as he intended (quite a few nights, in fact). If he had not, it would have been an idiot boy rather than a Cambridge philologist who met the Oyarsa of Malacandra and the good that came would not have come. Though his motives were mixed (as in this fallen world all motives are), his good intent brought goodness beyond man's dreams. Meanwhile, we see Ransom acting as we act; the picture is true to life (though such choice may not come to the more sedentary among us whilst on a walking tour). Similarly, when Ransom throws his pack over the hedge at The Rise, and then realizes he will have to follow it (thus being led to make up his mind by an unthought-out action of his own), when he clings to the (obviously improbable) belief that someone he knows cannot be involved in something shady, and when he realizes (too late for his immediate purposes) that just as he has detested Devine all these years, so Devine has detested him — in all this he is as much Everyman, or at least us, as he is Elwin Ransom.

By this we recognize a real (if academic or "Oxbridge") world, at the beginning of adventures that are, quite literally, out of this world. I am reminded again of Dr. Johnson's characteristic remark on viewing some of the wilder allegorical extravaganzas of the Swiss painter Fuseli, to the effect that he would rather see the picture of a dog he knew than all the allegories in the world. Like Johnson's, Lewis's imagination, even if it is down to Venus or down to Mars, is always down to earth. If he shows us the hounds of heaven and hell, they are still pictures of the dogs he knows. So here, using the opening pages of *Out of the Silent Planet* as a microcosm, we can expect to find, in whatever worlds Lewis brings us, detailed and realistic observation of daily life. That detailed and realistic observation may not be designed to point to a moral, but it surely adorns the tale. And not merely adorns. The movement of realistic figures through a pageant framework, with ironic or satirical intent, is at the root of the English novel, before its split into realistic novel and romance. The title, *Out of the Silent Planet*, reminds us that the completed Ransom novels are arguably science fiction. They are certainly part of the greater genre we have suggested above.

Perhaps, after all, we should do well to follow Professor Hillegas in his essay thirty years ago on "*Out of the Silent Planet* as Cosmic Voyage" (in *Shadows of Imagination*, 1969, pp. 41–58), and place *Out of the Silent Planet* in the tradition of Kepler, Godwin, and Cyrano de Bergerac's satire, *The Comicall Historie of the States and Empires of the Sunne and the Moone* (1650), verily antecessors of science fiction if not clearly the thing itself — but, like our later *Out of the Silent Planet*, coming out of the tradition of pilgrimage, pageant, and pastoral. *Out of the Silent Planet* would thus be the ultimate (or possibly penultimate) book in the series of which Wells's *The First Men in the Moon* is the penultimate.

Here I note remarks Lewis made in *Surprised by Joy* (1955, pp. 35–36) that are surely relevant to our inquiry. "The idea of other planets exercised upon me then a peculiar heady attraction, which was quite different from any of my other literary interests. Most emphatically it was not the literary spell of *Das Ferne*. 'Joy' (in my technical sense) never darted from Mars or the Moon. This was something coarser and stronger. The interest, when the fit was upon me, was ravenous, like a lust. This particular coarse strength I have come to accept as a mark that the interest which has it is psychological, not spiritual; behind such a fierce tang there lurks, I suspect, a psychoanalytical explanation. I may perhaps add that my planetary romances have not been so much the gratification of that fierce curiosity as its exorcism. The exorcism worked by reconciling it with, or subjecting it to, the other, the more elusive, and genuinely imaginative, impulse."

I have quoted the passage from *Surprised by Joy* at length because it enables me to bring in the subject of psychoanalysis, indeed almost demands its bringing in, which many of Lewis's admirers would otherwise take — and may still take (as I know full well) — pretty much as the insult direct and unforgivable. To be sure, whatever may be the science of his science fiction, it is not the science of psychoanalysis. But there is direct reference to psychoanalysis in all four books. We will come back to this later.

The science of the science fiction is not psychoanalysis, but is the "science" of *Out of the Silent Planet*, as one of Tolkien's characters asked (*Notion Club Papers*, p. 164) in fact science at all, or is it "scientifictitious bunkum"? "'But the trick in *Out of the Silent Planet*, getting the hero kidnapped by space-ship villains, ... was not bad.' 'Not bad ... still, it was, as you say, a trick. And not first rate, not if you want sheer literary credibility, the pure thing, rather than an alloy with allegory and satire.'" This is the "Lewisite alloy" (p. 165).

When Weston tells Ransom the ship works by exploiting some of the less observed properties of solar radiation, he is neither providing a scientific explanation (any more than Cyrano was in his catalogue of ways of reaching the moon) nor putting us in a science fiction story. Lewis himself observed he was wiser when he moved Ransom to Perelandra by angelic power. And even as he wrote *Out of the Silent Planet*, Lewis knew the *canali* on Mars were themselves a fiction. This is not space opera, feigned cosmic history (like Olaf Stapledon's *Last and First Men*), or a set of engineer's stories: it is not even space poetry like Bradbury's *Martian Chronicles*. Of all the more recent works of science fiction it may be most like James Blish's *A Case of Conscience*—but even so, it seems to bear almost as great an affinity to Eddison's *The Worm Ouroboros*, which (theoretically) takes place on Mercury, but is not science fiction at all. Like Arcturus in Lindsay's book, and Mercury in Eddison's, Malacandra and Perelandra are realms of the spirit, not of the solar system: the problem we will have to deal with in the third chapter is that so, likewise, is Thulcandra — Tellus — Earth. The "science" is part of a framework dictated by the conventions of the times. Unlike Swift, we can no longer put spiritual realms in the South Seas or on the Alaskan peninsula. We must put them in space, or separated in time. And to put them there, we must get them there.

Necessary though the scientific convention may be, it may also be a distraction. The otherworldliness, not the science, is the point. Lewis's eye for detail "saves" his otherworldly scenes "from the flatness of mere description" (his own phrase on Gavin Douglas). He has, as the French would say, "realized" the contours of Malacandra — especially the contours — and Ransom's initial reaction to them. "The air was cold but not bitterly so, and it seemed a little rough at the back of his throat. He gazed about him, and the very intensity of his desire to take in the new world at a glance defeated itself. He saw nothing but colours — colours that refused to form themselves into things. Moreover, he knew nothing yet well enough to see it: you cannot see things till you know roughly what they are. His first impression was of a bright, pale world — a watercolour world out of a child's paint-box; a moment later he recognized the flat belt of light blue as a sheet of water, or of something like water, which came nearly to his feet" (pp. 41–42).

And, a little later, on the contours of the planet, "even the smallest hummocks of earth were of an unearthly shape — too narrow, too pointed at the top and too small at the base. He remembered that the waves on the blue lakes had displayed a similar oddity. And glancing up at the purple leaves he saw the same theme of perpendicularity — the same rush to the sky — repeated there" (p. 48). It is interesting to see how Ransom's

increasing absorption into Malacandrian life is accompanied by his
increasing knowledge of the world of Malacandra (and therefore by
Lewis's increasingly far-reaching description), as well as being mirrored
in his increasing acceptance of Malacandrian mores — which, of course,
are much like those of any good Christian. And so, he begins to find his
Malacandrian experience increasingly "natural."

As more details of Malacandrian life are given, the more natural it
seems, and the more natural seems the underlying schema. Detailed
description becomes the mode of a convincing sermon. Eventually, of
course, Ransom, "for one privileged moment," sees "the human form
with almost Malacandrian eyes" — but this is to bring us to the climactic scene before our time. The implicit message of the first meeting with
the *hrossa* is made explicit in Chapter 12, where Ransom wonders how
their daily conduct so closely approximates the ideals of that far-sundered
species, mankind — until he rephrases the question in a sudden realization that it is his own species that is the anomaly. And in the end he learns
that the three Malacandrian species are, by the grace of their Oyarsa,
unfallen. (As we noted, the mixed morality of earthly pastoral may be
cleared up by a heavenly voyage.)

This unfallen state presents an artistic problem. We will see later
how, in *Perelandra*, once the temptation is removed, it is apparently
removed forever. On Malacandra it has apparently been removed forever
("One thing we left behind us on the harandra — fear" with "left behind
us" the operative phrase). We have thus a static, or largely static, world,
a backdrop (almost) for Ransom's spiritual journey. What does one do
with a backdrop? For answer (along Pevsner's lines), we can look at the
visual arts, and especially medieval and Renaissance visual arts, since they
are from the great ages of the pageant. Lewis himself, in his final scholar's
book, dealt with one particular adaptation of pageant to literature
(*Spenser's Images of Life*, edited after Lewis's death by his colleague Alastair Fowler) — but a quarter-century earlier he had put the technique to
work. The connection of Spenser to pageant and Spenser's images in particular are especially relevant to Lewis's time-fragment, but they are useful here with *Out of the Silent Planet*.

The answer to our question, what does one do with a backdrop? is
that one — especially if one is "English" in one's art — fills in the background

with a miniaturist's eye, gilds it, illuminates it, mixes detail from real life with a kind of heraldry (this is all part of Pevsner's definition of Englishness). That Lewis did this in *Perelandra* has been widely recognized: indeed, he himself refers to the heraldic dragon in the Garden of the Hesperides (on the floating islands). That he did it equally in *Out of the Silent Planet* has been less recognized, perhaps because the illumination and the heraldry do not so much outweigh the slices of "real life." Yet the technique is much the same. And it should be remembered that heraldry is the gift of the Middle Ages and the Renaissance.

All four books, as I say, fit Lewis's description of the fairy tale. All begin with scenes from or based upon his own experience. All progress to realms beyond our experience — but two of them to realms that are part of our traditional "mythic" consciousness — Mars and Venus. As Lewis observed in his "On Science Fiction" (*Of Other Worlds*, p. 69), the canals on Mars "were part of the Martian myth as it already existed in the common mind." So, of course, were the witches and ogres of the common fairy tale, to which Lewis refers in the preface to *That Hideous Strength*. In *Out of the Silent Planet* and in *Perelandra*, Lewis used detailed observation to "realize" the common myth (for Venus as paradise is a myth far older than the canals of Mars).

In *An Exchange in Time*, the "myth" was the medieval myth of Faerie, into which both Orfieu (Orfeo) and Scudamour must go, as we shall see. (Admittedly, what Lewis does in "realizing" — or perhaps it is "scientifictionalizing" — accounts of Faerie here may be more inventive, and more revealing, than we would wish.) In *That Hideous Strength* there was no such myth ready to hand, though we must give Lewis credit for trying to combine the English myth of Arthur with Tolkien's "Mythology for England" still in manuscript.

I am reminded here of a remark of Lewis's in his *OHEL* volume (*English Literature in the Sixteenth Century, Excluding Drama*, 1954), at a point when he was discussing the travelers' narratives in Hakluyt. One traveler succeeded in describing a coconut sufficiently well for someone who had not seen one to get a good idea what one was like. To describe with sufficient detail and sufficient imagination to achieve this, Lewis observes, is a very difficult thing indeed. The difficulty does not go away when the thing to be described is in one's imagination rather than having just fallen out of a palm tree. In fact, unless one is highly visually minded, the difficulty may be greater.

Lewis excels at the description, the visual imagination, the gilding, the illumination, the background detail, the "realization"—in short, the second part of the Englishness. He is very good at portraying the moral pageant through this description. Whether he is good enough at both to dispel our belief that what is of the earth is merely earthy (or even earthly)—and that earthly things are therefore the only "real" things on this earth—we shall see in the fifth chapter. For the moment, let us say that his success in this area is mixed: this is one of the flaws in *That Hideous Strength*. Meanwhile, back on Malacandra, we left Ransom noting the perpendicularity of the new planet. Shortly thereafter is a scene that calls echoes to my mind at least.

"The sound of his own voice yawning—the old sound heard in night-nurseries, school dormitories and in so many bedrooms—liberated a flood of self-pity ... he thought of men going to bed on the far-distant planet Earth—men in clubs, and liners, and hotels, married men, and small children who slept with nurses in their room, and warm, tobacco-smelling men tumbled together in forecastles and dugouts" (p. 50). The effect of the yawn on Ransom is brilliantly realized: it reminds me of myself yawning my first day at prep school, aged thirteen. For its trueness to life, it reminds me of quite another book. There should be no surprise that it is an eighteenth-century book.

When Ransom lays himself down to sleep I can see an earlier wayfarer—"having drank and put a little tobacco in my mouth to prevent hunger, I went to the tree, and getting up into it, endeavored to place my self so, as that if I should sleep I might not fall; and having cut me a short stick, like a truncheon, for my defense, I took up my lodging, and having been excessively fatigued, I fell fast asleep ... and found my self the most refreshed with it that I think I ever was" (*Life and Adventures of Robinson Crusoe*, Penguin ed., p. 67). But I think Lewis does the better job. And he does a good job also in conveying Ransom's surprise at simply being *on* Malacandra (p. 65). In fact, as one rereads *Out of the Silent Planet*, one is struck by just how good Lewis is at this sort of thing—that is, at making Ransom's presence on this other world convincing—and by the fact that his techniques are reminiscent not so much of the allusiveness of H. G. Wells or David Lindsay as of the detail of Defoe and Swift.

Partly, of course, this success is the result of Ransom's being on Malacandra for a considerable length of time: thus, when he reflects (or, rather, Lewis reflects from Ransom's experience) that it "was with a kind of stupefaction each morning that he found himself neither arriving in, nor escaping from, but simply living on Malacandra" (p. 65), we are much more in Swift's "I had now been two years in this country; and about the beginning of the third, Glumdalclitch and I attended the King and Queen in progress to the south coast of the kingdom. I was carried as usual in my traveling box..." (*A Voyage to Brobdingnag*, p. 141, Bantam ed.)—than in Lindsay's world. The key word in the passage from Swift is "as usual" and the key in Lewis's description is the "simply living"—after all, as we have noted, it is the description of the detailed minutiae of daily life that provides the mechanism for the "sermon" of English art.

Intermixed with the description (and I think this exemplifies the English moral imagination) are the philosophical conversations which, as with Swift, are the central part—or, perhaps, the formal cause—of the book. Indeed, it is just after Ransom realizes that he is "simply living" on Malacandra that he begins his discoveries in Malacandrian knowledge (pp. 66ff). Later on, in *Perelandra*, Lewis would pretty much successfully convert philosophy into the Great Dance, but here he is much more in the world of his predecessors.

There are some indications, by the way, that Lewis's earliest attempts at (adult) fiction were a kind of cross between a Socratic dialogue and *Tristram Shandy*: I do not know what this hybrid may have been like (it has not, so far as I know, survived—unless it was to be what happened in his "Ulster novel" of which we have a few pages in *The Lewis Papers*), but it is certain that the business of philosophy was, in Lewis's mind, very much mixed in with the business of fiction.

In fact, for the entire book, passages of detailed description (or "realization") alternate with passages of philosophical inquiry and conversation. It is far from accidental that (p. 40) "things do not always happen as a man would expect. The moment of his arrival in an unknown world found Ransom wholly absorbed in a philosophical speculation." Similarly,

Chapter XII (pp. 72–76) is a conversation between Ransom and Hyoi; Chapter XIII (pp. 77–84) is the history of the Hnakra-hunt and Hyoi's death; Chapter XIV (pp. 85–90) is partly travel and partly internal dialogue (thus repeating the pattern for the voyage to Malacandra); Chapter XV (pp. 91–96) is mostly conversation with Augray, and so on. For an author who once attacked the "scrappiness" of the chapters in *Tristram Shandy*, these are doubtless short and scrappy chapters indeed: what is more to the point, the plot (if that is the word) is carried on by the philosophy. In fact, to the degree that Chad Walsh is right and this is the re-education of the fearful pilgrim, the philosophy could almost be said to be the plot. In that it is indeed like *Rasselas*. But if the philosophy is the plot, what then of the heraldry (which goes with pageant)? Let me give some examples from this book (as I shall eventually for the apparently much more heraldic *Perelandra*).

Here is Ransom in Augray's tower, seeing the earth — Thulcandra — "He saw perfect blackness and, floating in the centre of it, seemingly an arm's length away, a bright disk about the size of a half-crown. Most of its surface was featureless, shining silver…" (p. 96). Or, as he is on his way to Augray, "the light was increasing, sharpening and growing whiter; and the sky was a much darker blue than he had ever seen on Malacandra. Indeed, it was darker than blue; it was almost black, and the jagged spires of rock standing against it were like his mental picture of a lunar landscape. Some stars were visible" (p. 89). Or, on Augray's shoulder, he contemplates his earlier vision of the *Séroni*: "The grace of their movement, their lofty stature, and the softened glancing of the sunlight on their feathery sides, effected a final transformation in Ransom's feeling towards their race. 'Ogres' he had called them when they first met his eyes as he struggled in the grip of Weston and Devine; 'Titans' or 'Angels' he now thought would have been a better word" (p. 101).

Surely a vision of the earth as a disk, argent, on a field, sable, is heraldry. Surely the brightness of the light, the blue-blackness of the sky, the pinnacles of rock, verge on heraldry. Surely the great feathered creatures with their august and titanic faces are from the same realm of experience that produced the dragon of the Hesperides in *Perelandra*. It will be recalled that on Perelandra, Ransom muses and remembers how in the "different world called Malacandra — that cold, archaic world, as it now seemed to him — he had met the original of the Cyclops, a giant in a cave and a shepherd" (*Perelandra*, p. 45). This musing is prompted by the first sight of the dragon of the Hesperides, nestling in the enchanted garden in the Islands of the Blest, which is also Enoch's Third Heaven, where trees bubble with fragrant exhalations: "And those men took me thence, and led me up on to the third heaven, and placed me there; and I looked downwards, and saw the produce of these places, such as has never been known for goodness. And I saw all the sweet-flowering trees and beheld their fruits, which were sweet smelling, and all the foods borne by them bubbling with fragrant exhalation" (*The Book of the Secrets of Enoch*, trans, W. A. Morphill, Chapter VIII, verses i–ii). When I suggested to Lewis that this was the origin of the bubble-trees, he responded, as I have noted (letter, October 22, 1963), that the proximate origin was the a childish mispronunciation of "laboratory" as "bubble-tree"—but he had read *Enoch*—and Enoch appears with Elijah and Melchidesec on Arthur's Avalon.

Ransom as Philologist

The plural of *sorn* is *séroni*: why? Because *séroni* (or *soroni*) was a philologist's plural—Tolkien's, to be exact. In *The Notion Club Papers*, the translation in the Elvish tongue of "The Eagles of the Powers of the west are at hand" is originally "Soroni numeheruen ettuler" (*The Notion Club Papers*, p. 290; n. 62). Doubtless there is something of the word (and idea) "Norn" in the sorns, the feathered Titans of the cold *harandra*, but there is also something of Tolkien's Eagles of the West. (And when Ransom considers these as angels, I wonder if there is a Tolkienian pun on eagles/angels.)

I said we would speak of Ransom as philologist, but up to this point we have been speaking of heraldry, when we were not speaking of mythology. There is, however, a connection. In fact, more than one, as we shall see. For the moment, however, let us ask, what is a philologist? In the Greek, a lover (or student) of words; in modern English, one who studies the history of words, their derivations, and their relationships one with another. The editors of the *Oxford English Dictionary* and their assistants (like Ronald Tolkien after the First World War) were and are philologists. Indeed, Tolkien was a philologist by profession, and Lewis's friend Barfield a student of words by avocation, one might say, an amateur philologist. Lewis was a voracious and retentive reader and listener, and he read and listened to Barfield and Tolkien as *Out of the Silent Planet* and its successors were taking shape. It would be surprising if philology were not on his mind.

What are the connections I alluded to, with heraldry and mythology? Heraldry is a kind of sacramentalism, an inheritor perhaps of Barfield's ancient unities. (We will note, later on, that Barfield's ancient unities appear in *That Hideous Strength*, in a passage I have been pleased to note turns up in a modern study of chaos theory.) Let me appeal here to *Poetic Diction* (1928), where Barfield is speaking of figurative expression (not "figures of speech"), and remarks that the word *figurative* "may justly be applied, owing to the perceptual or aesthetic, the *pictorial*, form in which these unitary meanings first manifest in consciousness." What we have is not "an empty 'root meaning to shine,' but the same definite spiritual reality which was beheld on the one hand in what has since become pure human thinking; and on the other hand, in what has since become physical light; not an abstract conception, but ... a living Figure" (*Poetic Diction*, 3rd ed., 1973, pp. 88–89). These ancient unities are reality, "Reality, once self-evident, and therefore not conceptually experienced, but which can *now* only be reached by an effort of the individual mind" (p. 88).

Lewis's friendship with Barfield, and Barfield's with Lewis, are well known, of course, and *Poetic Diction* is dedicated to Lewis with the quotation "Opposition is True Friendship" (which is from Blake's *The Marriage of Heaven and Hell*). Barfield's *History in English Words* (1926) has at least a family connection with Lewis's *Studies in Words* (1960), and there is something of Barfield in the Ransom of *Out of the Silent Planet*. There is also something of Ronald Tolkien in Ransom then (if not so much later), as well as of his languages from the world of *The Lord of the Rings* in Lewis's Old Solar. This was, indeed, my own introduction to much that then lay unpublished in his friend Professor Tolkien's manuscripts (*That Hideous Strength*, Preface — which was indeed the reference that led me to *The Lord of the Rings* when it first came out). But there were some less explicit references to the world of the Rings that I missed, back then. One of these less explicit references is Ransom's Christian name.

"His very name in his own language is Elwin, the friend of the Eldila" (*Perelandra*, p. 195). The speaker (on Perelandra) is the Oyarsa of Malacandra, at the beginning of the Great Dance, and when I first read the line (in 1951) I thought no more — and no less — of it than of "great syllables of words that sounded like castles" (*That Hideous Strength*, p. 228), or of the reference to "Ransom's *Dialect and Semantics*" (*That Hideous Strength*, pp. 189–90). This last, by the way, I now take to be a concealed reference to the book Lewis eventually planned to write with Tolkien, which by 1948 had the provisional title *Language and Human Nature* (W. H. Lewis, ed., *Letters of C. S. Lewis*, revised pb ed., ed. Walter Hooper, 1993, p. 399), and which would have dealt with the question of meaning and — for want of a better phrase — the *genius loci* of language. By this I mean the way in which the language of a place or a tribe (that is to say, a local people) mirrors their nature. The book will appear on the kalends of Greece, but the idea is important here.

Tolkien believed, with the Icelandic scholar Sjéra Tomas Saemundsson, that languages are the chief distinguishing marks of peoples (see my *England and Always*, Grand Rapids 1981, pp. 33–36, 88–89). As we noted before, Tolkien also believed, or else in the creation of his mythology for England he feigned a belief, that the earliest version of the English language, Old English or Anglo-Saxon, had some especial connection with the universal language of humankind beyond the moon or before the flood ("The Notion Club Papers" in Christopher Tolkien, ed., *Sauron Defeated*, 1992 [herein *The Notion Club Papers*], pp. 236–37 *et passim*): the "beyond the moon or before the flood" is, of course, a reference to the jewels of Logres in *That Hideous Strength* (p. 362).

The name "Elwin" or "Alwin" is from Old-English "Aelfwine" or "elffriend" (see *The Notion Club Papers*, p. 235) — not friend of the Eldila, but friend of the Elves, and this name is a material link in the action of Tolkien's unfinished philological romance, and in early versions of his mythology for England. This romance is the one provisionally entitled *The Notion Club Papers*: it had at one time the subtitle "Out of the Talkative Planet" and contains, as we have seen, much of Tolkien's literary criticism of *Out of the Silent Planet*. And some of his philological criticism, as well.

But before we get to that, we should note Lewis's version (*Out of the Silent Planet*, pp. 114–15) of connections between language and inner nature. Each of the three Malacandrian species has its own "old tongue" at home — "You can see it in the names. The *sorns* have big-sounding names like Augray and Arkal and Belmo and Falmay. The *hrossa* have furry names like Hnoh and Hnihi and Hyoi and Hlithnahi." Ransom asks, "The best poetry, then, comes in the roughest speech?" And the pfifltrigg answers, "Perhaps ... As the best pictures are made in the hardest stone. But my people have names like Kalakaperi and Parakataru and Tafalakeruf. I am called Kanakaberaka." The speaker is the pfifltrigg Ransom met at Meldilorn.

Once again, before going on to Tolkien's comments on Lewis's philology in *Out of the Silent Planet* (and in *Perelandra*), we ought to look at the particular significance of Ransom's philological study in the novel. Ransom, kidnapped to Malacandra by Weston and Devine, and having escaped from them, is "on the shore of a broad river, and looking out on a flat landscape of intermingled river, lake, island and promontory" (p. 54). Then the water heaves, and "a round black thing like a cannon-ball appears" — which turns out to be the head of a large aquatic creature: Ransom notes "in a dry objective way" that this is likely to be the end of his story. And then, "something happened which completely altered his state of mind. The creature ... opened its mouth and began to make noises. This in itself was not remarkable; but a lifetime of linguistic study assured Ransom almost at once that these were articulate noises. The creature was *talking*. It had a language. If you are not yourself a philologist, I am afraid you must take on trust the prodigious emotional consequences of this in Ransom's mind."

Let me set here a passage from *The Notion Club Papers* (p. 201). Ramer (Tolkien's equivalent of Ransom, I think) is speaking: "We each have a native language of our own — at least potentially. In working-dreams, people who have a bent that way may work on it, develop it ... it may be the invention of new words (on received models, as a rule); it may come to the elaboration of beautiful languages of their own in private: in private only because other people are naturally not very interested." Tolkien, of course, did precisely elaborate a beautiful language of his own in private, the language of the Elves of Middle-earth, abstracted or caricatured in Lewis's Old Solar. I am calling Ramer a Ransom equivalent partly because he seems to play much the role in *The Notion Club Papers* that Ransom plays in *An Exchange in Time*, and partly because the Middle-earth "raimen" means "ransom"— see Tolkien's *Glossary* to Kenneth Sisam's *Fourteenth Century Verse and Prose*—and I suspect some Tolkienian humor at work in the naming.

In *Perelandra* (p. 25) Lewis has Ransom assert that Old Solar (Hlab-Eribol-ef-Cordi) is the speech of the Hressa on Malacandra (Hressa-Hlab). But Ramer (and thus, I think, Tolkien) argues that the original human language on Earth could not well have been the "same as the Prime Language of other differently constituted rational animals, such as Lewis's Hrossa. Because those two embodiments, Men and Hrossa, are quite different, and the physical basis, which conditions the symbol-forms, would be *ab origine* different. The mind-body blends would have quite different expressive flavours…. Without symbols you have no language; and language begins only with incarnation and not before it" (*The Notion Club Papers*, p. 203).

Now Lewis had been admitted to the world of Tolkien's private mythology and its private languages as far back as the late 1920s, and the relations between and among language, meaning, and people were clearly a not-infrequent subject of conversation at the Cave of Adullam before the Inklings, and I daresay the Coalbiters before both (on the Cave, conversations with the late Cleanth Brooks, New Haven CT, Winter 1991-92). But evidently the lesson had not taken entirely, and it may be Lewis was aware of it: in the "Postscript" to *Out of the Silent Planet* (p. 155), Ransom refers to "the ruthless way" in which Lewis "cut down all the philological part … giving our readers a mere caricature of the Martian language." In fact, if it were not that Lewis says Ransom is a philologist, and that his being a philologist lies behind his revealing his presence to Hyoi (p. 55), we might have almost as much trouble in remembering Ransom's academic specialty as the Bursar's colleagues in *That Hideous Strength* (p. 36) had in remembering his. But it is nonetheless important that Ransom is a philologist, partly for what it does in this story and in the critical moment with the Voice in *Perelandra*, partly for its connection to Lewis's own real world.

Nevertheless, we may reasonably ask, What would Ransom's story have been like if it had indeed been written by a philologist? Tolkien's *Lord of the Rings* provides a clue. I have elsewhere noted (*England and Always*, p. 33) that, if "we assume there resides some kind of *genius* in a land ... then we would expect, as languages rise and fall within that land, that the peoples who speak them will not be unlike each other." To which I would add that the languages will in some ways be like each other. In Tolkien's world, sound and syntax both define the nature of the speakers of a language. (In Barfield's, the speakers of a language define its meaning over time — see his *Speaker's Meaning*, 1967 — which would mean that sound and syntax define meaning through the mind of the speakers.)

The Orcs speak without love of words or things, and this mode of speaking reveals the Orkish character. (Here is where the movie of *The Lord of the Rings* goes astray, I think, in substituting visual for berbal horror.) On the other hand, those who have skill with words seek to match the beauty of the words with the beauty of a thing or a person described. The old grammar books tell us that a noun is the name of a thing, but in this philologist's world to know the name is to know the inner nature not only of the thing but of the speaker. (And the identity of Name with Nature — of the thing — is one of Barfield's ancient unities.) Words in such a world, in their sound and their flavor, are objective correlatives for the things and actions of the material world, and their arrangement, their syntax, is its pattern. This is evidently not the kind of world Lewis brings us in *Out of the Silent Planet*.

Nevertheless, some of Tolkien's lesson took, though perhaps mostly that part relating to the mythology and heraldry of meaning — what we might call the pictorial part of the lesson. Doubtless Lewis was more visually minded than Tolkien (cf. "The Philologist's World of *The Lord of the Rings*" in my *England and Always*, esp. p. 45). Doubtless, also, this visual-mindedness is revealed in other ways, in the Ransom stories, and in Lewis's life. I have heard it said — and believe it — that Lewis feared madness. I know he had visions: he distinguished between vision induced by drugs in his treatment in summer 1963 and true mystical vision (according to Walter Hooper, and here certainly what Walter says rings true to me), and he reported, in saying how he came to write his stories, that "It all began with a picture" (in *On Stories*, New York 1982).

The Threat of Madness

For Ransom, the perilous realm in *Out of the Silent Planet* is not Malacandra but madness. This is "realization" with a sting in its tail. If we were to be taken to other planets — as, for example, Lindsay's Arcturus, or Eddison's Mercury, could we know it "really" happened? If we were to travel in time (except sixty minutes every hour into the future), could we know it had "really" happened? Even if we knew we had been in space, could we know that what we saw there was "really" there? Or is it the enchanted forest in which the mares have built nests in every tree?

We have noted how Lewis said the idea of other planets had exercised upon him a peculiar heady attraction, quite different from his other literary interests, and most emphatically not the literary spell of the far away. "Joy" (in his technical sense) never darted from Mars or the Moon. This was something coarser and stronger than joy, and his interest, when the fit was upon him, was ravenous, like a lust, meaning that the interest was psychological, not spiritual. "Behind such a fierce tang," he noted, "there lurks, I suspect, a psychoanalytical explanation" and went on to that his "planetary romances" were not so much the gratification of that fierce curiosity as its exorcism, worked by reconciling the curiosity with, or subjecting it to, the more elusive and genuinely imaginative impulse of literary subcreation. And here, though it is more fully dealt with in the next chapter, I should mention the attack of the dark eldila on Lewis at the beginning of *Perelandra*.

You will recall that he muses how "They call it a Breakdown *at first*" and then asks himself whether there isn't in fact a mental disease in which quite ordinary objects look unbelievably ominous to the patient — just as that abandoned factory looks to him then. "Great bulbous shapes of cement, strange brickwork bogeys, glowered at me over dry scrubby grass pock-marked with grey pools and intersected with the remains of a light railway." (*Perelandra*, p. 13). He sees a little empty house by the side of the road, with the windows boarded up except for one staring like the eye of a dead fish. "Suppose," he asks himself, "that real insanity had chosen this place to begin. In that case, the black enmity of those dripping trees ... would be an hallucination. But that did not make it any better.

To think that the spectre you see is an illusion does not rob him of his terrors: it simply adds the further terror of madness itself..." (p. 14). We shall see later something of Lewis's personal concerns with losing one's mind, and I will suggest a connection with Mrs. Moore and his diary.

It does not seem to have been widely remarked that early in Ransom's sojourn on Malacandra, he, like Lewis at the beginning of *Perelandra*, is skirting madness (p. 50): "The tendency to talk to himself was irresistible ... 'We'll look after you, Ransom ... we'll stick together, old man.' It occurred to him that one of those creatures with snapping jaws might live in the stream. 'You're quite right, Ransom,' he answered mumblingly. 'It's not a safe place to spend the night. We'll just rest a bit till you feel better, then we'll go on again. Not now. Presently.'" And then, the next morning (p. 51), picking up that same theme, Ransom "remembered with inexpressible relief that there was a man wandering in the wood — poor devil — he'd be glad to see him. He would come up to him and say, 'Hulloo Ransom' — he stopped, puzzled. No, it was only himself: he *was* Ransom. Or was he? Who was that man whom he had led to a hot stream and tucked up in bed, telling him not to drink the strange water? ... All that about the other Ransom was nonsense. He was quite aware of the danger of madness.... Not that madness mattered much. Perhaps he was mad already, and not really on Malacandra, but safe in bed in an English asylum.... He would ask Ransom —"

Eventually he learns "to stand still mentally" (p. 51) and let the delusions roll over his mind. But that does not prevent his wondering if it was all delusion. Even at the end (p. 152), when Ransom returns to Earth, he "was ill for several months and when he recovered he found himself in considerable doubt as to whether what he remembered had really occurred. It looked very like a delusion produced by his illness, and most of his apparent adventures could, he saw, be explained psychoanalytically...." This explanation, of course, would be an "explaining away" — as, for example, in Nevil Shute's *An Old Captivity* (1940), in which the aviator Donald Ross dreams (?) what later seems to be borne out as reality — only to have Oxford don Cyril Lockwood explain a Norse voyage in the "dream" (pp. 302–03) as the motion of a boat and sound of the oars penetrating Ross's sleeping mind, the Norse houses as recollections of Eskimo houses, and the vision of Vinland the Good as "what psychologists would call a contrast-impression."

Madness is, among other things, a matter of defining the bounds of the ordinary and extra-ordinary, or the normal and abnormal. Psychoanalytic or psychological explanations of the extraordinary or abnormal in terms of the ordinary or normal are in fact a denial of the actual existence of the extraordinary or the abnormal. When the apparently abnormal is really the supranormal, when the apparently unnatural is really the supernatural, psychiatry and psychoanalysis become denials of the transcendent, where even Jung plays the part of Aristotle to faith's Plato. It would have been so with Ransom. It might have been so with Lewis, as Mrs. Moore's brother went mad in 1922–23, but he kept a diary (perhaps at her urging), recorded ordinary events, and so was led to come to different terms with the extraordinary — not madness but faith.

But it was not so. In *Perelandra* (p. 21) Lewis comes through the "barrage" of doubts set up by the dark eldila — but there is no doubt that it is a barrage in a conflict, indeed in a war. In *The Screwtape Letters* (1941), Screwtape records his success in tempting his "patient" away from God by linking belief with the ideas that come to a man when he is shut away from the world with books, away from real life. But note the chapter title "Real Life Is Meeting" in *That Hideous Strength*. In *Out of the Silent Planet*, Ransom has decided to hold his tongue about the space voyage and his adventures on Malacandra, when Lewis writes him a letter (*Out of the Silent Planet*, p. 153) to inquire if he has ever heard a word like *Oyarses* or "can hazard any guess as to what language it may be?" He has decided to hold his tongue precisely because he believes that anyone hearing his story would psychoanalyze it away. It, too, does not agree with Real Life or the normal.

The "down-to-earth" quality of Malacandra as Lewis describes the planet and the flat quotidianity of the opening and closing passages of the book — a walking tour and an academic letter of inquiry — are guards against the belief that Ransom's adventures are an hallucination. As Lewis observed of that commonplace little girl, Alice, in her adventures in Wonderland, to have odd things happen to odd people is an oddity too much (Lewis, *On Stories*, 1982, p. 60). The quotidianity in fact endures on Malacandra: Ransom records the body temperature of the hrossa —

"because I always take a thermometer with me on a holiday (it has saved many a one from being spoiled) I know that the normal temperature of a *hross* is 103 degrees" (p. 155). But the quotidianity ebbs and flows. Here is Ransom almost on the *harandra* (p. 88).

He has become used to life on Malacandra, in the *handramit*. Now Malacandra is no longer *the* world or even *a* world, but a "planet, a star, a waste place in the universe, millions of miles from the world of men." He tries to recall his feelings about the *hrossa* or the *eldila*, or Oyarsa. He cannot. Indeed, it "seemed fantastic to have thought he had duties to such hobgoblins — if they were not hallucinations — met in the wilds of space." Here is the question of madness once again. But all this time — and here we are back to our own daily experience and the value of thinking on daily life — "the old resolution, taken when he could still think, was driving him up the road."

The little boy who makes up tales of wolves when there are no wolves will be left to them when they appear. No one will believe they are really there when indeed they are. How much more with hrossa and seroni and pfifltriggi, to say nothing of the Tutelary Intelligence or Angel of the planet Mars. So Ransom decides to have Lewis tell the story as fiction so as to have it believed. And eventually the rest of the story the same way, in *Perelandra* and *That Hideous Strength*, and in the time-fragment. But it is only because he has solved the problem or answered the question of madness to himself that he undertakes the project at all.

The Meeting with the Oyarsa as the Beginning of the Return

But before we turn our full attention to the fragment, then to *Perelandra*, then to *That Hideous Strength*, let me consider the climactic episodes of Ransom's sojourn on that very different world of Malacandra, in part because they are the beginning of the journey homeward to habitual self, in part because they more or less ideally illustrate the intermixture that makes up *Out of the Silent Planet*, and in part because they seem sometimes to have been misunderstood. These are in Chapters 17 through 20, the arrival at Meldilorn (including Ransom's meeting with the *pfifltrigg*), the meeting with the Oyarsa, the arrival of Weston and Devine (with Weston's "performance"), and the conversation of Weston and the Oyarsa. This last in particular has been attacked on what I take to be incorrect (though far from frivolous) grounds, by critics perhaps unaware of Swift; but all four need to be placed in proper context. One might say in proper eighteenth-century context. Let me begin by taking the objection commonly made to Weston's "conversation" with the Oyarsa.

In one form or another it is essentially that the whole affair is low comedy, even slapstick, inconsonant with the dignity of whatever proper role the critic is envisioning for Lewis (or for Ransom). But this is very like the kind of attack levied against Swift in Gulliver (leaving out the part of the attack devoted to Swiftian scatology) and indeed levied against Swift generally. What the critics seem (to me) to be missing is the fact that *Out of the Silent Planet* and the rest of the Ransom stories are no more realistic fiction than Swift's Gulliver or Johnson's Rasselas or even Defoe's Crusoe are realistic fiction. They are told realistically, to be sure. There is an accumulation of "realistic" details. But listen for a moment to Gulliver's departure from the Land of the Houyhnhnms (*A Voyage to the Country of the Houyhnhnms*, p. 265, Bantam ed.), and reflect on the question whether Swift or Lewis is painting in strokes of broader comedy. (And one might well reflect, at least in passing, on the question whether there is not indeed an obvious connection between the language of the Houyhnhnms, with its persistent initial "h," and the similar language of the *hrossa*— a point which I owe to my friend Charles Huttar.)

Gulliver departs. "I was forced to wait above an hour for the tide, and then observing the wind very fortunately bearing towards the island, to which I intended to steer my course, I took a second leave of my master: but as I was going to prostrate myself to kiss his hoof, he did me the honour to raise it gently to my mouth. I am not ignorant how much I have been censured for mentioning this last particular. Detractors are pleased to think it improbable, that so illustrious a person should descend to give so great a mark of distinction to a creature so inferior as I." Perhaps we should expand the question to include not only broader comedy but more savage satire. And perhaps, as Gulliver's canoe is made from the skins of the Yahoos, even these questions are mild.

Certainly the use of this kind of apparent satiric anticlimax as climax has perfectly respectable literary antecedents. They go back far beyond Swift, at least to the character of Herod in the medieval morality plays, or pageants. Now let us look briefly at the other chief elements in the scene on Meldilorn and the return to Earth by Oyarsa's doing — the vision of Meldilorn with the (anticlimactic) meeting with the *pfifltrigg*, the "trial" before Oyarsa, and the arrival of Weston and Devine, with its own attendant anticlimax in Weston's speech. The vision of Meldilorn is in some ways very much the vision of the earthly paradise, for all that it is on a world other than the earth. But it is a "classic" vision, which I take to be very much an eighteenth-century phenomenon: "He had not looked for anything quite so classic, so virginal, as this bright grove — lying so still, so secret, in its coloured valley, soaring with inimitable grace so many hundred feet into the wintry sunlight ... sweet and faint the thin fragrance of the giant blooms came up to him" (p. 105).

Then (and already the description suggests the "prospects" of the eighteenth-century garden) comes the gradual learning that, like the garden, this is an achieved paradise. The *pfifltrigg*, with his bag-wig (or the appearance of one), is rather like an eighteenth-century version of a nineteenth-century craftsman — "rather like one of Arthur Rackham's dwarfs ... and rather like a little, old taxidermist whom Ransom knew in London" (pp. 112–113). He is both artist and artisan, in a way more common in past centuries than in ours. More to our present point, it is his people who carved the great reliefs depicting the Malacandrian story, built (I believe) the guest-house, and decorated the great stones that lead Ransom to the grove for his "trial."

The decorations (so to speak) that surround the "trial" itself are, of course, medieval and of our own world: "He might, when the time came, be pleading his cause before thousands or before millions: rank behind rank about him, and rank above rank over his head, the creatures that had never yet seen man, and whom man could not see, were waiting for his trial to begin" (p. 119) The resemblance to the ranks of heaven in the medieval cathedral comes to mind. But the function of the trial, within the pattern or structure of the book, is within quite a different tradition. Here we have an author conscious of himself as author more than as redactor: here we have (so to speak) Fielding revealing the truth of Tom

Jones's parentage, thus putting an end to his adventures, Gay sending the King's pardon to Macheath. The sword that has apparently been hanging over the protagonist's head from the outset (or very nearly the outset) is neatly whisked away — indeed, it was never there at all.

The arrival of Weston and Devine, with Ransom's seeing "the human form with almost Malacandrian eyes" (p. 125), is essentially a Swiftian exercise. When Gulliver returns from Brobdingnag, he sees his surroundings with Brobdingnagian eyes: "My wife ran out to embrace me, but I stooped lower than her knees, thinking she could otherwise never be able to reach my mouth. My daughter kneeled to ask me blessing, but I could not see her till she arose, having been so long used to stand with my head and eyes erect to above sixty foot…" (Bantam ed., p. 149). And from this we pass into the comedy of Weston's conversation, ending with his attempt to entertain the Oyarsa as once he entertained a baby niece, followed by fourteen compulsory cold douches, his dismissal, and then the trip back to Thulcandra, a "conclusion, in which nothing is concluded."

Those six words are the title of the final chapter of Dr. Johnson's *The History of Rasselas, Prince of Abissinia*, which, despite obvious surface dissimilarities, has much in common with *Out of the Silent Planet* — or rather, *Out of the Silent Planet* with it. Not only are they much of a length, but the structures are remarkably like, both being travels intermixed with philosophy — with the story more in the philosophy than in the travels. Since a guided tour of *Rasselas* would be out of place here, let me, in its place, quote one of the book's more recent editors (from the Penguin edition, pp 9ff). He observes that "we read Rasselas for the solidity of its wisdom … and the verbal force and skill with which that wisdom is pressed home, out of our realization that the author is concerned with fundamentals rather than incidentals … and for its humour" (p. 9). And he goes on to remark (p. 11) that "Johnson's thought is drawn by the horses of instruction rather than the tigers of wrath, to use Blake's distinction" and then to quote John Wain's characterization of Rasselas as putting "one in mind of a dragonfly — a purposeful and powerful body moving on wings of gauze" (p. 12). All of which describes *Out of the Silent Planet*. This is the same John Wain who was a younger (and sometimes discontented) member of the Inklings after the war.

At the end of his pilgrimage, Ransom returns to Thulcandra, and walking (possibly naked but I have never been sure) into a pub, orders "A pint of bitter, please" — thus echoing (perhaps unconsciously) Johnson's stanzas in which he asks of the "Hermit hoar, in solemn cell," the question "What is bliss? and which the way?" and receives the answer "Come, my lad, and drink some beer." Even if the precise echoing is unconscious, Lewis's own Johnsonian character comes out in the conclusion. Or perhaps "conclusion" is the wrong word, since there remains Chapter XXII, in which Lewis the author comes out from the wings, and the postscript in which Ransom criticizes Lewis's auctorial effort and provides a brief first-person reminiscence of Malacandra. This is all, I believe, within the eighteenth-century tradition, more than the modern.

Yes, there are unquestionably echoes of Lindsay's *Voyage to Arcturus* in *Out of the Silent Planet*, as might be expected from Lewis's references to the earlier book. For example, the Rise, Ransom's dream, and the Dark Tower. And there may be a greater influence from Lindsay in the time fragment, as we shall see (and perhaps a little in *That Hideous Strength*). But the "ghastly vision" of Tormance (*On Stories*, p. 145) contributed neither to Lewis's technique, nor his invented worlds, nor the kind of book he was writing in *Out of the Silent Planet*: it left a small impress on his visual imagination, and that was all.

III

The Dark Tower, or *An Exchange in Time*

This chapter deals with the uncompleted second of the Ransom novels, the time fragment, or "Othertime" fragment, to which Walter Hooper gave the name *The Dark Tower,* and to the completed version of which (existing for the present only in my own mind) I have given the title *An Exchange in Time* (or, possibly, alternatively, *An Exchange with Time*). When he had finished *Out of the Silent Planet,* the visit to Malacandra, the problem Lewis faced was how to have Ransom, who has been given a special revelation on Malacandra, make use of that revelation in fulfilling God's saving purposes. Had Lewis finished the time fragment, this would, I believe, have been what it was "about"—and I can reconstruct roughly the theological line I think it would have taken. While my suggested title may recall J. W. Dunne's *An Experiment with Time,* the word "exchange" should not merely recall Charles Williams but give a strong indication of what Ransom's function might have been, and what the novel would have been.

The novel was begun before *Perelandra,* which came to usurp its place as the second book of the trilogy (a rightful usurper, one might say in Chesterton's manner). I believe Lewis tried again to finish it in 1944–45, as the second or third book in a tetralogy, after he had finished *That Hideous Strength* and while Tolkien was working on *The Notion Club Papers* (which can be used as clues here, though with occasional difficulty). Then he gave up on it a second time, perhaps in May 1945, immediately following the death of his instructor in the way of exchange, Charles Williams. Finally, I believe he fair-copied what he had (destroying the old text) and may well have written Chapters 5 through 7 sometime around 1956, before finally quitting the project.

I am aware that Kathryn Lindskoog thinks *The Dark Tower* is by a hand other than Lewis's. It may be by a hand other than Lewis's, of course ("Never say 'never'"), but it seems unlikely to me, on internal evidence and on the evidence of a Tolkien letter. I should here thank Mrs. Lindskoog for her counsel while I was writing this essay, and Douglas Gresham for his. I have already thanked Walter Hooper for his help. Obviously my conclusions are my own: they cannot be held responsible for them, nor do they in fact agree with all of them.

On the matter of internal evidence, we should note that Lewis was "a voracious and retentive reader" (letter JRRT to JCL, December 1963), who was easily influenced by his models and did not settle into his recognized style until the early 1940s at the earliest. In anything written before that time, it might be expected that he would be searching for a style. One of his letters to E. M. W. Tillyard in *The Personal Heresy*, as Owen Barfield has remarked (*Light on C. S. Lewis*, ed. J. Gibb, 1965, p. x), is virtually pastiche. If *The Dark Tower* is not so well written as other Lewis books, we might (1) consider under whose influence it was written, (2) note that the first three chapters seem to have been written in 1938, the fourth in 1939 (or 1944–45), the rest in 1944–45, or even 1956, and (3) take cognizance of the fact that he apparently wrote himself into a corner and, failing to find a way out, or growing bored with the project, or in the wake of Charles Williams's death, simply stopped. As we will see, it may be that the existing manuscript was fair-copied much later, perhaps in 1956, as a prelude to a continuation that never occurred. If this happened, it would not invalidate our conclusions, though we might want to seek an impetus for the planned continuation.

The date of composition is not to be determined by whether Gervase Mathew heard Lewis read the story or whether Lewis read it to the Inklings (being dissatisfied and not having a story that "went" anywhere, it would not be surprising if he read something else instead). The question of authorship is not to be determined by whether the story is inferior to Lewis's other long fiction (it is certainly not much inferior to *The Pilgrim's Regress*). Nor is the point at issue that the book shows a dark side of Lewis: it is hard for me to see how it is darker than some of *The Pilgrim's Regress*. My point here is simply that the beginning of the book fits not only as a first attempt at following up *Out of the Silent Planet*, but as a first attempt at a middle work between *Out of the Silent Planet* and *That Hideous Strength*. I would also say that, as I have said before, though there are arid stretches and places where Lewis is still seeking his own style, the parts that are good are too good and too "Ludovician" to be by another hand.

Moreover, it seems to me evident that the Othertime is an attempt at a "scientifictional" version of the Kingdom of Faerie, and later in this chapter I suggest some origins and even some episodes that Lewis did not write but (I think) intended. This is something the Lewis of the war years (and just before) might well have essayed, but with which the postwar Lewis might just as well have been bored. In any case, I think one fundamental weakness of *The Dark Tower* lies in the attempt to combine the novel of ideas with the allegory implicit (since Spenser) in Faerie, as though we could expect serious philosophical discourse in a medieval morality play. Another may lie in the influence of *A Voyage to Arcturus*.

The relevant Tolkien letter is one to Christopher Tolkien (in *The Letters of J. R. R. Tolkien* [1981], p. 105, 18 December 1944), in which he says Lewis's "fourth (or fifth?) novel is brewing, and seems likely to clash with mine (my dimly projected third)"—which is to say, with *The Notion Club Papers*. Now *The Notion Club Papers* is a time-travel story of a sort, beginning from an Inklings-like group including a man named Ramen (which I take to be a version of the Middle-earth "raimen" or "ransom"). It would certainly conflict with this fragment and equally certainly not with anything else Lewis wrote.

At least one knowledgeable observer — one who knows far more than I about the last ten years of Lewis's life — has suggested to me that the fragment was in fact written at one time, about 1956, and that Tolkien's letter refers to an idea that Lewis had discussed with Tolkien, but not to the story in this manuscript. If that is the case, the existing manuscript was not broken off because of Williams's death, but perhaps because Lewis's life had taken a new turn with the advent of Joy Davidman Gresham, and his interest in his story of a time-travel and scientifictional Faerie had declined. What is clear is that the story was in his mind in 1944–1945. I believe part of it was there earlier, and even written earlier. My friend John Rateliff says the manuscript shows no sign of discontinuity in the physical characteristics of the writing. A 1956 fair-copying or even a 1956 new attempt at writing up an earlier idea would fit in with this.

Dr. Rateliff also tells me that there is a date in the year 1945 on the back of one of the pages of the manuscript of *The Dark Tower*, suggesting that Lewis had returned to it at that time: I take it that the statement toward the beginning that the action takes place in 1938 suggests that was the year in which it was begun. Again, "Never say 'never'"—but the evidence suggests to me that the manuscript is Lewis's. I am forced to consider the question because it was recently in certain circles a *cause célèbre,* possibly through some misapprehensions as to what constitutes textual evidence of authorship, what parts of style are innate or perhaps genotypic, if any, and what parts are learned or acquired or perhaps phenotypic. It would never occur to me that the fragment was not Lewis's on internal evidence, and I believe that the tests Mrs. Lindskoog arranged showed that the later parts certainly were by Lewis. And then there is the external evidence of Tolkien's letter.

I said the book would have been a "scientifictional" version of Faerie, but what kind—that is, what genus—of book would it have been, beyond the simple designation as a "conversational" novel? It would, I believe, have been more like *That Hideous Strength* (and more like *Out of the Silent Planet*) than like *Perelandra*. The heraldry would have been there, to be sure, and indeed some of it is. The very existence of the Dark Tower and the White Riders, the stone seats and the dais in the Tower, the lances of the Riders—the curious medievalism of the "normal" life in the Othertime—all suggest a kind of heraldry (and "Englishness") not far from that of *That Hideous Strength*, and also Spenser's influence at work. Of course, the cruelty and bloodshed of the book, along with the medievalism—at least hinted at in the passages we have—reveal its origins in Faerie. Even so, the scientists of the Othertime, the jerkies, the Stingingman, have a considerable amount in common with the scientists, the dehumanized servants, and the Head of the N.I.C.E. One can easily imagine a "trilogy" in which the middle volume is not *Perelandra* but (to take my conjectural title) *An Exchange in Time*, with Ransom first traveling in space, then in time, and then staying put.

I think the book would have been more dry, perhaps more "rational" than *Perelandra*, in keeping with the picture that began it, and in keeping with the "scientific" or "scientifictional" nature of the time-travel problem. It is possible, even likely, that Lewis would have employed the same kind of parallelism between our time and Othertime that he subsequently used between Belbury and St Anne's in *That Hideous Strength*— though it may also be that reluctance to take on that kind of complex plot structure was part of what lay behind his putting the fragment aside (we have, I would say, perhaps a small third of the book). I would argue that he was prepared to write a "conversational" novel with more action than *Out of the Silent Planet*, but not yet (if ever) to write a novel of action. And here I had better pause to rebut a possible criticism of my views on Lewis's ability to plot stories.

Walter Hooper has commented on Lewis's juvenilia, the "Boxen" stories, that "There is not the slightest bit of evidence on a single page of the juvenilia that the author had to labour to find 'filling' for his really good plots; the stories seem to write themselves" (*Of Other Worlds*, p. vi). Here, of course, he speaks as the expert, and I under possible correction, but it does occur to me that a boy who entitles his juvenile creations *Boxen: Or, Scenes from Boxonian City Life*, or *The Life of John, Lord Big of Bigham, in 3 Volumes*, has fairly definite models before him, from precisely the sort of books we would expect to find on his father's bookshelves. (And was not Mr. Bigge then the secretary to the Prince of Wales?)

We should not be too far wrong, I think, if we traced the titles to such originals as, say, *The Life of Henry, Lord Brougham, in Three Volumes* (I pick this from my own father's books), and though I cannot just now trace the origins of the Boxen subtitle, I am sure others can, and they will be found in some English or Irish three-decker of the earlier nineteenth century. (Or perhaps something by Pierce Egan?) Well, perhaps not a three-decker; but the style of the title suggests an original from sometime between, say, 1710, and, say, 1860. In any event, we cannot say whether Lewis's juvenile plots were derivative, as I suspect they were, until someone with greater knowledge than mine turns his attention to the problem. But I doubt the juvenilia can, at the present time, be used as a case in point for Lewis's facility with plots. That matter aside, let me return to the time fragment, whether *The Dark Tower* or *An Exchange in Time*. Lewis has introduced us to six characters (or seven if one counts

Lewis himself), two of whom are known to have doubles in Othertime, and three of whom (counting Lewis) seem unlikely to have any major part in the book. MacPhee presumably will play much the same part he plays in *That Hideous Strength*—in fact, it has been suggested that he is already, in the fragment we have, playing that role at far too great a length (Owen Barfield, quoted by Walter Hooper in "A Note on *The Dark Tower*" in *The Dark Tower*, 1977, p. 97). Lewis is there to record the action, though, I suppose, he might have a double, as Scudamour and Camilla do, and Orfieu may. About Ransom we shall see.

It might be argued that Cyril Knellie is merely a portrayal of an academic "type" on a par with the portrayals of the Bracton Senior Common Room. Indeed, I detect a kind of academic pun in the fact that a man named Knellie is "nice in his eating," though I decline to believe he is there only for the sake of the pun, or only to the provide us with an academic portrait. In the fragment he does contribute to the confusion that allows Scudamour's double to escape, but he is not necessary for that purpose—though I think I know why he is there and what use Lewis intended to make of him. Lewis did from time to time in his books introduce us to characters who then do very little—Grace Ironwood is an example—and it may be that would have been Knellie's fate. But I think Knellie's character would have played a part—perhaps the drinks in his rooms also—in an exchange in time through the principle of resemblance invoked in the smokehorse and its house, as we shall see.

In the end, it may be, what produced the fragmentariness of the time-travel fragment was in part the fact that the framework on which the story is built—the machine, in the neoclassical sense—was difficult to work with: I think Lewis was going on to explore another machine more like the one originally used in the Othertime—that is how Cyril Knellie was going to be used. But I believe what stopped the book (if it was stopped in 1945) was in fact the death of Charles Williams. In a moment I will get to what I think was the picture of origin for the book, comparable to the bubble-tree for *Perelandra*. In the mean time, I do not want it thought that I believe *The Dark Tower* (which I am tentatively rechristening *An Exchange in Time*) to be generally "odd-man-out" among the Ransom stories: despite being a time story rather than a space story it is much more like the other three than it is unlike them. In fact, everything I know about *Perelandra* seems to suggest it is the "odd man out" in the Ransom books, and the "trilogy" might have been better ordered had the fragment been finished and been the middle volume. I think that true, though *Perelandra* is certainly closer to being a great work than the fragment would have been, and though I am far from wanting to give it up. I suppose I have reread it thirty times or more. I have reread *The Dark Tower* thrice.

The scenes and themes I have considered (and extrapolated) in *An Exchange in Time*, for the purposes of this essay, are (1) the academic beginning and particularly the "chronoscope" sections, noting the inspiration for the "chronoscope," (2) the discussion of the nature of time, with some comparison with discussion of time in *That Hideous Strength*, (3) Scudamour's visit to the place of the Stationary Smokehorses, implied in the text as we have it, with its origins and meaning, and (4) the return to our time, which is necessary for there to be a story at all, and which has at least partly taken place between the existing chapters four and five of the fragment. Of course, these latter two, though implied or necessary, are my extrapolations. In trying to reconstruct what Lewis might have done with the novel had he finished it, what comes first to mind is that the names of the characters provide us with a pretty good idea of the story Lewis would have told.

In particular, Scudamour will be a knight rescuing the true Camilla, Orfieu (Orfeo) will also be the rescuer of someone in Othertime (I can even suggest a name — Grace Hourday), Ransom will be the ransom for the person lost — all of which suggests that the book, when finished, would have been sufficiently "theological" in its concerns to take its place with the other Ransom stories.

In the Beginning: The Chronoscope

I would guess that the picture of origin for the book comes from Tolkien's "On Fairy Stories," where he refers to "a time-telescope focused on one spot" ("On Fairy Stories," as reprinted in *The Monsters and the Critics*, p. 147): wherever it may come from, it does not seem to have led readily to anyplace else, and the writing may have been hard slogging.

But let us look at that passage in "On Fairy Stories" where the phrase is used, because the way in which it is used may give us a clue to the effect it had on Lewis, when this story was beginning to take root in his mind.

It is a passage in which Tolkien is talking about *Mooreeffoc* or Chestertonian fantasy. *Mooreeffoc* is "a fantastic word, but it could be seen written up in every town in this land" (*Monsters and Critics*, p. 146), being "Coffee-room" as viewed from the inside through a glass door. It represents a kind of fantasy whose "recovery of freshness of vision is its only virtue" (p. 147)— but that is indeed a virtue. Here is the whole "time-telescope" passage (p. 147): "The word *Mooreeffoc* may cause you to realise that England is an utterly alien land, lost either in some remote past age glimpsed by history, or in some strange dim future reached only by a time-machine; to see the amazing oddity and interest of its inhabitants and their customs and feeding-habits; but it cannot do more than that: act as a time-telescope focused on one spot."

From this, I believe there came into Lewis's mind, first, a picture of a time-telescope focused on one spot, which is in fact the chronoscope; second, the idea of an utterly alien land sharing the location of the land of England; and third, as a twist on the second, the idea that the odd customs and feeding-habits of its inhabitants would be our own, or at least an imaginative picture and extrapolation of our own. And because the passage is from the lecture "On Fairy Stories," I think this utterly alien land sharing the location of England in Othertime was Faerie. Perhaps it is not coincidence that when (according to my conjecture) Lewis took his unfinished book off the desk in 1945, Tolkien was taking his unpublished lecture off his desk and setting about making it into the essay published in the Charles Williams *Festschrift*. Certainly when Tolkien mentioned Lewis's "fourth — or fifth" novel in a letter to his son Christopher, it was to deal with the descendants of Seth (that is, humankind) and the descendants of Cain (which is what the "good people" were argued to be in the Middle Ages).

The book begins (*The Dark Tower*, p. 17) in Orfieu's study, with those present being Orfieu (Orfeo?), a Cambridge philosopher, Scudamour, his assistant, MacPhee, (described as a sceptic and sceptical philosopher) from Manchester, Ransom (described as "the pale man with the green shade over his grey, distressed-looking eyes"), and Lewis himself, who owes his presence to Ransom. The description of Ransom makes it clear that this book is set after *Out of the Silent Planet* but before *Perelandra*. The discussion of the chronoscope (Ransom's word) is in fact a discussion of the impossibilities of sequential time travel, of J. W. Dunne's *An Experiment with Time*, and a brief reference to Orfieu's physiological research on the "Z substance in the human brain" which is the organ of memory and prevision (pp. 23–24). A Cambridge philosopher in the 1930s would be likely to be carrying out both philosophical and physiological research, and a Manchester philosopher would be likely to be a sceptic: the identifications are almost dictated by the characters. What universities would we expect but Cambridge and Manchester? Ransom was already identified in *Out of the Silent Planet* as a Cambridge don: so we are not surprised to find that Lewis is the only Oxford man present (p. 22). Note, by the way, the similarity to the opening scenes of H. G. Wells's *The Time Machine*, and even George Gaylord Simpson's later *The Dechronization of Sam Magruder.*

After some discussion of Dunne (pp. 20–23), we come to the chronoscope, in the next room to Orfieu's study (p. 24). This chronoscope's "most obvious feature was a white sheet about four feet square stretched on a framework of canes as if for a magic lantern performance." On a table immediately in front of the sheet "stood a battery with a bulb. Higher than the bulb, and between it and the sheet," there was hung "a small bunch or tangle of some diaphanous material, arranged into a complicated pattern of folds and convolutions, rather reminiscent of the shapes that a mouthful of smoke assumes in still air" — this tangle being the chronoscope itself. And this whole passage being, by way of disagreement with Mrs. Lindskoog, one of the passages I think too "Ludovician" to be by any other hand than Lewis's: to me it is both reminiscent of the description of the primitive computer or "pragmatometer" in *That Hideous Strength*, and (in the phrase "complicated pattern of folds") reminiscent of the description of Merlin shaven in the same book.

Note also the reference (p. 50) to the replacement of one Stingingman by another "according to the rules of some sort of diabolical civil service" at the discussion at lunch among the five scholars, when it is suggested that this Othertime is in fact hell. Ransom, of course (p. 49), argues that it is not hell but "our own world over again" and that it would need to be faced "even if one were taken there." When I think of a world in amidst our own to which one is taken, I think of Faerie and Thomas of Ercildoun. When I think of a diabolical civil service, I think of an idea followed out in *The Screwtape Letters* (1940–41), and note that the phrase occurs here in Chapter 3, which I believe was written in 1938. Perhaps at least one of Lewis's books began with a picture he himself created. In any case, let me note two points suggesting that Othertime is a scientifictional Faerie.

First, K, who first formulated the theory of time attraction, succeeded in exchanging a child from Othertime into our time, or as he put it from the Othertime perspective, he juxtaposed the this-time child with its Othertime counterpart when the Othertimer was asleep, and ordered the this-time child to escape if it could (p. 90)—which it did. This was K's "celebrated 'Exchange.'" And of course it provides a scientifictional controlled exchange that left a changeling child in our time, or, if you prefer, our world. But there had doubtless been uncontrolled exchanges before, as there have been changelings from "Faerie" throughout our history.

Second, the description of perpetual time (p. 87) gives a logical construct for an immortality in time, such as is popularly reputed to exist for Faerie (and perhaps for Tolkien's elvenkind). Since timelines can intersect in two-dimensional time, and one can pass endlessly from one timeline to another at these points of intersection (which have the same contents of past, present, and future), even though the box of time itself is finite. But with the chronoscope, one can slide from one timeline to another, even if the two do not quite intersect. This sounds rather like a present-day TV show. But to our point, like the changelings, the immortality of Faerie has been given a logical basis. I leave it for others more expert in the history of science fiction than I how much the Othertime time logic resembles the syllogismobile in the roughly contemporaneous Pratt and DeCamp *Incompleat Enchanter*. What is important here is that it is another pointer toward Othertime as Faerie.

We will see shortly whether these pointers can also be used, as I think they can, to suggest scenes and events that Lewis did not get around to writing. Here I believe we may find some help in the names of Scudamour and Camilla (from Spenser's *Faerie Queene*) and Orfieu. Orfieu, in this case, must have some relation to the version of the medieval "Sir Orfeo" translated by Professor Tolkien sometime in the 1930s, though the story of Orpheus and Eurydice is of course far older than the Middle Ages. From these clues, we will try to reconstruct two scenes Lewis did not write, after a look at the nature of time and Othertime in the existing fragment. And not only from these clues. I believe Tolkien's unfinished *Notion Club Papers* reflects the same discussions on time travel that Lewis's fragment reflects, and the completed work would have reflected more strongly. I believe the *Notion Club Papers* can therefore be used for additional clues on the mechanism of time exchange in Lewis's mind. Indeed, these are Tolkien's attempt to write the time-travel story that was to accompany Lewis's space-travel story back in 1938. What more natural than that Lewis would adapt Tolkien's notions to his own time-travel story?

The Nature of Time and the Nature of Exchange

Exchange is the link between our world and the perilous realms — being, in this case, a "machine" of the sort used by H. G. Wells in *The Time Machine*. I have ventured to suggest for the completed novel the title *An Exchange in Time*, or even *An Exchange with Time*. To see why — and whether there is any merit in the suggestion — we should look at the nature of time suggested in the novel, and the nature and meaning of the act of exchange, as Lewis would have understood it in 1945 (or even 1956).

In *That Hideous Strength*, written in 1943, Lewis remarks that Merlin had not died, but his life had been "sidetracked, moved out of our one-dimensional time, for fifteen centuries." The eldila had discovered his state "not from inspection of the thing that slept under Bragdon Wood, but from observing a unique configuration in that place where those things remain that are taken off time's main-road, behind the invisible hedges, into the unimaginable fields. Not all the times that are outside the present are therefore past or future" (pb ed., pp. 202–03). He later experimented, in the Narnia books, with the idea of separate time-streams for England and Narnia, for the Pevensie children, who were kings and queens in Narnia, but who did not live in this world past their young adulthood, and for Eustace Clarence Scrubb and Jill Pole, and Digory and Polly.

In *That Hideous Strength*, it was the same Merlin in the fifth century of our time and the twentieth. In the Narnia books, the children from our world had the adventures in Narnia, but was the Lucy who was a grown-up queen in Narnia when she welcomed Aravis in *The Horse and His Boy* the same Lucy who died in the train wreck in England in *The Last Battle*? In what sense the same? Lewis was (on my showing) writing the fragment that Walter Hooper calls *The Dark Tower* while he was writing on or at least thinking out *That Hideous Strength*, but the problem of Othertime is more like the problem of Narnian time than it is like Merlin (which might support the proposed 1956 date). Nevertheless, there is still a clue to the problem of *An Exchange in Time*—the Dunnean exchange — in *That Hideous Strength*. The clue is in the word "one-dimensioned"—the time in Lewis's Othertime is two-dimensioned (*The Dark Tower*, pb ed., pp. 85–88), with timelines running both backward-forward and andward-eckward. Moreover, they are wavy lines: backward-forward lines deviate from the straight in andward-eckward directions; andward-eckward lines deviate from the straight in forward-backward directions.

When two timelines intersect, the point of intersection will be a historical moment common to both timelines (*The Dark Tower*, pp. 83–84) — "in other words, the total state of the universe in time A at moment X [the intersection] will be identical with the total state of the universe in time B at moment X. Now like states or events have like results. Therefore the whole future of time A (that is, its whole content in the forward direction) will duplicate the whole future of time B (that is its whole content in the andward direction)." (But they are not the same timeline because one moves forward and one moves andward.) Finally, the practical application (p. 90), "The whole theory of time attraction was ... brought into being, and formulated in K's law that 'Any two timelines approximate in the exact degree to which their contents are alike.'"

As Hooper has pointed out in his "Note" to *The Dark Tower* (p. 93), Lewis seems to have combined — for the purposes of this book — J. W. Dunne's belief that dreams are composed of images of past experience and images of future experience, with the experience of "Elizabeth Morison" and "Frances Lamont" (Charlotte Anne Elizabeth Moberley 1846–1937 and Eleanor Frances Jourdain 1863–1924) recounted in *An Adventure* (1911). These two English ladies from St Hugh's College (Oxford) visited the Trianon on August 10, 1901, their first visit, and saw it — so far as anyone can tell — through the eyes of Marie Antoinette in 1792. Orfieu's remarks to MacPhee (p. 21) put it clearly: "If you'd read the story of the two English ladies at Trianon with an open mind, MacPhee, you would know there is on record at least one indisputable instance in which the subjects saw a whole scene from a part of the past long before their birth. And if you had followed up that hint, you would have found the real explanation of all the so-called ghost stories which people like you have to explain away.... I, at any rate, am perfectly satisfied that our experience of the past — what you call 'memory' — is not limited to our own lives."

The "scientifictional" basis of the "chronoscope" is also given by Orfieu, its inventor (pp. 23–24). "'We know that all the mind's perceptions are exercised by means of the body. And we have discovered how to extend them by means of instruments, as we extend our sight by the telescope or, in another sense, by the camera. Such instruments are really artificial organs, copied from the natural organs: the lens is a copy of the eye. To make a similar instrument for our time-perceptions we must find the time-organ and then copy it. Now I claim to have isolated what I call the Z substance in the human brain. On the purely physiological side my results have been published. But what has not yet been published [Orfieu continued] is the proof that the Z substance is the organ of memory and prevision. And starting from that, I have been able to construct my chronoscope.'"

I think it very likely that the invention of a chronoscope in the Othertime would have been recorded on the page immediately following the end of the existing fragment (*Dark Tower*, p. 91): "'Meanwhile,' the book continued, 'Q had been experimenting with the possibilities of some inanimate instrument which might give us a view of Othertime [here meaning our own time] without the need of the old precarious psychological exertions. In 74 he produced his'" (the manuscript breaks off here at the foot of folio 64). Given the rule of time attraction noted above, that any two time lines approximate in the exact degree to which their material contents are alike, the machinery is now in place for our *Exchange in Time*, with nearly identical chronoscopes here and in Othertime, along with the dark Tower, and the Smokehorses.

Of course, there is also the rule of psychological attraction between times and Othertimes. This would explain the presence of Cyril Knellie, the aged author of *Erotici Graeci Minimi, Table-talk of a Famous Florentine Courtesan,* and *Lesbos: A Masque.* As the fragment stands, he seems dragged in, particularly given the fact that folio 11 is missing, which contained an account of a visit to Knellie's rooms in the college. But the theory of time attraction holds that any two time lines approximate to the degree that their contents are alike: I suspect that Knellie's place in the *machina* was as a mind whose fantasies, Lewis would say, ran in the depraved patterns of the Othertime, thereby increasing the time attraction. This view would seem to be supported by the scene in which Knellie enters into the "observatory" (pp. 50–52) and then "appreciates" the "supreme genius to whom we are indebted for this fantasia" of the Stingingman in Othertime.

In the fragment we have, Scudamour (the Cambridge Scudamour) changes places with his Othertime double, who is the Stingingman (pp. 53–59). I would not be surprised if the Stingingman and his victims are in some way connected with Stalin's Russia, even though Lewis was known for having so little political knowledge that he thought the Yugoslav dictator Tito was king of Greece (in *Brothers and Friends,* p. 236). When we look at the description of the first Stingingman (*Dark Tower,* p. 32), yellowish complexion, the unmoving face, the stiff and lustreless hair, we see something of Oriental despotism. To be sure, readers of *That Hideous Strength* might say, "Francois Alcasan, to the life, (or, rather, to the death)," even to the reference to the blade of the guillotine (p. 32). But this is in what I believe to be the 1938 part of the book, and if I am right, Alcasan must come from this, not the other way 'round. I think the Stingingman and the Jerkies have an origin in political satire — though I admit that sounds more like George Orwell than C. S. Lewis — and I think that while the original satire may have been based on Nazi Germany, it would have been based in the end at least in part on Stalinist Russia, because Stalinist Russia was the totalitarianism available for the satirizing. And while Lewis may not have known what country Tito was tyrannizing over, he did unquestionably recognize the characteristics of tyranny, by whomever practiced. Nonetheless, the trappings seem to be largely those of Nazi Germany.

The presences in Othertime are still, in some sense, "there" in the Othertime, and possibly in ours (p. 32)—because time has more than one dimension. Now what of the nature of the exchange? Here Williams is important, but more important may be some of Tolkien's reflections in *The Notion Club Papers*. Still, let us look first at Williams: I note that the mention of the word "exchange" in connection with Charles Williams calls to my mind some of Williams's phrases and titles: "The Way of Exchange"—"The Doctrine of Substitution"—"your life and your death are with your neighbor"—"at the hand of every man's brother will I require the life of man"—the single word "coinherence." These are keynotes to the mystical theology of romantic love preached by Charles Williams to his co-workers at the Oxford University Press, his friends, and the Companions of the Co-inherence. When Lewis mentioned "K's celebrated 'Exchange'" in the fragment (if indeed he was writing the continuation in 1944–1945), Charles Williams and his "Way of Exchange" were very much in his mind: I think it probable that the fragment was put aside for the second time because Williams's death intervened, and there was work to do on the *Festschrift* (which was already begun) and the *Arthurian Torso* (which was not). And if Lewis was looking forward to working out the implications of his exchange with Williams, that alone might have sufficed for him to break off when Williams died. I think it likely that much of Chapters V through VII was first written sometime before Williams's death on May 13, 1945 — even if (as I am increasingly convinced), the fragment was written in four installments, the last in 1956, at which time, as preparation for his continuing the story, Lewis fair-copied (and then destroyed) all he had written before.

We can see how the book might go on. Someone from our time may go into the Othertime to deliver someone there, a perfect exchange and substitution. Who better than the man whose name shares Christ's nature — Ransom? We remember the passage in *Perelandra* (pb ed., p. 147): "'It is not for nothing that you are named Ransom' said the Voice" — never mind that the name is from Ranulf's son — and then (p. 148) "'My name also is Ransom' said the Voice." But if Ransom stays behind as ransom (and given the description this is clearly Ransom before he came back bursting with new life and strength from *Perelandra*), how will he travel to Perelandra and how become the ageless young-old Pendragon and Fisher King in *That Hideous Strength*? Or are we here treading close to a miracle so great it would wrench the story apart? Could this be one of the reasons the time fragment remained a fragment?

It is worth noting that the language of Othertime contains no word for God (*Dark Tower*, p. 89) — another indication that we are in Faerie, and also setting the scene for a coming of a Christ-figure. Not Lewis surely, not the sceptic MacPhee, not the non-believer Orfieu, not Scudamour who has a double and has traveled through the linked chronoscopes: the only ransom can be Ransom himself. Acting, as it were, for Ransom Himself. Or Ransom's double in Faerie, bringing souls to those who have none, the people of Faerie, the descendants of Cain. To be sure, I believe Orfieu will go — but not as the Ransom.

I thought of Orpheus going after Eurydice and then looking back and failing. But as we will see, that is not the story in "Sir Orfeo" — there the good knight brings back his Heurodis (ll. 593–594, in J. R. R. Tolkien, trans., *Sir Gawain and the Green Knight, Pearl, Sir Orfeo* (pb ed., p. 148). And by the way, I believe, though this is highly speculative, that as Orfeo became Orfieu in the fragment, so Heurodis would have become "Hourday" or "Miss Hourday" (perhaps even "Grace Hourday") — a character not yet introduced in the fragment as it stands, but one perhaps in Lewis's mind from the time he named his characters. Now what light can *The Notion Club Papers* cast on all this?

As Tolkien's idea of the time-travel or time-exchange mechanism progressed, he came to a time exchange through names, inheritance, poetry, and dreams. His time-travellers, who bring an Atlantean storm to our time (but Tolkien's future time — 1987) out of the ancient past, are Alwin Arundel Lowdham (son of Edwin Lowdham), and Wilfrid Trewyn Jeremy. But when they travel to the days of King Edward, Alfred's son, they are Aelfwine, Eadwine's son, and Treowine — and Arundel is not from the Sussex coast but from Earendel, the Morning-Star, and Earendil, the Mariner. Tolkien postulates a connection between the Anglo-Saxon (and Lombard) peoples, and the downfall of Atlantis

(Numenor). That is properly the subject for a paper on Tolkien: what is important here is that Alwin Arundel Lowdham in the 1900s and Aelfwine in the 900s are not the same person, but Lowdham sees with Aelfwine's eyes and in a sense is in Aelfwine's body to such a degree that it is *his* body. And if a connection of this sort suffices for an exchange along time, by a rule of time attraction, it should suffice for an exchange across time. Tolkien makes it clear that storm and battle can travel out of the past, and we can travel to them in the past: what is needed is the link.

In the time fragment the link is deliberate physical imitation by Othertime of our time. The mechanism is the construction of the storage house for the Stationary Smokehorses. I believe this would have been the scene in the perilous realm of the spirit, where the physical similarities of the places within our time and Othertime make it possible for someone to be dragged into Othertime if that person relaxes spiritual vigilance — though I do not know whether that would have happened in this case.

Scudamour and the Stationary Smokehorses

In Othertime, "In the year 60, Z, who had come to chronology from the study of folklore, propounded the theory that certain fabulous creatures, and other images which constantly appeared in the myths of widely separated peoples and in dreams, might be glimpses of realities which exist in a time closely adjacent to our own. This led to his famous experiment with the Smokehorse. He selected this familiar horror of the nursery because it is almost unique among such images in having arisen in historical times — no evidence having been found of its existence before the last century" (p. 88). When Z induces dreams and waking hallucinations of Smokehorses in children, he finds them much altered from the Smokehorses of tradition — to be expected since they are now the gleaming green ten-wheelers of the L.N.E.R. and other lines of modern (1945) England.

The next stage of discovery had to do with observation of Stationary Smokehorses in the southwestern region of the Othertime "England" —

which I take to be (at least putatively) the mining engines of Cornwall, though they could be locomotives in a roundhouse. K, the Othertimer who formulated the law of time attraction, succeeded in constructing a replica of the building where the stationary Smokehorses were stored. Now Lewis visited Cornwall sometime in 1944–45 (letter to the author from A. K. Hamilton Jenkin ca 1978). In his friend Jenkin's *The Story of Cornwall* (London 1934), we learn that James Watt's stationary steam-engines were used in the Cornish mines in 1777, that the first high-pressure steam-engines were developed by Richard Trevithick in Cornwall in 1801 (pp. 141–143), and the principle of the steam-blast locomotive adopted in 1829 by George Stephenson for the *Rocket* was first established by the Cornishman Goldsworthy Gurney (pp. 143–145). It is my belief that Lewis read this short history of Cornwall on his visit, perhaps on the train back home, and this was in his mind when he was writing about the Stationary Smokehorses (mine engines, though — as noted — perhaps simply line locomotives in a roundhouse).

But it may be that the mining scene was implicit in his choice of the name Scudamour in the first place, back in 1938. Certainly I would argue the likelihood that there was implicit in it the scene described in *The Faerie Queene*, (Book IV, Canto V, ll. 294ff): "Whereto approaching nigh, they heard the sound / Of many iron hammers beating rank / And answering their weary turns around, / That seemed some blacksmith dwelt in that desert ground /..../ In which his work he had six servants pressed / About the anvil standing evermore / With huge great hammers, that did never rest / From heaping strokes which thereon soused sore: / All six strong grooms, but one then other more; / For by degrees they all were disagreed; / So likewise did the hammers which they bore / Like bells in greatness orderly succeed / That he which was the last, did far the first exceed/..../So dreadfully he did the anvil beat, / That seemed to dust he shortly would it drive / So huge his hammer and so fierce his heat / That seemed a rock of diamond it could rive / And rend asunder quite, if he thereto list strive / Sir Scudamour there entering much admired / The manner of their work and weary pain / And having long beheld, at last enquired / The cause and end thereof, but all in vain / For they for nought would from their work refrain / Ne let his speeches come unto their ear...."

It is not unimportant for our purpose that the blacksmith is Care and the bellows weary sighs (this is a realm of the spirit), but it is less important than that Scudamour, in search of Amoret, enters the din of a forge, even a forge whose heat brings forth a mining simile, "It seemed a rock of diamond it could rive." True, this is not a mine, but here for comparison is Hamilton Jenkin's description of a Cornish mine (in *The Story of Cornwall*, 1934, p. 105): "In the United Mines, near St. Day, the temperature in the deep levels was nearly 115 degrees Fahrenheit, whilst the water was so hot that men were in danger of being scalded if they slipped into it. In some places the air was so bad a candle would scarcely burn. The holes which had to be made in the rock for blasting were drilled with a round iron bar. Two of the miners would beat this with heavy hammers, whilst another turned it." Here are the hammers and the heat, and with Lewis's voracious and retentive memory, and all being grist to his mill, I think we have a clue to one scene he did not write — a scene in the Othertime equivalent of Cornwall: Scudamour in the mines. Let us look at the original Scudamour.

Why was Scudamour travelling in Faerie in *The Faerie Queene*? He seeks his lady, fair Amoret (Book III, Canto XI, ll. 91ff): "My lady and my love is cruelly penned / In dolefull darkness from the view of day / Whilst deadly torments do her chaste breast rend / And the sharp steel doth rive her heart in tway / ... / Yet thou, vile man, vile Scudamour, art sound / Ne canst her aid, ne canst her foe dismay / Unworthy wretch to tread upon the ground / For whom so fair a lady feels so sore a wound." In the first draft of the fragment, Camilla (as of 1945 surnamed "Bembridge") was named Camilla Ammeret (Hooper, "A Note on *The Dark Tower*," p. 97), and while this Ammeret was not enchanted by Busirane and rescued by Britomart, I believe she was enchanted and was to be rescued.

In *The Faerie Queene*, Britomart had rescued Amoret from Busirane, then fallen asleep (Book IV, Canto VI, ll. 217–234), and while Britomart slept, Amoret disappeared: "I found her not where I left her whilere, / But thought she wandered was, or gone astray: / I called her loud, I sought her far and near; / But nowhere could her find, or tidings of her hear." Britomart and Scudamour return to the deserted forest where Amoret was lost. Actually, Amoret had been taken by "a wilde and salvage man; / Yet was no man, but only like in shape / And eke in nature higher by a span; All overgrown with hair…" (Book IV, Canto VII, ll. 37–40). She escapes, over leaping hedge and ditch, hill and dale, pursued by her raptor, until she chances on Belphoebe and is rescued. Then (in Canto VIII), Britomart and Scudamour come to the tournament, finally address the fighting knights, and then follows this passage (Book IV, Canto VIII, ll. 341–352): "Certes her loss ought me to sorrow most / Whose right she is, wherever she be strayed, / Through many perils won, and many fortunes wayed; / For from the first that I her love professed, / Unto this hour, this present luckless hour, / I never joyed happiness nor rest; / But thus turmoiled, from one to other stour / I waste my life, and do my days devour / In wretched anguish and incessant woe / Passing the measure of my feeble power; / That living thus a wretch and loving so, / I neither can my love ne yet my life forgo."

Then Sir Claribell entreats Scudamour, "That, as we ride together on our way, / Ye will recount to us in order due / All that adventure which ye did assay / For that fair ladies love…" (ll. 358–361). And then (ll. 362–364), "So gan the rest him likewise to require: / But Britomart did him importune hard / To take on him that paine…." The pain in question is the task of recounting the adventure, but to Lewis, rereading the passage with Charles Williams in mind, taking pain — any pain — on oneself would have had the added meaning of substitution and exchange. In passing, let me note that one of the essays Lewis or Williams ought to have written was a consideration of exchange and the famous "No man is an island" meditation, with its explanation of the uses of pain as treasure.

There follows, in Book IV, Canto X, Scudamour's account of his conquest of the virtuous Amoret, which seems a straightforward allegory of love, until the last stanza of the Canto, after which Spenser shifts to another tale (Book IV, Cantos XI and XII), before going on to Book V ("The Legend of Artegall, or of Justice") and the rest of his (incomplete) twelve books "fashioning XII moral vertues" as his title page tells us. Here is Scudamour's last stanza (Canto X, ll. 514–522): "'No less did Daunger threaten me with dread/ Whenas he saw me, maugre all his power, / That glorious spoil of beauty with me lead / Than Cerberus, when Orpheus did recower [recover] / His leman from the Stygian princes bower. / But evermore my shield did me defend/ Against the storms of every dreadful stour: / Thus safely with my love I thence did wend.' / So ended he his tale, where I this canto end." Here is Orpheus in Hades as counterpart to Scudamour in *The Faerie Queene.*

The guide that Spenser provides for what would have happened in Lewis's book is as incomplete as *The Faerie Queene,* but I have little doubt that the scene of the smithy, reinforced by Jenkin's descriptions of the Cornish mines, provides us with Scudamour's way back to our time — perhaps in connection with the White Riders. Surely as the Stingingman he would be able to devise a reason for going there, and there ought to be some hair's-breadth adventures on the way. (Will *they* or won't *they* suspect? Can he carry it off?) I think someone dear to Orfeo may be exchanged during Scudamour's exchange — necessarily, I think, whoever plays the part of Orfieu's Eurydice. The final return to our time would then be Orfieu's return with his Eurydice. (I have toyed with the idea that the character of this Eurydice became part of the character of Grace Ironwood.)

The scene when Scudamour as Stingingman visits the place of the Stationary Smokehorses would emphasize the heat and din and weary pain. The Othertimers have constructed their smokehorses from the nightmares of our children, and Lewis's Faerie (land of the descendants of Cain) is soulless, cruel, and bloody. In our world and time the heat and cacophony and pain are bad enough, but there they would be deliberately worse, so the children of Othertime would want to escape.

The idea (what Spenser would have called a conceit) that we have doubles in Othertime, in Faerie, is parallelled by a set of doublets in Genesis, for the descendants of Cain and the descendants of Seth. In Chapter IV of Genesis, the line from Cain (Adam's disinherited eldest son), living east of Eden in the Land of Nod, goes to Enoch, Irad, Mehujael, Methusael, Lamech, and then three sons, Jabal, Jubal, and Tubal-cain. In Chapter V the line from Seth (Adam's third son and heir) goes to Enos, Cainan, Mahalaleel, Jared, Enoch, Methuselah, Lamech, Noah, and then three sons, Shem, Ham, and Japheth. I think those doublets were in Lewis's mind when he was working on this book, as *The Book of the Secrets of Enoch* had been in his mind when he was working on *Perelandra.*

Now when Scudamour returns to our time (as he evidently does from the fragment we have in *The Dark Tower*), it could be that he returns without his Camilla (exchanging in the process with the Othertime Scudamour), then goes back to rescue her (setting the Stingingman back in our own time), then returns with her in a double exchange. But this is too complicated a plot. Perhaps Ransom will go into Othertime with Orfieu and they will bring back the Eurydice. Perhaps Orfieu will return first and Ransom will seem to be lost, then will return unexpectedly. But until someone tries to finish the novel, we do not need to know exactly how the plot line would go. There is certainly one return to our time — Scudamour's. I think there are two — Scudamour's and Orfieu's. That is what the names suggest, and I believe that is what is necessary to round out the story and link it with what comes after.

The Return to Our Time

Here our text is the medieval ballad of *Sir Orfeo*, which Tolkien translated into modern English about 1938. (Like the discovery of the "P" substance in Cambridge in the 1930s, this date suggests a 1930s start for the book.) The lines that follow might be used to describe the carnage of war in Othertime: in the ballad (ll. 387–400) they describe the scene within the walls of the proud castle of the king of Faerie: "Then he began to gaze about / and saw within the walls a rout / of folk that were thither drawn below / and mourned as dead, but were not so. / For some there stood who had no head, / and some no arms, nor feet; some bled / and through their bodies wounds were set. / And some were strangled as they ate, / and some lay raving, chained and bound, / and some in water had been drowned; / and some were withered in the fire, / and some on horse, in war's attire. / And wives there lay in their childbed, / and mad some were, and some were dead." I recall a scene of two aged hands withering in fire in *The Lord of the Rings*, which may have its distant origins here, but I think the madmen bound in chains caught out of our world and time into Faerie would be more in Lewis's mind. In any case, this whole scene would provide appropriate *Grand Guignol*—or First World War trench realism, like Frodo and Sam in Mordor — for Orfieu's visit to Faerie.

III. The Dark Tower, or An Exchange in Time

Are there any clues in *The Dark Tower* as we have it — besides the names — that there was more than one exchange between our time and Othertime (the one we are sure of being Scudamour's exchange in the fragment)? I just now suggested a possible second exchange with Scudamour and Camilla, but the passage at the beginning of Chapter 5 in the fragment seems to show only one Scudamourian trip to Othertime (*The Dark Tower*, pp. 61–62): "At this point it will be convenient if my narrative turns to Scudamour. The reader will understand that the rest of us heard his story much later; that we heard it gradually and with all those repetitions and irruptions which arise in conversation…. No doubt I lose something from the purely literary point of view by not leaving you for the next few chapters in the same uncertainty which we actually endured for the next few weeks, but literature is not here my chief concern."

This single trip by Scudamour may however have been followed, in Lewis's original plan, by a similar trip by Orfieu, as the name implies. Lewis's literary use of myth and legend was (except for the slightly slapdash character of the earliest Narnian stories) generally complete and detailed — Psyche's palace in *Till We Have Faces* is a good example, Yellowhair in *After Ten Years*, the Medusa in "Forms of Things Unknown" — and if we have a character named Orfeo (Orfieu), it is likely he would play Orfeo's role, just as Scudamour will have played Scudamour's.

Perhaps the section on Scudamour's reading the time-theory of Othertime, to the point of the invention of the chronoscope in Othertime (which would have been right after the existing fragment breaks off), would have been followed by his attempt to return with the Othertime Camilla to Cambridge. This would have involved the principle of affinity in time attraction, in the place of the Stationary Smokehorses, which would have been an appropriate setting for someone's being snatched into Lewis's scientifictional — one might even say, industrialized — Faerie.

In the convoluted plot that would have seen Scudamour and the Othertime Camilla exchange with Camilla Bembridge and the Stingingman, another exchange would have been necessary, with Orfieu (and Ransom?) going into Faerie to rescue the Eurydice. Just as in *That Hideous Strength* Merlin's return to our time is not the end of the story but only of one part of the story, so in *An Exchange in Time* Scudamour's return to our time would end one part and not the whole. If Orfieu's name is a clue — and Ransom's. I believe they are. But even if this conjectural reconstruction is not correct, I believe *Sir Orfeo* provides some evidence for a comprehensive vision of Faerie, and of rescue from Faerie.

Orfeo goes before the King of Faerie, who says (ll. 421–428): "The King replied: 'What man art thou / that hither darest venture now? / Not I nor any here with me / have ever sent to summon thee, / and since here first my reign began / I never found so rash a man / that he to us would dare to wend / unless I first for him should send.'" Then Orfeo begins to tune his harp, and then to sing, and when his song is through (ll. 448–452), "this speech the king to him then made / 'Minstrel, thy music pleaseth me. / Come ask of me whate'er it be / and rich reward I will thee pay. / Come speak and prove now what I say.'" So Orfeo asks for "that very lady fair to see / who sleeps beneath the grafted tree" (ll. 455–456).

It has occurred to me that in Genesis, Chapter IV, verse xxi, Lamech, of Cain's line, had a son Jubal, and "he was the father of all such as handle the harp and organ" — and as one of Kipling's poems reminds us, and Genesis V:xxii tells us, his half-brother Tubalcain was "instructor of every artificer in brass and iron." As of December 1944, Lewis's projected fourth or fifth novel was dealing with the children of Cain: in the common knowledge of Kipling's day and Lewis's youth, the two best-known of Cain's descendants were Jubal and Tubalcain. We have suggested the scene from *The Faerie Queene* and the Cornish mines, blended into the place of the Stationary Smokehorses, as a pivotal scene in *An Exchange in Time*. That is for Tubalcain, instructor of artificers in brass and iron. And, though I have missed any indication that Orfieu is musical, it may be so, and his visit to Faerie and release of his Eurydice (Heurodis), in the traditional mode, would be for Jubal, father of all such as handle the harp and organ.

My extrapolation from the existing fragment would be that the coming of the White Riders would bring war to Faerie — that is, Othertime — and there would be, as Lewis might say, some rattling good adventure-story writing here, with martial music. (There was also a third brother, Jabal, father of such as dwell in tents, including, perhaps, the White Riders.) There is a clue on the music given in the existing fragment (p. 40) where Lewis remarks of Othertime that "what between the bands [which accompany even the details bringing dinner to the workers] and the noise of the workmen, it must have been dinning with sound."

The scenes of carnage from *Sir Orfeo* could be worked in as the battles' aftermath. If the book was started in 1938 and restarted in 1945, a reconstruction of the part unfinished could involve concentration camps and prison camps. Indeed, both kinds of camps antedate the Second World War, and were thus part of Lewis's own military experience, though given added meaning by what happened between 1938 and 1944. After all, as Lewis says (*The Dark Tower*, p. 32), the evil in Othertime is still in some sense "there" (or even "here"): "the things I am describing are not over and done with." But perhaps for the final return to our time, in the wake of a White Rider's attack, we should know more of these White Riders. Who are they?

When Z was doing his research, in the year 70, "the White Riders had not yet reached even the continental coast" (p. 89) — meaning the northern coast of what in our time is Europe. While Scudamour is in Othertime, in the person of the Stingingman. "The Lord of the Dark Tower and the Unicorn of the Eastern Plain" (p. 65), the White Riders attack the Dark Tower: they try "to spare the workmen as they always do" (p. 75), the Jerkies cannot get out of the way of the Riders' horses — "Do what we will, we cannot make them move like real men and change their direction" (*ibid.*) — and after apparently attempting to batter down the door, the Riders leave a message (p. 75) that "whoever comes to them with a sting in his hand, cut from a Unicorn's head, shall have a good welcome, he and all his party, and be a great man among them."

These are medieval knights seeking a unicorn in the enchanted forest: but Faerie has been modernized and rationalized. And all its horror has been brought to the surface as the horrors of human nature were brought to the surface in the days of Auschwitz and Bergen-Belsen and Dachau and the Katyn Forest massacre — which are the days when Lewis was writing. Just as *The Screwtape Letters* tell of hell's defeat from the vantage point of hell, so here the morals of the year 70 (when Z was experimenting) were low (sic!), and Z was forbidden to maim and torture children and drive them insane (p. 89). That was before the threat of the White Riders. And from the same inverted point of view, the

White Riders are Man-Eaters (p. 72): in a language that has no word for God (p. 65) they could not be God-eaters, and I think it likely that the "Man-Eater" refers to their eating the flesh and drinking the blood of God at Mass. As I say, they are medieval knights. Possibly they have an origin in Tolkien's world, as well as in the medieval world Tolkien and Lewis shared. They may also have some origin in stories of the last cavalry charge of the Polish army in the early days of World War II, against a mechanized enemy. Given Lewis's insulation from current events (Tito was king of Greece!), that may not seem likely—but if he had heard of it, it would have attracted him, and been germane to his story.

Not all of the Othertime doubles need have been in the ranks of the Dark Tower: perhaps Orfieu's double is with the White Riders. Perhaps Ransom's double is their king, or the king of Faerie. The story would hang together better if Orfieu goes (*sans* double) as self-proclaimed envoy from the Dark Tower to the king of the White Riders, plays his music, and brings back his Eurydice, with the king's permission. But perhaps indeed the king is Ransom's double. Perhaps indeed he is Ransom. We know something about the king of Faerie as Christ-figure from Tolkien's later *Smith of Wootton Major*, and about Ransom as Christ-figure from *Perelandra*. If our Cambridge Ransom does not himself go into Othertime, then we have no problem in getting him back, and this can be the second volume of a tetralogy (as the description of Ransom suggests), with *Perelandra* the third and *That Hideous Strength* the last. When Ransom changes appearance in *Perelandra* it could be to resemble the king that Orfieu has seen. It would be Orfieu's visit to the White Riders in the aftermath of battle that would produce the climactic return, after Scudamour has returned to our time.

The Arcadian mode of the completed novel would lie in part, of course, in the contrast of "virginal" nature and the world of the machines. But adventures in Arcady demand the judgment that follows them, so this *Exchange in Time* will end with judgment, from the king. If ever I were given leave to finish the novel, I hope I would live up to Alastair Fowler's judgment (*TLS* 1 July 1977, p. 795) that it has the same compulsive readability as the rest of the Ransom stories, and that "finished, it might have been his best." It would almost certainly have been his most science fictional and (as James Blish has suggested) thus his most satirical novel. Thus his most political. Thus his strongest lesson against the politics of the twentieth century. Or the nineteenth. Or the twenty-first.

IV

Perelandra, or Paradise Retained

As I noted above, Lewis apparently began his time-travel story that I would like to call *An Exchange in Time* in 1938, the year *Out of the Silent Planet* was published, as a kind of sequel to his space voyage. Whether he had *That Hideous Strength* in his mind then I am not sure, but the references to Bernardus Sylvestris and the concomitant linkage of our present-day war in heaven with the medieval times suggest that he might. In any case, the fragment that makes up the first few chapters of Walter Hooper's *Dark Tower* (and therefore of my putative *An Exchange in Time*) was the first swerve at a sequel to *Out of the Silent Planet*. But the swerve went off course, and the sequel was the very different (and much better) *Perelandra*.

In the second chapter we looked at some eighteenth-century antecessors for *Out of the Silent Planet*. Both of the possible sequels follow the eighteenth-century techniques, though both have (in my view) more nineteenth- and perhaps (with *Perelandra*) even seventeenth-century connections than eighteenth-century. Even so, though in *Perelandra* Lewis carries the eighteenth-century technique about as far as he can, I believe it is still eighteenth-century technique, with eighteenth-century antecessors. To be sure, *Perelandra* pushes the form of the eighteenth-century novel so hard as to come up with a genuinely new thing. The newness — perhaps one should say the "differentness" — has been recognized by recent critics, but the eighteenth-century origins have not, which has led to a curious feature in the criticism, a looking away from what we recognize as sources and analogues for the other books in looking at this. It is this feature I would like to begin with here.

The scenes and themes I am considering in *Perelandra*, as I noted in the introduction, are (1) the framework, including the prologue, and also including the mythic framework, (2) the pageant of what I call the Great Conversation, much of it Miltonic in inspiration, though not at all Miltonic in style, (3) linked with the mythic framework, the descriptions of Perelandra (the planet) and in particular the floating islands and the caves on the fixed land, and (4) the Great Dance at the end. In connection with the second of these, I should say I believe it a general rule that if one looks at Lewis's *Preface to Paradise Lost* when looking for the origins of *Perelandra*, one will see Milton everywhere, but if one looks at Milton himself, one will not.

One of the best of the more recent books of Lewis criticism notes that Lewis, in *Perelandra*, has turned to a mechanism more supernatural and less scientific than in *Out of the Silent Planet*, and finds this linked with the novel's differences in tone, though I do not recall that he quotes Lewis's own statement that he was wiser when he sent Ransom to Perelandra by angelic power than when he sent him to Malacandra in a spaceship. But in *The Notion Club Papers* (p. 168), there is a conversation in which one of Tolkien's characters comments that "Lewis used a spaceship [in *Perelandra*] but he kept it for his villains, and packed his hero the second time in a crystal coffin without machinery" — to which another member of the club responds, "Personally, I found the compromise very unconvincing. It was willfully inefficient, too: poor Ransom got half-toasted, for no sound reason that I could see. The power that could hurl a coffin to Venus could (one would have thought) have devised a material that let in light without excessive heat. I found the coffin much less credible than the Eldils, and granted the Eldils unnecessary."

That the "machine" in Perelandra is less mechanical is certainly and obviously true, and that fact may indeed be tied to the greater theological content of the book, as Lewis suggested. But I doubt it is very much tied to differences in tone — they are essentially the differences between the mythic Mars and the mythic Venus — and, in any case, whatever it is tied to, the tie is more complex than any relatively simple statement would suggest. After all, before we examine Lewis's answer to a particular auctorial problem, we should certainly know what the problem is, and should very probably know in what tradition he approached it.

Knowledge of the problem is essential — but knowledge of the tradition is at least useful.

Now the problem, on one quite obvious level, is what we do with Ransom now that we have him back from Mars — to which the obvious answer is, we send him to Venus. (Just so might Swift, having Gulliver back from the land of the Lilliputians in the South Pacific, decide he should next send him to the land of the Brobdingnagians in the North Pacific.) But this was not the original question or the original answer, which were, "What do we do with Ransom now that he has traveled in space?" and "We have him travel in time."

On another level, the problem is how to have Ransom, who has been given a special revelation on Malacandra, make use of that revelation in fulfilling God's saving purposes. Had Lewis finished the time fragment, this would, I believe (as I have suggested), have been what it was "about" — and in Chapter II I have reconstructed roughly the theological line I think it would have taken. Of course he did not finish it (even though he tried a second time, and perhaps a third), and instead of answering the question, "What do we do with Ransom now that he has traveled in space?" — he answered (as we have noted) the question, "What do we do with Ransom now that we have him back from Mars?" The form of the question demands the Gulliverian answer: we send him to Venus, which we already know as Perelandra. If I seem in what follows to dwell overmuch on the question, "What is *Perelandra?*" it is because the true nature of the book explains much, not only about immediate reader reactions and the reactions of nearly sixty years later, but also about problems of critical analysis of the Ransom stories as a whole, and as science fiction, Arcadian or otherwise.

Yes, *Perelandra* is different from the other Ransom stories, though it is counted as part of a "space trilogy" and therefore found on bookstore shelves with science fiction. When I read it and reread it in my teens, I found it to be poetry, in comparison with the prose of *Out of the Silent Planet* and *That Hideous Strength*. In the first chapter of this book, I noted that it is the "odd man out" of the Ransom stories, though it has some of the eighteenth-century markings that characterize *Out of the Silent Planet* (Ransom looking over his floating island like Robinson Crusoe, for example). But it is the odd man out not because its antecedents are earlier than those of *Out of the Silent Planet* and even (in some ways) *That Hideous Strength*, but because they are later.

Lewis's area in scholarship was the Middle Ages and the Renaissance. His own literary antecedents run from the age of Queen Anne to the age of Victoria, from Swift to Wells. He is, in fact, a satirist. (Doubtless that is part of a link with Dryden.) But *Perelandra* is not a satire — at least, we surely do not think of it as a satire, and resent any satirical passages. What is it? What happens? These are not the same question, but recent studies of the nature of genre have led us to conclude that they are more closely related than we have at times been willing to admit.

What the reader perceives to be happening — which is, in one sense, what "happens" — in a book is partly determined by the genre of the book. If there is a clock running slow on the mantelpiece at the beginning of a *Bildungsroman*, it is perhaps to be read as an indication of the type of household in which the hero is growing up, but if in a mystery, as a clue. The interpretation of events, and thus in an important way, their perception, depends in part on a knowledge of what kind of book the author was writing. What is *Perelandra*?

I suggest that we do not have sufficient evidence on that question without looking at what happens in the book, even though looking at what happens to find out what genre we are dealing with, and then looking at the genre to find out what happens, may seem to be a prime case of *petitio elenchi*, or at least circularity. But we can sketch a series of events and look at the way the story is told, to see where this leads, even if we have a particular idea in mind as to the genre we are dealing with. If need be, we can do the same thing with a different genre in mind, to see if that makes a difference — but perhaps there will be no need of that. In any case, we begin by asking again, "What happens in *Perelandra*?"

Perelandra: *Events and Framework*

We begin with Ransom as, in some way, a mediator, a type of Christ (a view strengthened if we take *Perelandra* as the third volume in the tetralogy), or at the very least as a servant of Maleldil, and in the first few pages, we learn that he is going to Venus. Or rather, to Perelandra, since we have already been introduced to that name in *Out of the Silent*

Planet, p. 91, as we have been introduced to a man whose name is Ransom, and not — for example — Unwin, or something else less suitable. Will he then have, on Perelandra, a series of adventures interspersed with philosophical conversation, where a pageant is played out across a heraldic but detailed landscape, as we had on Malacandra? Just so. But something happened in the writing.

Before we get to that, we should mention that what I have called "realization" — and which might be called "imaginative reconstruction" — is a key to Lewis's fiction. It is also, of course, part of the science fiction mode. "What would it be like if..." is the operative phrase, and of course this explains why these interplanetary or intertemporal romances are enough like science-fiction (given the scientifictional machinery) to be given its name without any notable protest. To this there may be two reactions. First, it holds for stories which are clearly not science fiction: "What would it be like if you were inside the Trojan Horse?" or "What would it be like if Psyche were telling the truth?" Second, it looks as though the machinery of science fiction is extraneous to the story and in fact weakens it. Tolkien's spokesman in *The Notion Club Papers* uttered the earliest and most fervent protest on this point, on Ransom's journey to Venus, on the discord between machinery and story (*The Notion Club Papers*, p. 168): "this impossible sort of parcel post did not appeal to me as a solution to the problem ... I doubt if there is a solution. But I should prefer an old-fashioned wave of a wizard's wand, Or a word of power in Old Solar from an Eldil. Nothing less would suffice: a miracle.'" If Lewis was wiser in *Perelandra*, he was wiser yet in *That Hideous Strength*, and very much wiser with Narnia. But for all the strength of this view, the fact remains that as "what-if?" pageant, these books are in fact very closely related to science fiction, the present intracultural form of a "what-if?" (and eclectic) pageant through the realms of the spirit.

The book begins with Lewis's setting a scene including himself as author, a kind of prologue. This is not an unusual device in medieval literature — as Chaucer and Langland attest — but the use here is more akin to the Victorian convention as seen in Rider Haggard's *She*. To be sure, Haggard is not a character in the same way Lewis is in *Perelandra*, but then Lewis is certainly not a character in *Perelandra* in the same way Chaucer is in *The Canterbury Tales* or Long Will in *Piers Plowman*.

The Scientifiction Novels of C. S. Lewis

Neither parallel is exact, but the Victorian is the closer to exactitude. There is some attempt to set up a persona for Lewis, as Ransom's friend: but the persona is part of the framework, not part of the story. The Lewis persona serves as a foil to Ransom, reminding us in the process that, though it comes through Lewis, Ransom is the real narrator of the story. He is the real narrator here even more than in *Out of the Silent Planet*, where Lewis has "written up" the story as fiction, with the devices of fiction, including the opening reference to the Pedestrian: Ransom would scarcely begin his own story in that way himself.

It has been argued (by Professor Percy Adams, among others) that the English novel has its origins in the English traveler's tale. The style of these most generally is first-person narrative by the traveler, which is not quite what we have here. I mention this to suggest that the "traveler's tale" is *not* the genre with which we are dealing in *Perelandra*: let us see now what clues we can develop toward determining what the genre is. Continuing with the progress of the book, we find that, with the first chapter serving as both foreword and afterword to Ransom's story, we move into the story proper — Ransom's landing on Perelandra, in the sea, his struggle ashore onto "his" floating island, and his first waking, seeing reality and thinking it was a dream.

Ransom meets the Lady (if "meets" is quite the right word). She names him "Piebald." They talk. It has turned out that the language of the Hrossa on Malacandra, *Hressa-Hlab* is really "Old Solar" — *Hlab Eribol ef-Cordi* — or, in other words, Tolkien's language of "great words that sounded like castles" — though Tolkien himself thought this impossible. Weston's spaceship lands, and Ransom helps him set up camp in the Fixed Land. Weston makes the acquaintance of the Lady, then, in argument with Ransom, proclaiming "I, Weston, am your God and your Devil," invites the force (has that word changed meaning?) into him, and is unmanned. He becomes, in fact, the Unman — is taken over by a devil, perhaps the Devil.

Thereafter ensues the temptation of the Lady by the Unman (to spend the night on the Fixed Land, which Maleldil has commanded her not to do). Ransoms argues against her doing what the Unman tempts her to do, and Ransom fights the Unman after Maleldil has cast an enchanted sleep over the Floating Islands. Eventually Ransom and the

Unman (in whom Weston once or twice briefly resurfaces) are submerged and come up in a seacave within the Mountain of Perelandra, a seacave with no exit back the way they came, and no certain exit through the mountain, though that is the way they go. "He and his enemy, when they sank, had clearly, by some hundredth chance, been carried through a hole in the cliffs well below water level and come up on the beach of a cavern. Was it possible to reverse the process? He went down to the water's edge — or rather, as he groped his way down to where the shingle was wet, the water came to meet him. It thundered over his head far up behind him, and then receded with a tug which he only resisted by spread-eagling himself on the beach and gripping the stones. It would be useless to plunge into *that*..." (p. 174). And then, "he came to another cliff. There appeared to be a shelf on this about four feet up, but this time a really shallow one. He got on it somehow and glued himself to the face, feeling out to left and right for further grips. When he found one and realized that he was now about to attempt some real climbing, he hesitated.... For some minutes he did things which he had never done on earth.... Doubtless if anyone had seen him he would have appeared at one moment to take mad risks and at another to indulge in excessive caution" (pp. 175–176). I will forbear quoting the whole, but it brings to my mind Buchan's description of the climb out of the cave in *Prester John* (quoted below, p. 100).

In the course of all this (before the cave), we see in the Unman what Lewis has described as the nature of Satan, attacking those who see him as Milton's hero. The Unman has been torturing frogs (*Perelandra*, pp. 110–111). "It looked at Ransom in silence and at last began to smile. We have often spoken — Ransom himself had spoken — of a devilish smile. Now he realized that he had never taken the words seriously. the smile was not bitter, nor raging, nor, in an ordinary sense, sinister; it was not even mocking. It seemed to summon Ransom, with a horrible naiveté of welcome, into the world of its own pleasures.... It did not defy good-ness; it ignored it to the point of annihilation. ... The extremity of its evil had passed beyond all struggle into some state which bore a horri-ble similarity to innocence."

Ransom escapes through the caves, the Unman (in Weston's body) limping after him, until, after signs and wonders, Ransom casts the body into the fires in the center of the mountain, escapes from his underworld, and comes out into a second infancy, breast-fed by the planet Venus herself. The king finds his queen, unfallen, they are crowned, there ensues the Great Dance, and the world begins not anew, but for the first time (p. 197) "Today for the first time two creatures of the low worlds, two images of Maleldil that breathe and breed like the beasts, step up that step at which your parents fell, and sit in the throne of what they were meant to be."

I have considered the nature of mythopoeic writing in my essay, "C. S. Lewis and the Myth in Mythopoeia," which has become Chapter VII in this book. It is my belief (as will be seen there) that "atmosphere" or "flavor" is a needed part of successful mythopoetic creation, and I believe therefore that considering the atmosphere or flavor of *Perelandra* is a part of looking at the book's mythic framework. Now the flavor of Perelandra is ceremonial, a flavor of pageantry, a flavor also of traveler's tales (which is a part of science fiction, of course): what it is not, and so far as I know makes no attempt to be, is a Christian flavor. The story is Christian, but the flavor — no more than the rest of the mythic framework — is not. It is pagan, of the fields: here is the description of the unfallen Adam and Eve of Perelandra (p. 207): "The blood coursing in the veins, the feeling trembling on the lips and sparkling in the eyes, the might of the man's shoulders, the wonder of the women's breasts, a splendour of virility and richness of womanhood unknown on earth, a living torrent of perfect animality...." That is the flavor and that is part of the pagan framework.

Milton and the Great Conversations

We have noted that it is a commonplace of Lewis criticism — and particularly of critical biography — that *Perelandra* was at least midwifed, if not begotten, by Lewis's work on *A Preface to Paradise Lost*, and that, of course, is true. And one part of the truth is that neither has any domesticity, any quotidianity, any ordinary quality of daily life. All is powers and principalities and fighting depraved hypersomatic beings at great heights. That is important. But we cannot let this lead us astray in our analysis. We must not think that the deep roots of *Perelandra* lie somewhere in the seventeenth century, a century in which Lewis was somewhat ill at ease, except perhaps with authors who carried over from the century before (Raleigh, Shakespeare, Donne), or who notoriously anticipated the age to come (Dryden).

This part of this chapter was first conceived as part of a conference (never held) on "C. S. Lewis, Medievalist and Victorian," and it is the Medieval and Victorian periods that provide the more important clues to what goes on in *Perelandra*, both in the book and in its creation. Lewis was a medievalist by trade and Victorian by birth: at the risk of indulging once again in the personal heresy, I suggest that his understanding of the sixteenth century in the best of his books — I mean the *OHEL* volume — has its roots in the peculiar sympathy of the Victorian for the Elizabethan era, a sympathy extending to widespread emulation. These are times of England's expansion, of great flowerings of English literature in Eliza-bethan plays and Victorian novels, of English hymns and anthems, and (not coincidentally) of English pageantry. This Elizabethan-Victorian nexus is in a place far from Milton.

At least, it is a place far from most parts of Milton, though *Lycidas* finds Victorian echoes — and certainly far from what Lewis (in *That Hideous Strength*) speaks of as the "sweet Protestant" world of John Bun-yan. "Sweets to the sweet" doubtless — but it would not be my choice of phrasing, and Lewis's emulation of Bunyan in *The Pilgrim's Regress* is not entirely happy and almost entirely unlike Bunyan. Lewis did not under-stand Bunyan well, I think. He understood Milton well — as continuing earlier tradition. He disliked Congreve and that ilk. The seventeenth-century author with whom Lewis in his writing seems eventually most sympathetic is Dryden (it was not so originally), whom he finds medieval, and who leads to his favorite Swift, and the next century.

I have toyed with the thought that the true analogue to *Perelandra* — in its form — is not to be found in the late eighteenth-century novels that pushed the form to its bounds, but in some nearly forgotten Romantic novels of the century after. But I think not. *Out of the Silent Planet* is classical; in *Perelandra* the Romance pushes against the classical bounds, but the bounds are still there. It is not, I believe, accidental that when Ransom is on his first floating island, the simile Lewis uses is "looking down like Robinson Crusoe on field and forest to the shores in every direction" (p. 41); certainly Lewis must have had Crusoe in mind as he was writing.

Is this of importance to an understanding of the Ransom stories, and of *Perelandra* in particular? I think it is. We have already seen some of the origins — or at least the antecessors — of the stories, particularly *Out of the Silent Planet,* in the eighteenth century, and we will see more in our analysis of *That Hideous Strength.* But *Perelandra* is not a work whose roots lie quite so deep in the eighteenth century (even mediated by the Victorians), and over the years I have observed the tendency in meetings discussing Lewis to extend the obvious consanguinity of *Perelandra* and the *Preface to Paradise Lost* into an argument for Lewis's book as an answer to Milton — *Paradise Retained* answering *Paradise Lost* and making *Paradise Regained* unnecessary. Yes, it is Paradise Retained: that is the subtitle of this chapter. But surely there is a loss of perspective in this claim. For all the great untransmuted lump of futurity in the last two books, for all Milton's flaws, *Paradise Lost* is a great work, and *Perelandra* is not. In fact, at best, it bears the same relation to its Miltonic antecessor that Victorian Arthuriana bears to Spenser or Malory, particularly Spenser.

It would be too severe here to appeal to the language of Thomas B. Macaulay's attack on the poems of Mr. Robert Montgomery, but there is something to the appeal, and the temptation is great. And like Oscar Wilde, I can resist everything except temptation. You remember that Macaulay attacked Montgomery's "Turkey carpet" style of writing: there are colors in a Turkey (that is, Turkish) carpet that have before made and will again make works of art, and there are words in Montgomery's writing that have before made and will again make poetry. Just so. And there are themes and motifs in *Perelandra* that have before made and will again make (we hope) an epic, but *Perelandra* is not therefore an epic just because those themes and motifs are present.

These themes were triumphantly present in Milton — but also in Genesis and the strange once–Scriptural literature collected under the name of *Enoch*, which I have already mentioned. There is an Arthurian subtheme — Arthur is with Enoch in the cup-shaped land of Abhalljin or Aphallin (that is, Avalon, and the cup whose shape it is would be the Grail) — and we remember that Milton originally thought of an Arthuriad as his secondary epic (see *A Preface to Paradise Lost*). No one denies the Miltonic midwifery, but *Perelandra* is not therefore either Miltonic or epic. Milton, particularly in *Paradise Lost*, is creating a poem, a secondary epic, a *poiema*, a made thing, to embody a story his prospective readers know already, the story "Of man's first disobedience and the fruit...." The one possible similarity with *Perelandra* as a literary creation — and it's a little far-fetched — is that Milton's style pushes as hard against the bounds of syntax and grammar as Lewis's story pushes against the bounds of the novel of ideas, or indeed of the novel at all. But they are not writing the same kind of work, nor telling the same story (quite the contrary), nor is Lewis telling a story his audience already knows, nor are there any similarities in their style. To be sure, the Unman reflects Lewis's reflections on Milton's Satan, but that is all the influence I can see, unless (not likely!) Lewis broadened his scope in *Perelandra* simply because he was writing a book on *Paradise Lost*.

The second chapter mentioned Lindsay's *A Voyage to Arcturus* as a point of origin for some of the scenes and attributes of *Out of the Silent Planet* (nothing brilliant in that, since Lewis himself had pointed the way). I will suggest that E. R. Eddison's *The Worm Ouroboros* has something of the same relationship to *Perelandra*. No more than *Arcturus* is like *Out of the Silent Planet* is *The Worm* like *Perelandra*— on the face of it, perhaps less — but there is nonetheless a significant similarity: both are furnished with the mental furniture of a writer both medievalist and Victorian.

For all his salutary study of *Paradise Lost* as a secondary epic, and his brilliant analysis of the progress of the poem and of Satan in the poem, Lewis fundamentally sees Milton as a Victorian medievalist might be expected to see him — as a writer of pageant ("A thousand liveried angels lackey her" is an indicative line quoted in *The Great Divorce*), as a writer of great surging lines of emblematic words that escape syntax (which is how I also see him), as pictorialist. The furniture of Lewis's mind determines his artistic reaction to Milton, if not his critical reaction, which may be largely that of Charles Williams. Lewis's intention in writing his *Voyage to Venus* may well have been satiric (that was the title of the shortened paperback version, as *The Tortured Planet* was of its sequel), but he sat down to write with a Victorian pictorialist's mind steeped in Milton's classical and medieval inheritance, in pictures from *Paradise Lost*. The result is unlike anything else Lewis ever wrote, though it is not entirely unlike books we know he read. For the moment, however, let us consider *Perelandra* as a pageant play written by a man who would not or could not write a play, except as a small child, and even though the most important scenes could not be realistically staged.

This consideration at least underlines a certain kinship with the Canterbury plays of Charles Williams, and Dorothy L. Sayers, perhaps even with T. S. Eliot. And it explains (if it does not quite justify) my original impression of *Perelandra* as poetry. Such a poetic play might well be framed in a more realistic prologue and epilogue — though I am not sure I would care to call the opening of *Perelandra* purely realistic, or at least to have experienced what it describes as reality (pp. 13–14): "'They call it a Breakdown *at first*,' I thought. Wasn't there some mental disease in which quite ordinary objects looked to the patient unbelievably ominous? ... looked, in fact, just as that abandoned factory looks to me now? Great bulbous shapes of cement, strange brickwork bogeys, glowered at me over dry scrubby grass pock-marked with grey pools and intersected with the remains of a light railway.... There was a little empty house by the side of the road, with most of the windows boarded up and one staring like the eye of a dead fish.... We have all known times when inanimate objects seemed to have almost a facial expression, and it was the expression of this bit of road which I did not like. 'It's not true,' said my mind, ' that people who are going mad never think they're going mad.' Suppose that real insanity had chosen this place to begin. In that case, the black enmity of those dripping trees — their horrible expectancy — would be an hallucination. But that did not make it any better. To think that the spectre you see is an illusion does not rob him of his terrors: it simply adds the further terror of madness itself...."

That way, quite literally, madness lies, a surrealist madness: perhaps that also is pageant, like a Breughel painting. In any case, we have summarized the events in *Perelandra*, suggesting what is the genre they suggest, and suggesting what went into Lewis's mind in the creating. We have already noted that the content of the book presses against the form — the form of the novel, and particularly the novel of ideas. I am aware that a case could be made for considering *Perelandra*, like *Out of the Silent*

Planet and even *That Hideous Strength*, as a Menippean satire, but if it is, then the content presses even more violently against the form than we have suggested. It could be read as such a satire, but my experience suggests we read it for the pageantry (certainly not for a description of Lewis's going mad), and whatever it was intended to be, the terms in which it should be judged are those relating to pageant or — as I will suggest a little later on — cantata.

Lewis did not meet E. R. Eddison till after *Perelandra* was done, but he read *The Worm* when it came out in 1922, and when he met Eddison he found him in some ways a kindred spirit. He praises Eddison (*On Stories*, p. 29) for his "blend of hardness and luxury, of lawless speculation and sharply realized detail, of the cynical and the magnanimous." If we substitute "lawful" for "lawless" and "satirical" for "cynical" we shall be closer to *Perelandra*. But there is a good deal else as well: indeed, we might reasonably claim that *The Worm Ouroboros* is a Victorian child of the *sogur* out of Elizabethan theatre, and indeed Elizabethan (or at least sixteenth-century) poesie generally. We might also make the same claim for *Perelandra*, though it is more medieval, perhaps, than Renaissance — if, in the face of *De Descriptione Temporum*, it is still proper to make the distinction. The transition in *Perelandra*, in any case, is by way of mythology into a perilous realm of the spirit only slightly less bookish than the mythology. But how wonderfully done.

The Descriptions of Perelandra

If *Perelandra* started as satiric pageant (which is a principal form of science fiction as well as what underlies the beginnings of the English novel), something happened in the writing. In one sense, of course, what happened was that the description of Perelandra ran riot: the pictures with which Lewis's writing "all began" came tumbling over one another in such profusion that they could not fully be brought into the story. The background and the heraldry threatened to overwhelm the pageant — the travels — and the philosophic story. The visions of landscape cease to exist for the sake of the story: instead they begin to have a life (perhaps it is a Jungian life) of their own. They are what make Perelandra memorable. But they are not what make it go. They are not even there to adorn the tale.

Certainly Defoe (in *Robinson Crusoe*) added much in the way of corroborative detail not strictly required by the story: he was far from following that Chekhovian economy of line whereby a gun hung above the mantel must go off before the story is over. Nevertheless, even as Defoe describes the "pleasant savannas or meadows" he notes in them "a great deal of tobacco, green, and growing to a great and very strong stalk" (Penguin ed., p. 112). His description of his island (or rather, of Crusoe's) is very much that of a nonconforming political economist in the days of King George I or of Queen Anne. But Lewis's description of Ransom's islands is neither fully subordinated to the character of his hero nor the demands of the story — nor, evidently, to the demands of political economy. Admittedly they illustrate his view of mythology, but it is highly unlikely that was their design. For indeed, something else happened in the writing. The "conversations" became a battle — not with humour or comedy or satire, as in Weston's "conversation" with the Oyarsa of Malacandra, but in deadly earnest, and not for the sake of the reader, with the author coming onstage at the end, but for the sake of the whole world. Since theology (as I have elsewhere argued) begets mythopoeia, this may go some way toward explaining the descriptive mythological passages in *Perelandra*: what is more important is that it forces Lewis to approach, if not transcend, the bounds inhabited by his predecessors, and thus to make the final "conversation" visual and operatic both.

It is important to recognize that the final "conversation" — the Great Dance — is not unearthly, and neither, indeed, is the rest of Perelandra. The Venus it takes place upon (to the extent that the Great Dance is taking place *there*— but the statement certainly holds for the rest of the story) is a Venus drawn from earthly images, far more than Malacandra is a Mars drawn from earthly images. If there are new creatures, they are like those to be found in medieval bestiaries. If there are new landscapes, Lewis has given us their origin; "He opened his eyes and saw a strange heraldically coloured tree loaded with yellow fruits and silver leaves. Round the base of the indigo stem was coiled a small dragon covered with scales of red gold. He recognized the garden of the Hesperides at once" (*Perelandra*,

p. 45). *Perelandra* is, to be sure, mythological, but it is a well-established earthly mythology. After all, when the author of *The Book of the Secrets of Enoch* wrote of being carried up into the Third Heaven and seeing the trees "bubbling with their fragrant exhalation," he was speaking of earthly things far more than Ezekiel was speaking of earthly things with his wheels within wheels. Yet this very mythology, which provides the transition from the quotidian to the realms of the spirit, is what — with the description — plays against the traditional form of *Perelandra*, the Swiftian or Johnsonian form.

In *Out of the Silent Planet*, Swiftian form and Swiftian humor go together. Here, though there are occasional passages — the description of Weston's arrival on Perelandra, for example, or "Weston's" lecturing to Ransom after his arrival — and though the leisure-time activities of the Unman have a Swiftian ring, the book is escaping its bounds. I should note, by the way, that my linking of Lewis's humor with Swift's is not purely idiosyncratic, as Professor Derek Brewer's contribution — p. 49 — to *C. S. Lewis at the Breakfast Table* should make clear: "He enormously enjoyed Swift's humour and thought his work fuller of real laughs than almost any other...." The appreciation of Swift's humor is very much an eighteenth-century characteristic, not so much a modern one.

And as *Perelandra* escapes its bounds, it becomes, as we have said, a new thing, rather (though the parallel may seem forced) as Beckford's *Vathek*, or even Walpole's *Castle of Otranto*, became a new thing. Unlike Walpole's work, it has had no imitators; like it, it had an immediate effect in the world of letters — from the 1945 *Atlantic Monthly* poem (by Father Berrigan) referring to "Sun of shadow and light / On a lost Perelandran lane" to the paean in Marjorie Hope Nicolson's pioneering work on interplanetary voyages. The effect shows the strength of *Perelandra*, and the lack of imitators testifies to its singularity.

Even *The Lord of the Rings*, *sui generis* at its publication, has had its imitators — too many for my taste — but this has not. And looking at it without our views of Tolkien or Charles Williams in the way, we can see why. Tolkien's books grew out of the Edwardian adventure story, Williams's out of the popular novel of the 1920s and early 1930s: both are part of the immediate literary heritage of the twentieth century. Both came from popular story-telling, and were thus ripe for imitation by popular story-tellers — though only Madeleine L'Engle comes to mind as following in Williams's way.

But Lewis, though he made himself into a story-teller, did not come by it naturally: the great conversation, the scenery, the "realization" of different worlds (and these three not only in the Ransom stories, but in *Screwtape* and *The Great Divorce* and *The Pilgrim's Regress*), these are his strong points. He could not see how to finish the time fragment; he set an overschematic plot line for *That Hideous Strength*; he had trouble finishing his narrative poems; he eventually turned to "realizing" mythic stories in the Narnia books and in *Till We Have Faces* — in which, of course, he was learning from his medieval rather than his eighteenth-century predecessors.

In short, for a man who sang the beauties of "story" he had grave difficulties in producing one. His short stories include two "realizations," one mythic story (also a kind of "realization"), and one science-fiction story that is at least as Johnsonian, to my mind, as *Out of the Silent Planet*. I do not say this to denigrate Lewis. It was once said of him (*Breakfast Table*, p. 65) that "he was a very good man, to whom goodness did not come easily" — and equally, in the end, a very good story-teller, to whom story-telling did (or at least had) not come easily. But when we examine the Ransom stories as stories we must recognize that they are from a tradition we have largely left behind us, a heritage that — far from having squandered — we have put away in storage. At least these two are. But as a descriptive poet, well, that is quite another story. Let us return to the story line of *Perelandra* and to the pictures in Lewis's mind as he set up that story line. We left off with Ransom's physical contest with the Unman, after the Lady's Temptation.

After the fight and the escape on the sea-horses, Ransom, with Weston (or the Unman) following him, climbs slowly up the insides of the mountain where they have come ashore in a cave where no day ever reaches. Here let me quote a passage from a book published at the end of Lewis's boyhood, by an author whose influence on the Inklings has been too little noted: "There were only two outlets from that cave — the way I had come and the way the river came ... I sat down on the floor and looked at the wall of water. It fell ... in a solid sheet, which made up the whole of the wall of the cave. Higher than the roof of the cave I could not see what happened, except that it must be the open air for the sun was shining on it ... I began the climb ... almost before I knew I found my head close under the roof of the cave.... Just below the level of the roof—say two feet — I saw the submerged spike of rock.... To get to my feet and stand on the spike while all the fury of the water was pluck-ing at me was the hardest physical effort I have ever made ... a slip would send me into the abyss...." And so on, until "not suddenly as in romances but after hard striving and hope long deferred, I found myself on a firm outcrop of weathered stone. In three strides I was on the edge of the plateau ... I managed to stumble a few steps forward on the mountain turf and then flung myself on my face. When I raised my head I was amazed to find it still early morning..." (John Buchan, *Prester John*, 1910, Popular Library ed., pp. 230–34).

This is not the only cave we know of in Lewis's early reading: he himself has recorded the impact made by Rider Haggard's *King Solomon's Mines* and the scene in the caves. Moreover, if some of the origins of the caves and river of Perelandra lie here (as I believe they do), they have been greatly transmuted in Lewis's mind. Still, there are the caves, the river, the climb, the springtime morning on the mountain outside. Lewis wrote with pictures in his mind, and I am arguing that, just as the bubble-trees have an eventual origin in *The Book of the Secrets of Enoch*, so the caves within which Weston's body was burned have their origin partly in the cave wherein the Reverend John Laputa leapt to his death. Davy Crau-furd crawls out only to high hillside and recovers from his madness and his struggle with Laputa; Ransom is "breast-fed by the planet Venus in a second infancy." To be sure, the circumstances are different — not so the emotions implicit in the pictures.

After the emergence from the caves, Ransom eventually stands in the valley where the Green Lady and her Consort, the king and the queen, are to be crowned by the gods or angels, Perelandra, and Malacandra, and Ransom the Man of Thulcandra. The great struggle is over; the coro-nation proceeds; and the conversation of men and angels is transmuted (or taken up) into the Great Dance. Then it is a year later, and Ransom steps into his celestial packing-box for his return to Earth, flowers are put in, and the lid closed, which is the last thing he knows before his return (which has already been recounted in the combined foreword

/afterword at the beginning of the book). Now what kind of book is this?

One of my friends, a devote of Dumas and Walter Scott, claims that it is a book in which nothing much happens: certainly, by the standards of Dumas and Walter Scott, that is true. Whatever origins some of its scenes may have in adventure stories, it is not itself an adventure story. Unlike *Out of the Silent Planet* and *That Hideous Strength* (whatever we may think of the fragment), it is not a satire, though Lewis is pre-eminently a satirist (viz, besides those just mentioned, *The Screwtape Letters*, *The Great Divorce*, and much of the "business" of the Narnia stories). It is indeed essentially a pageant, a Medieval (and Renaissance, even Elizabethan) genre on the one hand, and revived in the Victorian period on the other. It is not allegory, though we might think it well on the way, with Ransom, the Lady, the UnMan, the King, Ares and Aphrodite, Singing Beast and Giant Insect, not to mention location in the Third Heaven and the Hesperides, and on the Fixed Land. But though this may sound like allegory, it is really something else. I have called it pageant, which is accurate as far as it goes, though it suggests Christmas pageants in graded schools or Sunday schools, with a pillow or light bulb playing the baby Jesus. We might, at the risk of misunderstanding, call it a cantata without the music, because a cantata is a kind of pageant with music.

It was a Victorian view that religious pageant involved a kind of allegory. The stylized external event that was enacted in the Greek Theater — the *dromenon*, the play — with its chorus, its Eumenides, its Erinnyes, its stylized costumes, has allegorical affinities (or perhaps pageant and allegory are the two parts of an ancient unity). But, curiously, the principal area in which the idea of religious pageant as allegory permeated the Victorian consciousness — I came across it in a boys' book by G. A. Henty — was in connection with Egyptian religion. (Lewis echoes this kind of thing, for satiric purposes, in Bree's denial that Aslan is really a lion, in *The Horse and His Boy*, pb ed., 1970, pp. 192–93.) If the different "divine masks" really reflect different attributes of divinity, the lion for strength and so on, then the pageant in which the masks are carried or worn takes on allegorical qualities. This happens in *Perelandra*, if at all, only in the Great Dance, in which all the speakers, Ransom included, can be taken as voices of God (and we are prepared for it, if at all, by the Voice in the Darkness the night before the battle, "My Name also is Ransom"). But that it happens, here or elsewhere, is indicative of the tie between allegory and pageant — I believe Lewis's appreciation of Edgar Wind's *The Pagan Mysteries of the Renaissance* involves this point.

Pageants are solemn — *solempne* in the medieval sense — and are re-enactments of the sacred or sacral, as with the pageant of the Mass. Historically, and perhaps necessarily, they involve music and dance — *melopoeia* and *choreography*. When we think of it, this is a very odd thing for a satirist like Lewis to be writing — Lewis whose dislike of hymns and church music is well known, Lewis with his putative "North-of-Ireland scunner" against the stage. Perhaps this was tied to his own shyness and his acute embarrassment at failed variety "turns" — but he would find *that* an unprofitable line of inquiry. Lewis believed himself a boor and, as Joy doubtless said, a "klutz" in such affairs. What is he doing writing a pageant, with all the kettles and bells and trumpets and gold and silver, marching and masks and obeisance, that implies? Yes, Charles, the Omnipotence does indeed have a sense of humor, and Under the Mercy all things are possible. But how did it come to be? Doubtless "it all began with a picture" — and here the picture or pictures took over.

It might be said that I began writing this chapter in 1953–54, when I was a fifth-former in school. My term-paper that year for my combined English/History course was titled "A Chosen Vessel: C. S. Lewis in *Perelandra*" and I wrestled manfully if unsuccessfully with the paradox that Lewis, whom I saw as a successful poet in *Perelandra* (I quoted the passage on climbing the mountain to the crowning of the king and queen at length), was in fact in his poetry a highly unsuccessful poet, and I was reduced to saying that the small amount of his poetry that was effective was "fairly definitely so" (and no, I will not footnote that quotation: I no longer have a copy of the paper, but one was bound and placed on the shelves of the Library at the Wooster School in Danbury, Connecticut; it may still be there). What I did not realize, at the age of sixteen, was that Lewis's art, like any satirist's (except, perhaps, Blake's), was likely to be derivative even when he was not being satirical, and of course I did not then know the originals from which his art was derived. Of course, the game of *Quellenforschung* is a dangerous one, but if we know what works a writer has in mind when writing, we can know more about what that writer is trying to write, and why the writing is or is not successful. Obviously, the nature of the particular writer's mind is also important.

The Great Dance

Let me turn now to what Lewis does when he is forced beyond the bounds. The best case is, as I have noted, the Great Dance, and we shall be considering that, but it is important to note that this is far from the only case. In the early part of the book, we are still by and large following the form of *Out of the Silent Planet*, though the chapters are longer and the machine for getting Ransom to the planet better chosen (and the Swiftian humor less evident). Then, at a particular point, the change comes; when the Voice speaks to Ransom in the darkness, a Voice revealing its reality by saying, "It is not for nothing that you are named Ransom" (p. 147). We have moved from conversations with men or angels (the Oyeresu) to conversation with God. We have left the Augustan world and entered the Romantic. From this point on, we are in Lewis's vision of Paradise — or, to be accurate, of hell, of Purgatory, of Paradise, and at the last (if the distinction can be made), in the Great Dance, of heaven.

I do not know if Lewis's words in Chapter 3 (or Ransom's words quoted by Lewis), "The reason why the thing can't be expressed is that it's too definite for language" (p. 33), were written before or after the Great Dance, but they are a useful lead-in to the Dance and to the more purely visionary part of *Perelandra* (though of course it is all "visionary"). In the Great Dance, it will be remembered, "The voice that spoke next seemed to be that of Mars, but Ransom was not certain. And who spoke after that, he does not know at all. For in the conversation that followed — if it can be called a conversation — though he believes that he himself was sometimes the speaker, he never knew which words were his or another's, or even whether a man or an eldil was talking. The speeches followed one another — if indeed they did not all take place at the same time — like the parts of a music into which all five of them had entered as instruments or like a wind blowing through five trees that stand together on a hilltop" (p. 214).

And then, "by a transition which he did not notice, it seemed that what had begun as speech was turned into sight, or into something that can be remembered only as if it were seeing. He thought he saw the Great Dance. It seemed to be woven out of the intertwining undulation of many cords or bands of light, leaping over and under one another and mutually embraced in arabesques and flower-like subtleties. Each figure as he looked at it became the master-figure or focus of the whole spectacle, by means of which his eye disentangled all else and brought it into unity — only to be itself entangled when he looked to what he had taken for mere marginal decorations and found that there also the same hegemony was claimed, and the claim made good…. He could see also (but the word "seeing" is now plainly inadequate) wherever the ribbons or serpents of light intersected, minute corpuscles of momentary brightness: and he knew somehow that these particles were the secular generalities of which history tells…" (p. 218). And then —

And then "the thing must have passed altogether out of the region of sight as we understand it. For he says that the whole solid figure of these enamored and inter-animated circlings was suddenly revealed as the mere superficies of a far vaster pattern in four dimensions, and that figure as the boundary of yet others in other worlds; till suddenly as the movement grew yet swifter, the interweaving more ecstatic, the relevance of all to all yet more intense, as dimension was added to dimension and that part of him which could reason and remember was dropped farther and farther behind that part of him which saw, even then, at the very zenith of complexity, complexity was eaten up and faded … and a simplicity beyond all comprehension, ancient and young as spring, illimitable, pellucid, drew him with cords of infinite desire into its own stillness" (p. 219).

I shall forebear further quotation — this being sufficient to demonstrate just how hard Lewis's substance is pressing against his form. It also, by the way, demonstrates a certain Johnsonian Latinity in his style, which may or may not be relevant to our concerns. I am not sure to what degree Lewis himself knew what was happening here, but we know that by November 1941 (Lewis finished the book by May 1942), he had "got Ransom to Venus and through his first conversation with the 'Eve' of that world; a difficult chapter"— going on (in the letter quoted) to say how what he was trying to do must "combine characteristics which the Fall has put poles apart" (quoted in Donald Glover, *C. S. Lewis: The Art of Enchantment*, p. 93). It is evident that he knew there would be difficulty in any literary expression of what he wanted to say, and given his concern at the time with the problems of literary form (as, specifically, in the *Preface to Paradise Lost*), I think it likely he knew perfectly well where the sticking point was. Certainly I (who share Lewis's problems with plots) could predict precisely this difficulty — in fact, my predictions of it are what keep me at the critical last — and he was a far more accomplished, and deliberate, writer than I. Be all that as it may, the difficulty was real, and Lewis found a way to handle it, or his genius (old sense) found a way for him. At least one contemporary reader has asked me if I thought Lewis had come on his description of the Great Dance through taking drugs, since in some drug-induced states sound does appear as light: the answer is, one assumes, *no* (and one might quote here Lewis's distinction, when his final illness necessitated his being drugged, between the passing nature of the drug-induced state and the lasting nature of the truly mystic).

Nevertheless, since Lewis apparently distrusted — and rarely experienced — mystical visions, we may reasonably ask where the Great Dance came from. The answer, I believe, is twofold. First, this too is "realization" — the imaginative reconstruction and filling out of what someone else's experience "must have been like," which is of course the quality Lewis has particularly singled out for praise in Malory, and which we have already noted as characteristic of the "Englishness of English art." What I believe Lewis has done here is take descriptions — stories — of mystical experience and "realize" them; whose stories I do not know, but it is unlikely they come from the eighteenth century. Or perhaps they do. Perhaps the Great Dance is a "realization" of what things must be like if the plain and practical advice of, say, William Law is to be followed. To put the matter briefly, I am reasonably sure what Lewis has done, but not what his original materials were.

Let me introduce my second point by way of a digression. I recall that many years ago, the late John Kirkpatrick spoke at the New York C. S. Lewis Society on the Great Dance as illuminated by music theory. I tried, over the years, to get him to expand his talk into an essay, but he never did. I also asked him where Lewis, who was notoriously unmusical in church, would have absorbed any music theory: the answer came to me the other day and is noted earlier in this chapter—from Maureen Moore and W. H. Lewis, who was studying music and composing in the latter 1930s at least (and from Nevill Coghill). For our purposes, what is important is John Kirkpatrick's analysis and the music lessons at The Kilns, and the suggestion these make as to the genre of *Perelandra*.

Lewis had the assistance of his more musical brother, his much more musical "sister"—Maureen—as well as of his dancing friend, Owen Barfield, or more accurately, his dancing friends, Owen and Maud Barfield. Here I have recourse to Major Lewis's diaries and to a recollection of a long-ago conversation with the Barfields, as well as to conversations with the late John and Hope Kirkpatrick—for my own musicality unaided is far less than my eighteenth-century expertise, and that is little enough. In this conversation with the Barfields, the picture of the Lewis/Moore household at The Kilns in the 1930s became clearer to me than it ever had been. A number of the household friends were musical, particularly "Smudge" (Vida Mary Wiblin, the musical director of the Magdalen College School 1926–37), and I am told Mrs. Moore had a good voice and liked to sing. Lewis, as a schoolboy, had learned the requisite popular songs, and of course been instructed in dancing (*Surprised by Joy*, pp. 68–69), but he was the unmusical one of the brothers, an unmusical, undancing man in a musical, even a dancing, household.

To be sure, he had not grown up in a musical household. Music was not a major part of the house at Little Lea. But it was not unknown. The figure of Fanny Burney comes in here briefly. One of the *dicta* in *Pudaita Pie* (no. 86) is Albert Lewis's reaction to a mention of the reception of Signora Agujari by the Burney family, in a way suggesting some knowledge of that incident and of the Burney family household. This speaks not to musical knowledge. In the household of CSL's youth musical knowledge almost certainly did not extend beyond music hall, and Gilbert and Sullivan, and Irish airs (his father was surprised when CSL appeared to be surprised that the Connaught Rangers had a bagpiper). But it speaks at least to some knowledge of the history of music, and particularly the eighteenth-century social history of music. I think this mixed with the "musicality" of the Janie King Moore years at The Kilns, and Lewis's ability as *réalisateur*, to produce at least the frame of reference in which the Great Dance could be conceived. But there was one musical area in which Lewis had at least some claim to expertise, and though I cannot of my own knowledge speak to its relevance, I have what I think excellent authority for believing it highly relevant.

It was thirty years ago that I asked John Kirkpatrick how he would define the Great Dance in musical terms. At the New York C. S. Lewis Society he had spoken of the operatic structure of that part of *Perelandra*, and my question was, "What operas are we talking about?" He gently pointed out the obvious, that CSL was for much of his life a *dévoté* of Wagnerian opera, particularly the Ring Cycle. He briefly — and quite extemporaneously — sketched a view of *Perelandra* as Wagnerian opera: it was this sketch I tried to get him to expand. One thing he made clear. With the Great Dance, at least in its musical form, we have left the Augustan age, and entered the Romantic.

The Dance reaches its crescendo: "complexity was eaten up and faded ... and a simplicity beyond all comprehension ... drew him with cords of infinite desire into its own stillness ... at the very moment when he stood farthest from our ordinary mode of being he had the sense of stripping off encumbrances and awaking from trance, and coming to himself" (*Perelandra*, p. 219). With a gesture he looks around him ... to find it is a year later, the animals have gone about their business, and his casket awaits him for his trip back to Thulcandra, back to the silent planet. The king and queen and the Great Eldila bid him farewell. "Then came the great cumbrous noise of the lid being fastened on above him. Then, for a few seconds, noises without, in the world from which he was eternally divided. Then his consciousness was engulfed" (p. 222). And those are the last words of the book.

This has passed beyond *recitatif*, beyond cantata, beyond any pageant, musical or not, to the effect of great music. To me, it awakens thoughts of Beethoven beyond Wagner, and I have sought evidence that CSL's was listening to Beethoven's Ninth in the late 1930s. But all I can find in Warren Lewis's diaries is that he and CSL listened to Holst's *The Planets* in 1935 (*Brothers and Friends*, p. 169), at the same performance with a Vaughan Williams symphony that CSL thought quite the best he had ever heard. And there, till there is further research carried out by someone more expert than I, the matter of Lewis's (and *Perelandra*'s) musicality must needs rest. Yet I am sure that the Ninth played a part. And perhaps it is also worth noting that one of the definitions of *pastoral* is a song.

V

Thulcandra, or
Our Time Under
That Hideous Strength

Whereas *Perelandra* does not stick entirely to the fairy-tale mode (although it is a — slightly lopsided — "there and back again" story), *That Hideous Strength* defines and is defined by that mode. Of course, *Perelandra* has more of Elvish enchantment in it (you recall Tolkien's phrase in "On Fairy Stories"), while *That Hideous Strength* is a university novel. Lewis claimed that the outer edges of his "fairy tale" of deviltry had to be shown touching a workaday world he knew — which was the university world. But if he had not seen the university world as rife with the promise of deviltry, he would not have written the book he wrote. The great versions of the story of Faust were written in the sixteenth century by Christopher Marlowe and the nineteenth century by Goethe: there is a Faustian element in *That Hideous Strength*, but I would be hard put to link it to any one century. A combination of the eighteenth and the twentieth, perhaps?

In one sense, any eighteenth-century novel is analogous to the university novel, inasmuch as the purpose of the satirical pageant is instruction — as with *That Hideous Strength*. Note (as I have elsewhere pointed out) that the kind of things one says to praise this novel are the kind of things one says to praise any old-fashioned novel. The characters are well-drawn ("realized" in our sense); the action follows logically (that is, the characters act "in character" and their action in character is the action of the book); the story is clearly told; the people are "real"; the book "overflows with life." My point is not that all these are true all the time —

there are certainly weak passages — but that these are the kind of statements whose degree of truth determines the book's success. Though it speaks with the tongues of men and of angels, it is rarely mythopoetic (Lewis once remarked that he was not very good at "Archangelese" — whether that is true or no, he, like Johnson, is showing us pictures of the "dogs he knows").

In fact, one of the difficulties Lewis's admirers seem to have with the book is that it remains resolutely earthbound until Ransom is ready to leave the earth. Then the sudden transformation from serious novel to farce and vision (pretty much simultaneously) leaves a number of readers cold. The farce is, of course, well within the Swiftian tradition: what may be harder to recognize is that so also is the sudden vision. If we are unprepared, it is because we understand both "realism" and the function of the novel in ways different from the ways they were understood at least through Dickens, when (witness *Pickwick*), the novel was still in part satirical pageant.

We expect (if subconsciously) that the fairy-tale mode will not obtain — that humdrum scenes will lead to further humdrum scenes, not to pantomime animals and planetary angels. Do we then prefer the humdrum to the visionary — "O tedium, tedium, tedium ... the frenzied ceremonial humming of the humdrum"? No, but we like to know where we stand. A mystery writer who introduces a coincidental solution to the mystery is not playing fair: he is instead changing the rules in midgame. So here — or at least so we think here. That Lewis knew we might think so is shown by his initial warning in the preface: "I have called this a fairy-tale in the hope that no one who dislikes fantasy may be misled by the first two chapters into reading further, and then complain of his disappointment" (p. 7).

He put that warning in its most easily understandable form, of course, much more understandable than if he had said, "I have called this an eighteenth-century English novel in the hope that no one who dislikes the intermixture of *didache*, comic characters, "real life," unreal estates, pageant, detailed observation, realization (and so on) that characterizes the form may be misled...." But I think the latter form would itself have been much less misleading.

That Lewis mixed heraldry and detailed observation in *That Hideous*

Strength as in its predecessors may explain some of the resistance to that book — we do not think of our earth as heraldic. I suggest we confront this problem head-on. What we feel is appropriate to other worlds — the pageant background, the heraldic blazonry — does not seem fitting to our own. The reverse of this is that when the heraldry is absent in other-worldly description, as some have suggested it is in the Othertime of *The Dark Tower* (but this is a misapprehension), we feel cheated, or at least let down. But the detailed observation is there, no less in *That Hideous Strength* and *The Dark Tower* than in *Out of the Silent Planet* and *Perelandra*. After all, *Out of the Silent Planet* begins in Much Nadderby and Sterk (or in between them), *Perelandra* begins with a country cottage, *That Hideous Strength* begins with a small university — and all progress to the depths of heaven and the descent of the gods.

This chapter focuses on four matters. The first is the "humdrum" opening of *That Hideous Strength*, the college meeting, as an example of moral imagination in which the imagining and the "realization" are good but in part mere reporting. The second is Denniston's "Distributivism" as one part of the transition from humdrum beginning to unreal estates — though a part in which Lewis has not perhaps projected his imagining to its full Euclidean conclusion, which some might call an extreme. The third is what I have called the Last Dinner, the disastrous banquet at Belbury, when it happens that *qui Verbum Dei contempserunt, eis auferetur etiam verbum hominis*, them that have contemned the Word of God, from them also shall the word of man be taken away. I know several Christian scholars who think this scene a blight and a travesty. I do not think it is, but I think I had best be about showing why that is the case. The fourth, for the journey homeward to habitual self, is Curry and his (temporal) salvation, one of the best examples of fully developed (and this-worldly) moral imagination in the book. Let us look at these four matters.

The College Meeting: Frenzied Humming of the Humdrum

"O! tedium, tedium, tedium. Te-di-'um te-di-'um te-di-'um! The frenzied ceremonial humming of the hum-drum." Does anyone now recognize the words of Christopher Fry? Perhaps not, but they are applicable here. There is a kind of frenzied nature to Lewis's reaction to the Oxford common-rooms (visible in his diaries), that perhaps interferes with the purity of his moral imagination. We have known for a while that T. D. Weldon of Magdalen (1896–1958) was the model for Lord Feverstone. Now we have Lewis's sketch of Weldon (in *All My Road Before Me*, ed. Walter Hooper [1991], pp. 482–83):

"*Determined to be a villain.* He is a man of the melancholy complexion: his face very pale, his hair very black and streaked down with oil over his head without a parting: his mouth long and thin: his features clear cut, and very little flesh on the face. He is a frequent and loud laugher, but the expression of his face in repose is fierce and sullen. He carries a great deal of liquor without being drunk. His light talk is cynicism and bawdy: when he grows serious without anger (which is seldom) he likes to rap out his sentences very sharply and close his mouth after them like a trap. In anger ... he is not at all hot, but grows paler, smiles a great deal and is powerful in dialectic. He is insolent by custom to servants and to old men, yet capable of kindliness, though not to be depended on. He showed himself courageous in the war and is so in peace. He has great abilities, but would despise himself if he wasted them on disinterested undertakings. He gives no quarter and would ask none. He believes that he has seen through everything and lives a rock bottom. He would be capable of treachery, and would think the victim a fool for being betrayed. Contempt is his ruling passion: courage his chief virtue."

This was written about 1928. Though he appears in *Out of the Silent Planet* (1938), Feverstone is the more full-blown villain in *That Hideous Strength* (1943). Our concern with him here is his actions at the college meeting, and with the college meeting generally (*That Hideous Strength*, pp. 23–28). "The most controversial business before the College Meeting was the question of selling Bragdon Wood. The purchaser was the N.I.C.E., the National Institute of Co-ordinated Experiments.... The N.I.C.E. was the first-fruits of that constructive fusion between the state and the laboratory on which so many thoughtful people base their hopes of a better world. It was to be free from almost all the tiresome restraints — 'red tape' was the word its supporters used — which have hitherto hampered research in this country" (pp. 23-24). Now, watch the maneuvering (and the perfect recapture of donnish ways)—as well as the delineation of Feverstone—"Dick Devine as he used to be" (p. 18).

"The Progressive Element managed its business really very well. Most of the Fellows did not know when they came into the Soler that there was any question of selling the Wood. They saw, of course, from their agenda paper that item Fifteen was, 'Sale of College Land,' but as that appeared at almost every College Meeting, they were not very interested. On the other hand, they did see that item One was 'Questions about Bragdon Wood.' These were not concerned with the proposed sale" (p. 23). In fact they were concerned first with the preservation of Bragdon (from a society concerned with the preservation of ancient monuments), then from a society of Spiritualists who wanted leave to investigate "reported phenomena" in the Wood—"a letter 'connected,' as Curry said, 'with the next, which, with the Warden's permission, I will now read to you'"—from a firm wishing to make a film, "not exactly of the phenomena, but of the Spiritualists looking for the phenomena" (p. 24).

"Then came a new voice from a quite different part of the Soler"—Feverstone apparently "leading a revolt against 'Curry and his gang'" (p. 24), and asking whether something should not in fact be done about the wall and the well and the Wood. Eventually the matter of preservation was tabled till the next meeting, there was discussion of the N.I.C.E. (item Two), and then item Three, "Rectification of an anomaly of the stipends of Junior Fellows," was taken up, with the Bursar pointing out that this was the second question of major expenditure to come before them that day (the preservation of the Wood being the first). "A great deal more was said, but the Bursar remained unanswered, the matter was postponed, and when, at a quarter to two, the Fellows came out of the Soler, hungry and headachy and ravenous for tobacco, every junior had it fixed in his mind that a new wall for the Wood and a rise in his own stipend were strictly exclusive alternatives" (p. 26). There follows what I take to be a case of Lewis's unforced, but donnish, sense of humor.

"'That darn Wood has been in our way all morning,' said one. 'We're not out of it yet,' said another." I think this came to Lewis spontaneously as he wrote his account of the meeting: it is in the same vein in which Lewis once responded to a Portuguese guest at high table who said, when served haggis, that he felt like a gastronomic Columbus: "The comparison is wayward in your case — why not a vascular da Gama?"

"It was not until six o'clock that all the converging lines of thought and feeling aroused by the earlier business came together upon the question of selling Bragdon Wood. It was not called 'the sale of Bragdon Wood.' The Bursar called it 'the sale of the area coloured pink on the plan which, with the Warden's permission, I will now pass around the table.' He pointed out quite frankly that this involved the loss of *part* of the wood" (p. 27). In the end, "the advantages of the sale discovered themselves one by one, like ripe fruit dropping into the hand" — the Diehards to whom Bragdon Wood is a fact of life cannot believe what is happening — and when "old Jewel, blind and shaky, and almost weeping, rose to his feet, his voice was hardly audible.... At this moment Lord Feverstone sprang to his feet, folded his arms, and looking straight at the old man said in a very loud, clear voice: "If Canon Jewel wishes us *not* to hear his views, I suggest that his end could better be obtained by silence" (p. 28).

Now I wonder if that was something Harry Weldon once said in the Magdalen Common Room. Recall Lewis about Weldon: "He is insolent by custom ... to old men." What is certain is that this is not, for Lewis, the spontaneous overflow of powerful emotions recollected in tranquility. Emotions, yes. Tranquility, no. If the moral imagination is expressed in the activity of the secondary imagination, rather than the passivity of the primary, I am not entirely certain how much of the moral imagination is at work here. There is an uncomfortable sense that this is reporting (though rather good reporting), rather than imagining. I do not see that this strides beyond the barriers of private experience and events of the moment, nor does it cover the defects of our naked shivering nature, nor is Lewis's own experience yet seen *sub specie aeternitatis*. But it is very good reporting.

It will be recalled that Lewis goes on from this point to reflect that Jewel had already been an old man in the days before the First War, when old men were treated with respect — and then to report Feverstone's response to Mark's expression of pity for Jewel — that (like Clausewitz) he believes that total warfare is the most humane in the long run. And here, and perhaps here only in this scene, we verge on the moral imagination with esemplastic force, in this kind of reminder that we are at war, and this college meeting is one more campaign in the history of the war. The humdrum begins, however faintly, to sound as a war drum.

Economic Theory: C. S. Lewis, Distributist

Oddly, the nexus (or one of them) that brings us into the realm of the spirit in *That Hideous Strength*, a bridge — so to speak — between the humdrum beginning and the deviltry of the N.I.C.E. — is a doctrine in economic theory. To be sure, not a well-known economic theory, and one which attempted to apply spiritual principles to economics, but finding economic theory in Lewis is rather like finding knowledge of political events.

"One sees now that Denniston would never have done. Most emphatically not. A brilliant man at that time, of course, but he seems to have gone quite off the rails since then with all his Distributivism and what not. They tell me he's likely to end up in a monastery" (*That Hideous Strength*, p. 9). The speaker is Curry, the listener Mark Studdock, and the unflattered subject, of course, Arthur Denniston, who had so nearly received Studdock's fellowship at Bracton.

Now Denniston does not, at least in the book, end up in a monastery, though the Manor at St. Anne's has certain similarities to one, and though it is likely (I have never been quite sure) that he becomes Pendragon of Logres — at least as holy a state. (I might mention here that, to the best of my knowledge, and of Walter Hooper's, Lewis never explicitly said who was to follow Ransom as Pendragon [letter WH to me, 15 March 1970], but Mr. Hooper agrees with me that Denniston probably was the choice.) Nor has Denniston truly gone off the rails. But we may assume that Curry has been accurate (or almost accurate) in calling him a Distributivist, if indeed we know, or can find out, what exactly it was that he was calling him. The "almost accurate" comes from the fact that the doctrine is correctly Distributism rather than Distributivism. The importance of this subject for us is that Distributism comes precisely from the artistic apprehension of right order applied to the subject of economics — to be exact, from the artistic apprehension of right order by G. K. Chesterton.

Distributism was an economic and political polity proclaimed and supported by the League for the Defence of Liberty by the Distribution of Property, chiefly (though not only) in the 1920s. It was, as noted, the brain child and ward of G. K. Chesterton, and the only lengthy exposition of the principles of Distributism I have come across is to be found in his book, *The Outline of Sanity* (1926). A reading of that book, while it has not convinced me that Distributism is a workable economic doctrine, has convinced me that Denniston's "Distributivism" is not accidental and that, as of 1943, Lewis's own economics were essentially Distributist.

It will be remembered that Lewis, in another context, once gave something of his view of a fully Christian society. "We should feel that its economic life was very socialistic and, in that sense, 'advanced,' but that its family life and its code of manners were rather old-fashioned — perhaps even ceremonious and aristocratic" (*Mere Christianity*, 1952, p. 66). But I find it hard to take the word "socialistic" to be exactly meant unless it is the socialism of William Morris's *Dream of John Ball*, socialism intended (one might say) in a purely Kelmscottian sense: not that the State should own factories but that Everyman should own his own land.

Likewise, though St. Anne's might be called "socialistic" or even "communistic" — for the property is held by the Company of Logres and the work is shared — it has little enough to do with the Socialism of the Fabians, and nothing at all to do with that of the present Labour Party. It is difficult, however, not to convict Lewis of semantic inexactitude here: at the very least, I wonder if his desire to speak colloquially did not lead him astray. Of course, it is quite possible that Lewis's listeners understood "socialistic" simply to mean "modern" or "nonfeudal" or something of that sort. He may have gauged his audience more accurately than I can now. In any case, however they understood "socialistic," it is clear that not a tithe of them — not yet a tithe of a present-day graduate seminar in economics — would have understood him had he said that the economic life of the Christian society would be Distributist. Yet if we are interested in Lewis's imaginative perception of right order, we should be able to understand such a statement.

Distributism, as Chesterton preached it, was essentially a doctrine that between the very similar evils of monopoly (the end result, in Chesterton's view, of private enterprise) and Communism (as practiced, the end result of government control), there is very little to choose — and that, moreover, both private enterprise and government control hastened to their end result. Accordingly, it becomes necessary to resist both, and the means of resistance lie in the widest possible distribution of private property (*The Outline of Sanity*, pp. 9, 11–12 *et seq.*). This means that the small shop should be preserved as against the large one, the small farm preserved as against the large one (indeed, if necessary, the small farm created), the small factory — the true *manu*-factory — preserved as against the large one (*Outline*, esp. pp. 61–69, 115–27, 141–50). It sounds, on the surface, rather like the program for an Industrial Counter-Revolution, and that was indeed almost exactly what it was. We can begin to see, I think, how this inspired Lewis's vision of St. Anne's, and how it serves as a link between our world and the perilous realms of the spirit.

In passing, one curious thing may be remarked. Chesterton, writing in 1926, or rather up to 1926 (for the book is made up, in general, of earlier newspaper articles), has an oddly modern sound in much of what he says. "I think the monster emporium is not only vulgar and insolent, but incompetent and uncomfortable; and I deny that its large organization is efficient. Large organization is loose organization. Nay, it would be almost as true to say organization is disorganization" (p. 62). But, save for its suggesting the strength of Chesterton's moral imagination of order, this is a digression: the point at issue here is not so much the truth of what GKC said, but what precisely Distributism entailed, and how it formed Lewis's moral imagination, and thus how it serves to link our world and the realms of the spirit (I have toyed, also, with the thought that Lewis might have absorbed some of Rudolf Steiner's economics from Owen Barfield, who translated Steiner on economics — but, on reconsideration, I think not).

The basic tenet, beyond the small shops and small factories, was the need for small landholdings, for a stable peasantry tied to their own land. Chesterton argues (perhaps with justice, but again, that is not the point) that capitalist monopoly is a weed that grows in the waste places: it will not grow up where there are industrious small farmers owning their own farms, planting and harvesting their own crops (*Outline*, p. 12). This, as

I suggested immediately above, is what Lewis envisioned in the Manor of St. Anne's, almost precisely a Distributist economy in microcosm.

To begin with, the company raise their own vegetables — and, for that matter, their own bacon at least as well (*That Hideous Strength*, pp. 190 ["trenching celery"], 306 ["the pigs are kept in a stye and killed for bacon"]). And on this, Chesterton is clear. "Exchange and variation can … be given their reasonable place … but there would be somewhere in the centre of civilization a type that was truly independent; in the sense of producing and consuming within its own social circle" (*Outline*, p. 136). That is exactly what happens at St. Anne's, center of the civilization of Logres: the production and consumption goes on within that circle only.

Moreover, none of the company, except perhaps MacPhee, has any background in country living. Ransom is a don, Grace Ironwood a doctor, Dimble and his wife scholars (don and don's wife), Arthur and Camilla Denniston also, Jane Studdock a scholar, if "not perhaps a very original" one (*That Hideous Strength*, p. 2), Ivy Maggs a housekeeper; MacPhee, one supposes, was a tutor, like his model, the Great Knock, but perhaps the Great Knock could trench celery with the best of them. In any case, one turns to Chesterton and finds that the nucleus of his England of small farms comes from the cities. "We have to consider whether there are any materials out of which to make peasants to make a peasantry … the number of people who would like to get out of the tangle of mere ramifications and communications in the town, and get back nearer to the roots of things, where things are made directly out of nature, I believe to be very large" (*Outline*, p. 123). In yet a second way, then, St. Anne's is a microcosm of Distributism at work, and this microcosm has its birth in Lewis's faculty of moral imagination of the ordering of things.

In addition, though this does not deal directly with St. Anne's, there is an instructive comparison to be made between the "no doubt recalcitrant and backward" laborers enjoying their thick sandwiches and mug of beer at the Two Bells in Cure Hardy (*That Hideous Strength*, p. 93), and the imported impersonal workmen hired by the N.I.C.E. at Edgestow. The scene at Cure Hardy is precisely idyllic. The scenes of the workmen at Edgestow are like something taking place on the outskirts of hell — the scrum that breaks Henrietta Maria's window, the raucous voices disturbing the funeral, and, of course, Miss Hardcastle's riot (*That Hideous Strength*, pp. 100, 140, 172 *et seq.*). The idyll is a Distributist idyll (though it is more), and the outskirts of hell are the outskirts of a Socialist experiment, the N.I.C.E. — remember how, in Mark's editorial, he accuses the enemies of the National Institute of being in favor of the Liberties of the capitalists (p. 149).

One must be careful not to belabor the point. Evidently there is much more to St. Anne's and to this part of the book than Distributism. But in view of the fact that this has not often been a point of concern, and in view of the fact that this clue to Lewis's own economic views has been widely overlooked (many years ago, in August 1970, I believe, I heard him described at a New York C.S. Lewis Society meeting as a Socialist) — and particularly in view of its significance in Lewis's artistic apprehension of right order, and as a link between the beginning of the book and its climax in the perilous realms — it seems to me worthwhile to point all this out. And before we leave this section, one other passage ought to be noted.

Mark, it will be remembered, had "recommended that certain classes of people should be gradually eliminated: but he had never been there when a small shopkeeper went to the workhouse or a starved old woman of the governess type came to the very last day and hour and minute in the cold attic. He knew nothing about the last half cup of cocoa drunk slowly ten days before" (*That Hideous Strength*, p. 212). I have seldom heard the anger in Lewis's voice more clearly than I hear it in these words: reflect for a moment on the fact that the elimination of certain classes is part of the modern Socialist dogma, and then ask if Lewis is a Socialist, if it is still necessary to ask. To say that he was is to play Humpty-Dumpty's game with words — and it is his moral imagination which keeps him from it. (Yet somehow this anger is less personal than Lewis's anger against Weldon/Feverstone, an anger both feverish and stony, if not entirely well-done.) For some (doubtless odd and personal) reason, I connect this passage with the remarkable book *God Calling*, by Two Listeners (1938).

Lewis was not, to be sure, a capitalist, and certainly not an advocate of that unrestrained pursuit of profit in a laissez-faire economy some consider the capitalist ideal. But in *That Hideous Strength* as elsewhere he was Chesterton's disciple in many ways (note the similarities between the robing scene at the end of *That Hideous Strength* and that before the meeting with Sunday in *The Man Who Was Thursday*), not least in the application of moral imagination to economics.

The Last Dinner: *Qui Contempserunt Verbum Dei*

One point should be dealt with at the outset. I have referred to the Last Dinner at Belbury as *Grand Guignol* and I have used Julien Benda's *Trahison des Clercs* in my discussion of Curry. As one friend observed of this chapter, "a lot of French around for a book that concerns the Englishness of C. S. Lewis." (And we note that Dimble quotes the Frenchman, Brother Lawrence, in *That Hideous Strength*, p. 224.) The point is valid, but the implication is not — or not entirely. First, an appeal to the Arthurian legends is an appeal to what comes to us in part through French literature. Second, France was evidently on Lewis's mind, as in the passage in *That Hideous Strength* about the Goddess Reason being enthroned in France and "then it will be Spring" (*That Hideous Strength*, p. 371). Third, this book was written when Warren Lewis's long study of seventeenth century France was beginning to bear scholarly fruit. The presence of what is French is easily explained — and, of course, Lewis's art would be not much less English if he wrote in French. Nonetheless, there is something of a problem that this leads us into.

Briefly, as we have noted, Lewis's realm of the spirit here is Thulcandra, Tellus, Earth. Specifically, that part of Earth that is England — perhaps forever England. We can use the English technique for making the unfamiliar — the space voyage — into the familiar, but how do we make the familiar into the unfamiliar? The answer Fielding gave us in *Tom Jones* and Gay in *The Beggar's Opera* is to put the story of familiar events into the form of pageant, and that is not unlike the answer given on the other side of the Channel by Savinien-Hércule de Cyrano de Bérgerac in his *Comicall Historie of the States and Empires of the Sunne and the Moone* (1651) and by several generations of science fiction writers in their satires — Menippean or otherwise — as James Blish reminded us in his definition of science fiction. Or the formalist critic Darko Suvin in call-ing science-fiction the literature of cognitive estrangement.

Be all this as it may, let us return to the matter of the novel's cli-max. There is some question in my mind whether the true climax of *That Hideous Strength* is the dinner at Belbury and the events in the chaos immediately afterward, or the visitation of angelic powers at St. Anne's (or can they be separated?). Artistically (if they can), the climax is, I think, the dinner, though spiritually it is the visitation: here we will stick with the artistic climax. Now, two charges are frequently leveled against Lewis's treatment of the diners at Belbury. The punishment is absurdly mismatched with the crime: Wither and Frost and Feverstone survive the dinner and are given another chance to choose salvation — a chance denied to lesser evildoers like Jules, not to mention the anonymous (but recog-nizable) diners:

"There were the placid faces of elderly *bons viveurs* whom food and wine had placed in a contentment which no amount of speeches could violate. There were the patient faces of responsible but serious diners, who had long since learned how to pursue their own thoughts, while attending to the speech just enough to respond wherever a laugh or a low rumble of serious assent was obligatory. There was the usual fidgety expression on the faces of young men unappreciative of port and hun-gry for tobacco. There was bright over-elaborate attention on the pow-dered faces of women who knew their duty to society" (p. 343).

What have these people done to deserve what befalls them? Is there not something repellent in the carnival of gore, the elephant with Steele grasped by its trunk, the tiger worrying Fairy Hardcastle into a bloody wreck, the fatal scrum, and particularly the death and destruction of these *bons viveurs* and serious diners and young men and young women? In this case it will not do to say, as Grace Ironwood said of Edgestow, "that nearly everyone except the very good (who were ripe for fair dis-missal) and the very bad, had already left Edgestow" (p. 371). Yet, as she continues, we find the answer: "I agree with Arthur. Those who have for-gotten Logres sink into Britain. Those who call for Nonsense will find that it comes" (pp. 371–72).

Granted, this is neither a lovely nor a lovable passage, and it fairly reeks of blood and gore — and Lewis could well have carried it off better —

I think it important to see the tradition that lies behind it. Before getting back to that tradition, I would like to turn for a moment to the morality of that poem of pure imagination, *The Rime of the Ancient Mariner*. We ask whether the punishment of the mariner fits the crime of killing the albatross, and whether the sea snakes of redemption are not a bit peculiar — a bit disordered, even, or at best like Mrs. Barbauld's genie.

The answer is that these are symbols participating in the moral unity they represent. Listen to Ransom in almost his last words in *That Hideous Strength*. The animals are freed and Perelandra returns for him (pp. 378–379). Mr. Bultitude finds a Mrs. Bultitude; the mare finds a stallion; there are revels among the mice in the wainscoting. MacPhee asks, "In the name of Hell, where's all them beasts coming from?"

"'They are the liberated prisoners from Belbury,' said the Director. 'She comes more near the Earth than she was wont to — to make Earth sane. Perelandra is all about us, and Man is no longer isolated. We are now as we ought to be — between the angels who are our elder brothers and the beasts who are our jesters, servants, and playfellows.'" Then there are elephants in the garden, and Grace Ironwood speaks: "How light it is! Brighter than moonlight: almost brighter than day. A great dome of light stands over the whole garden. Look! The elephants are dancing. How high they lift their feet. And they go round and round. And oh, look! — how they lift their trunks. And how ceremonial they are. It is like a minuet of giants. They are not like the other animals. They are a sort of good daemons."

Now one of these at least is presumably the elephant rampaging with Steele in his trunk. And we recall Merlinus's prophecy (p. 282) that "before Christmas this bear would do the best deed that any bear had done in Britain except some other bear that none of us had ever heard of" (the speaker is Dimble). This is presumably the killing of Wither by a "huge bear, rising to its hind legs ... its mouth open, its eyes flaming, its fore-paws spread out as if for an embrace" (p. 355). This is after Merlinus has laid his hand on Mr. Bultitude, and the bear's "dark mind was filled with excitement as though some long forbidden and forgotten pleasure were suddenly held out to it" (p. 351). As with Ransom's righteous anger at the Unman on Perelandra, so here is just and righteous war.

Before coming to any conclusion on Lewis's moral imagination as revealed in the last dinner and the other parts of the killing of Belbury, let me suggest again that Lewis is in the tradition of Dean Swift and Dr. Johnson, and also that this tradition has Rabelais not far in its background. In particular, the dialogue of order and carnival, the tradition of the *serio ludere*, seems to me relevant here. Here is Professor Jan Kott on Marlowe (*The Bottom Translation*, p. 13): "Throughout the entire *Tragicall History*, at least from the first through fourth acts, *buffo* follows *serio*. After Faustus's incantations and the summoning of Mephistophilis, Wagner, Faustus's servant and pupil, threatens to change Clown, his hungry colleague, into a dog, cat, mouse, or rat.... In *serio ludere*, whose patrons in antiquity are Apuleius and Lucian [and — author's note — Lucian is the patron of science fiction], *serio* is *buffo* and *buffo* is *serio*. There is seriousness in the laughter and laughter in the seriousness. The high and the low ... the inflated and the shriveled ... the face and the mask, the refined and the vulgar, the learned and the rude, reflect and ape each other as in a fun-house mirror." And he goes on to observe that "This medieval hell and the vulgar adventures of a folk magus have never been read from the perspective of carnival laughter and popular wisdom" (p. 13).

The *Tragicall History* is a history of damnation, but it is, on this showing, part of the same tradition that gives us *Grand Guignol*. The gorilla (quite literally) apes Jules at the banquet; the tramp is dressed as a doctor of divinity; and (in a kind of turn-about on Wagner and Clown) the beasts are turned into demons, as the people have been turned into beasts. Now, is this last dinner a disproportionate punishment for the diners? To this there are two different answers. First, I daresay it is — but that this is scarcely a complaint, in this context. The antics of a Punch-and-Judy show are disproportionate. *Grand Guignol* is disproportionate. Punch's very nose and chin are disproportionate. Second, I daresay it is, in much the same way that the Mariner's punishment for killing the albatross is disproportionate (a disproportion implicit in "Inasmuch as ye have done it unto the least of these My brethren, ye have done it unto Me"). Lewis has taken his moral imagination to extremes — an extreme of carnival and an extreme of holy order. We think of this last dinner as only an extreme of carnival, and yes — it is Rabelaisan, I suppose. The *serio* is *buffo* and the *buffo* is *serio*. There are revels among the mice in the wainscoting, "So geht es in Snutzeputzhausel / Da singen und tanzen die Mausel" (*That Hideous Strength*, p. 378), and that is part of the serious passage in the *serio ludere*. When Mr. Bultitude kills Wither (if indeed Wither was "alive" as we use the word), that is part of a humorous (*buffo*) passage in the *serio ludere*. This, too, is a drama of damnation, and it is all quite appropriately medieval.

It may be that the nonsense words in the speeches at the last dinner can be taken as a kind of indication what was in Lewis's mind at the time he wrote *That Hideous Strength*. Consider the three full sentences from the speech by Jules. First, "The madrigore of verjuice must be talthibianised." Second, "The surrogates esemplanted in a continual of porous variations." Third, "We shall not till we can secure the erebation of all prostundiary initems" (all from *That Hideous Strength*, p. 344). There are clues also, of course, in trusting to Calvary for salvation in modern war, and in the word *aholibate* (was Aholibah not the daughter in Egypt who committed whoredoms and whom Ezekiel likens to Jerusalem in *Ezekiel* 23:4, 36?), but let us look at the three full sentences. Or rather, let us look at four words in these sentences (though not all are existing words). Let us look at *madrigore, verjuice, esemplanted,* and *erebation*.

We have reminiscences of mandrake, Coleridge's *esemplastic* faculty, the gates of Erebus — and one actual though uncommon word, verjuice, sour green grape juice. I think "talthibianising" the madrigore of verjuice, the esemplanting of the surrogates in a continual of porous variations, and securing the erebation of all prostundiary initems, all suggest a mad garden and rank growth of legal nonsense — and this is the same Lewis who wrote the nonsense poem "Awake My Lute!" and at about the same time. More to our point, perhaps, a man who uses the word "esemplanted" has Coleridge on his mind. And all these words are from a mind very well-stocked with medieval furniture.

I am arguing that, far from being a failure, these scenes, like his "realizing" Curry's salvation, are really a highly successful projection of the moral imagination, whereas the projection of the Distributist vision is incomplete, and the college meeting mostly reporting. Let me return now to the matter of the disproportionate punishment for the (assumed or known) transgressions of the diners. Admittedly, the scenes may not be to our literary taste (we may not like *Grand Guignol* or even Rabelais) — but there is still the matter of philosophy. Whatever our reaction to the blood and gore and low comedy, we must still consider whether there is a sense in which the diners deserved what they got. Consider the Mariner's killing of the albatross (and here I am quoting Robert Penn Warren):

"Many critics, even [John Livingston] Lowes, for example, dismiss the matter [of the Mariner's killing the albatross] with such words as *wanton, trivial, unthinking.* They are concerned with the act at a literal level only.... This literal-mindedness leads to the view that there is a monstrous and illogical discrepancy between the crime and its punishment.... But we have to ask ourselves what is the symbolic meaning of the act. In asking ourselves this question, we must remember that the symbol, in Coleridge's view [as in Lewis's], is not arbitrary, but *must contain in itself, literally considered, the seeds of the logic of its extension — that is, it must participate in the unity of which it is representative.*" (The emphasis is in the original.)

Now what is the symbol? Merlin's cry over the tumult and hubbub, quoted in part in the title to this section, gives the answer. The symbol is the Word, just as when Dimble speaks the Great Tongue before going out (as he believes) to meet death or Merlin (*That Hideous Strength*, pp. 228–29): "And Dimble ... raised his head, and great syllables of words that sounded like castles came out of his mouth.... The voice did not sound like Dimble's own: it was as if the words spoke themselves through him from some strong place at a distance — or as if they were not words at all but the present operations of God, the planets, and the Pendragon." It is not mere chance that Ransom is a semanticist — were he not he would not have known that Hyoi on Malacandra was speaking a language, indeed (a dialect of) this language of words that sounded like castles. These are the words of God, as Maleldil the Young is the Word of God, and *qui Verbum Dei contempserunt, eis auferetur etiam verbum hominis.* The symbol, quite literally considered (letter by letter?) holds in itself the seeds of its extension and indeed participates in the unity of which it is representative. That is a successful exercise of the moral imagination.

Petty Curry: Salvation by a Taste for Tripe and Onions

What I have to say on Curry's importance in the machinery of *That Hideous Strength*, and particularly on the journey homeward to habitual self that ends the story in the fairy-tale mode, may seem a little tendentious. After all, Jane Studdock goes through many of the events, far more than Curry does—indeed her story is pretty much half the story of *That Hideous Strength*—and the final scene suggests she is returning to her habitual domestic life with Mark (though Mark, of course, is changed). But she is in the ogre's castle briefly, is rescued, and then in the idyllic realm of St Anne's—where, however domestically, it would seem she stays, when her friend Arthur (Mark's friend, too) becomes Pendragon.

Finding a link between the opening and the return to habitual self is complicated by the fact that, in *That Hideous Strength*, almost everyone connected with Bracton College (and a good many connected with the University of Edgestow, but not with Bracton) perishes either at the hands of the N.I.C.E. or in the general holocaust at the end when the N.I.C.E. is overthrown. The singular exception is the Subwarden of Bracton, Curry—and a very singular exception it is. Even the "wholly innocent Warden" of Bracton, Charles Place, is missing and presumed dead in the course of the action; but Curry, the very leader of the Progressive Element, is spared. It seems a strange choice. (On Place, see *That Hideous Strength*, pp. 122 ["wholly innocent Warden"], 221 ["why Place and Rowley and Cunningham ... have been arrested, and where they are"].)

Curry is a military historian who will almost certainly never put college politics aside and get down to writing his book on military history. He loves business and wire-pulling for their own sake. He is a bore. He is "so used to superintending the lives of his colleagues that it [comes] naturally to him to superintend their deaths." He regards his survival as providential—because it means there is a responsible person left to deal with the refounding of Bracton College. He is, in short, rather a pompous ass, and more than a bit of a fool, though we are assured he is not a hypocrite. (*That Hideous Strength*, pp. 36 [military history], 40 ["loves business and wire-pulling for their own sake"], 83 ["a pompous fool"], 92 ["the fantastic suggestion that he, Curry, might be a bore"], 126 [the passage quoted], 374 ["Providential"].)

The point about hypocrisy is interesting, and one is inclined to think it important. It is made twice, once when Curry is present at Hingest's funeral, once when he hears the news that Bracton is destroyed. In the first case, he is "stricken by a heavy blow but still mindful that he [is] the father of the College and that amid all the spoils of mutability he, at any rate, must not give way" (*That Hideous Strength*, pp. 125–126). In the second, "without the least hypocrisy, habit and instinct had given his shoulders just such a droop, his eyes such a solemn sternness, his brow such a noble gravity, as a man of good feeling might be expected to exhibit on hearing such news" (p. 374). The two passages may be taken together to suggest that Curry in fact has grown into what he has been pretending to be. Lewis elsewhere makes the point that, if pretending to be better than one is can be called hypocrisy, then hypocrisy (of this sort at least) is half a virtue; one becomes what one pretends to be (*Surprised by Joy*, p. 192). It is not hard to see Curry as an example of this.

Walter Hooper once noted (in a letter to me 15 March 1970) that "Curry represents the kind of ass we shall always have to endure: he is a common fixture in almost every Oxford common-room, and Lewis was marvelously charitable in enduring such self-complacent bores." One thinks of Lewis's comment, in a letter to his publishers (quoted in Chad Walsh, *C. S. Lewis: Apostle to the Skeptics*, 1949, p. 162): "I have all the usual vices: the only virtue (if it is a virtue) which I can claim in any marked degree is a patience, amounting almost to a liking, for bores." One notes elsewhere in his work, especially in the 1940s, a preaching of patience for bores. It would in fact be possible to see in Curry's survival (as in Lewis's own patience) a sort of corollary to that passage in *The Screwtape Letters* where his Abysmal Sublimity remarks that "if the Enemy appeared to [the patient] in bodily form and demanded that total service for even one day, he ... would be greatly relieved if that one day involved nothing harder than listening to the conversation of a foolish woman" (pp. 107–08). It is not a mortal sin to be a bore, whatever the common-rooms say, and I think Lewis's moral imagination has accurately perceived the place of such a bore in the eternal order.

Yet, when all this is said, and one realizes that Curry is certainly not so bad by a long shot as he might be, one might still question whether this is his right place in the eternal order. Why was he preserved? To this there are two answers, one dealing with the function of his salvation in the machinery of the book, one with the spiritual argument of the book. For the second, our immediate concern here, it may be suggested that the key lies in Dimble's words (already quoted in a different context). His wife asks, "Aren't Merlin and the eldils a trifle ... well, *wholesale?* Did *all* Edgestow deserve to be wiped out?" He answers, when Denniston presents a kind of bill of indictment, "I'm afraid it's all true, my dear" and then "*Trahison des clercs*. None of us is quite innocent" (*That Hideous Strength*, p. 371). The reference to *Trahison des clercs* should repay attention.

That, it will be remembered, is the title of a book by the essayist Julien Benda, published in English in 1928 under the title, *The Treason of the Intellectuals*. Benda's influence on Lewis does not seem to have been generally noticed, though a comparison, for example, of the summary chapter in *La Trahison des clercs* with Lewis's remarks in his *Rehabilitations and Other Essays* is highly revealing, especially in the passages relating to the difficulties in achieving civilization — the more so since Lewis's strictures on the philosophy of history in *De Descriptione Temporum* echo Benda. We will return to this later. (See Benda, *The Treason of the Intellectuals* [New York 1928], pp. 195–97. The relevant part of the essay from *Rehabilitations* is quoted in C. S. Kilby, ed., *A Mind Awake* [New York 1969), p. 238. Cf. "De Descriptione Temporum" in Walter Hooper, ed., *Selected Literary Essays* [1969], pp. 1–14, esp. p. 3.)

The essential question here is whether Curry is guilty of the *trahison des clercs*. In order to answer this question, it is necessary to discover what it is Benda and Lewis were attacking. The conclusion of Benda's summary chapter is obviously relevant to one of the themes of Lewis's entire Ransom sequence: "Above classes and nations there does exist a desire of the species to become the master of things, and, when a human being flies from one end of the world to the other in a few hours, the whole human race ... adores itself as distinct from the rest of creation" (*Treason*, p. 201). He goes on (p. 202), "Sometimes one may feel that such an impulse will grow ever stronger, and that in this way inter-human wars will come to an end.... But far from being the abolition of the national spirit with its appetites and its arrogance, this would simply be its supreme form, the nation being called Man, and the enemy God." This is Benda's prediction: his evidence, in the earlier chapters, is relevant here, and his prediction relevant to our considerations in the next section.

Benda finds the psychological foundation of politics to lie in two desires: the will of a group of men to get hold of (or retain) a material advantage, and the will of a group of men to become conscious of themselves as distinct from other men (*Treason*, p. 33). The treason of the intellectuals consists in their preaching the goodness of these aims. This preaching is peculiar to the present time: "Our age has seen a fact hitherto unknown ... in metaphysics preaching adoration for the contingent and scorn for the eternal" (*Treason*, p. 100). Moreover, "it is impossible to exaggerate the importance of a movement whereby those who for twenty centuries taught Man that the criterion for the morality of an act is its disinterestedness ... that his will is only moral if it seeks its law outside its objects, should begin to teach him that the moral act is the act whereby he secures his existence against an environment that disputes it, that his will is moral insofar as it is a 'will to power'" (*Treason*, pp. 124–25). It should not be necessary to labor the point — this is precisely the treason of the N.I.C.E., and Benda's participation in the moral imagination supplies the ordering for Lewis's.

Note that Curry is not involved in this treason in any great degree. He is not a "clerk" — he thinks that the "traditionalists and research beetles" affect to look down on him (*That Hideous Strength*, p. 92). He neither wants any material advantage (Feverstone notes that he can be persuaded to drive the train but has no idea where he is going), nor is he quite wholeheartedly convinced of the "dimness of the outsiders" in the Bracton common-room (*That Hideous Strength*, pp. 40, 92). Like the man who is "defended from strong temptations to social ambition by a still stronger taste for tripe and onions" (*Screwtape Letters*, p. 69), Curry is defended against the *trahison des clercs* by a taste for wire-pulling and superintending the lives of his colleagues. He preaches neither adoration for the contingent nor scorn for the eternal (unlike Busby, the Bursar), and (unlike Mark Studdock) does not seek to justify his actions on moral grounds (*That Hideous Strength*, pp. 37, 41). In fact, he neither preaches nor seeks to justify at all. In this, I think, lies his salvation. Perhaps that may seem to be overstating it. There is no guarantee, after all, that his temporal salvation will lead to eternal life.

But Walter Hooper (letter to me, 15 March 1970) has pointed out that Curry "thought the saving of his life was 'Providential'" and asked "Might he possibly go on to understand that in the religious sense?" The answer, to my mind, is "Yes," even though there is no guarantee. His preservation takes place in the midst of an apocalyptic vision in which temporal and eternal salvation are virtually synonymous, or at least, though "there will be pain and heartaches yet, for the moment, near enough" (the reference, as my readers will recognize, is to the closing sentence of Williams, *The Greater Trumps*). It does not seem unreasonable to refer to Curry's "salvation."

Nor does it seem unreasonable to use the word "trivial"—especially when Lewis writes of Wither's damnation, "some tiny habitual sensuality, some resentment too trivial to waste on a blue-bottle, the indulgence of some fatal lethargy, seems to him at that moment more important than the choice between total joy and total destruction" (*That Hideous Strength*, p. 353). Just as damnation rests on trivial choices, as "the safest road to Hell is the gradual one—the gentle slope, soft underfoot, without sudden turnings, without milestones, without signposts" (*Screwtape*, p. 65), so, it would appear, may salvation. That is implicit in the idea of growing into what one is pretending to be. And Curry seems to be a case in point.

To sum up thus far (and we are here dealing with the spiritual argument of the book), Curry seems to have been saved (or, if one wishes, preserved) in part because being a bore is a very minor sort of irritation (and may even be funny, as in Lewis's poem: "I stood in the gloom of a spacious room / Where I listened for hours (on and off) / To a terrible bore with a beard like a snore / And a heavy rectangular cough"), in part because he is protected against the *trahison des clercs* more or less "by a still stronger taste for tripe and onions." (The poem "Awake, My Lute!" is quoted in full in Walsh, *Apostle to the Skeptics*, pp. 62–63.) It is possible to see in the very triviality of these things not only a characteristic working out of Lewis's moral imagination, but also an answer to a question of great concern for Lewis.

The terms of the question may be taken from Screwtape, except that he asks how one is to damn, whereas Lewis is asking how may salvation be given, creatures "hardly worth damning," souls "so passively responsive to environment, that it [is] hard to raise them to that level of clarity and deliberateness at which mortal sin becomes possible" ("Screwtape Proposes a Toast" in *The World's Last Night*, 1960, p. 54). The importance of Curry lies not in his part in *That Hideous Strength*, in which he is tangential to the main story or stories, but in the fact that he alone in Lewis's fiction provides an answer to this question — and that the answer he provides represents in clear the working out of Lewis's moral imagination. One does not suppose he would have found this importance very flattering: one is reminded (as Walter Hooper noted long ago) that this novel did not make Lewis popular in the Oxford common-rooms (letter, WH to me, 15 March 1970). But for all that, the importance is there.

Curry is almost a candidate for limbo, a "failed human" (*World's Last Night*, p. 56). Yet, in the end, for every one who is called upon to combat "depraved hypersomatic beings at great heights" (like Ransom, *Perelandra*, Macmillan pb, p. 24), there are dozens who approach God through the almost unconscious imitation of virtue, whose way is open because they innocently produce boredom rather than intentionally producing harm (Curry does not seem to be malicious), and who are defended against great evil (the *trahison des clercs*) because it is beyond their capabilities, or because they have a still stronger taste for something (comparatively) innocent. One finds Curry, somehow, a comforting example. And, finding him so, one comes to think his preservation less strange. And his example not only comforting, but important.

The figure of Curry has one additional value, this in the machinery of the book. He is the lasting link between the humdrum beginning, the college meeting, and the return to habitual self at the end. He is not part of Belbury and the N.I.C.E.; he is not part of the Last Dinner. Mark is, but Mark does not return to his habitual self. This is the only book in which Lewis does not appear as a character, and the story clearly could not have been told him by Ransom: if he is indeed telling the story (and it sounds like him) I suppose it was told him by Jane and Mark, by the Dimbles — and by someone who knew Curry. In a way Curry is like the Centurion Proclus in Dorothy Sayers's *The Man Born to Be King*, on the edge of unimaginable events, touching the story at its major points, but only briefly part of it (though Proclus is a better man and a more likeable character).

In that also, one comes to find his preservation less strange. And his example comforting. And his presence an important part of the machinery of the fairy-tale mode. I believe Lewis used the phrase "the journey homeward to habitual self" in connection with Keats's visit to perilous seas in faerie lands forlorn. That is part of what Curry does in this fairy-tale mode — though, of course, Jane's seeing Mark's shirt over the window sill does something of the sort on a more domestic level: "how exactly like Mark — obviously it was high time she went in."

VI

Lewis's Arcadian Science Fiction

Arcady — Arcadia — is, as Lewis said of David Lindsay's Tormance, a realm of the spirit. Not solely an English realm of the spirit, to be sure, but in this case, precisely that. This chapter properly includes a reminder of the Englishness of Lewis's art, then of the characteristic fairy-tale mode and movement from daily life through a connecting link or nexus into the perilous realms of the spirit, through the climactic moment (which involves a threat within or to the realms of the spirit), and then the journey homeward to habitual self, or the realms we know. Perhaps it will be as well to begin with a brief discussion of Arcady as a realm of the spirit, and the pastoral belonging to it. Then we can get on to the pattern in each of our four books.

A realm of the spirit? Perhaps the characteristic figure in the traditional Arcadia is the shepherd, the pastor of the pastoral, with his shepherd's crook. Now there was some kind of spiritual significance to Arcady and the signs of Arcady even in Greek times, though we cannot be entirely certain what exactly that spiritual significance was. In the Judeo-Christian tradition, of course, there is no doubt of the spiritual significance of the sheep and the shepherd, the pastor who is also a priest, the shepherd's crook that is also the bishop's crozier. But when the revived classical tradition mixes with the Judeo-Christian in the Renaissance, there comes ambiguity, most especially in the famous Arcadian (or pastoral) paintings of Nicolas Poussin. The Ransom stories are pageant and pastoral and — in short — Arcadian science fiction. Moreover, as we noted in the introduction, the fairy-tale mode informs the Arcadian pattern of pageant and makes this Arcadian science fiction a somewhat more complex thing

than Blish's (or Frye's) ironic and hivernal literature of religious syncretism. That is, what is going on is not merely religious syncretism, but
also and especially exploration of the realms of the spirit, even though
the symbols used in that exploration may be taken from more than one
religious tradition.

In fact, in general, they are not, in *Out of the Silent Planet* or (mostly)
in the scene-setting of *Perelandra*. Both come from the classical tradition
that was part and parcel of the eighteenth century. And even the story
of *Perelandra* comes from the co-equal antiquity of the Old Testament,
rather as Ossian (in the eighteenth century) organized his Celtic fragments — whatever they were — in classical mode with biblical references.
That Hideous Strength is perhaps more medieval: though the *eldila* are
the classical gods, Lewis's coign of vantage is set largely in the Middle
Ages. Perhaps *The Dark Tower* (*An Exchange in Time*) is, except — it may
be — for the opening of *Out of the Silent Planet*, the most like ordinary
Wellsian twentieth-century science fiction. Until, of course, we get to the
ironic realization of Faerie as a modern (Fascist?) industrial state, and con-
currently, the pageant quest of Sir Scudamour, Sir Orfieu, and (I think)
the king. Here we are largely divorced from the classics, as Faerie is
divorced from the classics.

One reminder here on the Englishness of English art, and how this
has fitted in with our inquiry. The point is that, in the English tradition,
art exists to preach, and the best preaching is done by rehearsing the
details of daily life, whether pictorially or verbally. If verbally, then there
is of course a story, but the story, if not simply pilgrimage or travel, must
be one of two things. Either it must be a story dictated by the symbols,
or it must be an existing story or at least a commentary on an existing
story. Most likely it will be both. It cannot be a story dictated by per-
sonalities — by the characters in the story. In short, in the twentieth-century dichotomy, it will be romance rather than novel. Of course, science
fiction need not be in this mode, though I believe most of it is. It can be
Bildungsroman. It can be fiction whose pattern is determined by extrapolation of theory, the pure form of science fiction (according to its prac-
titioners) where the science is not merely the machine — though this too
is very often a kind of pageant.

It does not much matter, I believe, whether the science fiction in question is time travel or space travel: so long as it is travel, it will have a pageant quality. That is, it will center on the pictures, the detail, the mysteries — in the sense Edgar Wind uses that word in his study on *The Pagan Mysteries of the Renaissance*, which Lewis admired. There is, perhaps, a small subsection of these travel stories (apart from the humorous variety) where this is not the case. In these, what is important is the sense of travel. In the space-travel narratives, this is a kind of nautical sense — one thinks (though they are not very good books, in my view) of the novels of the late A. B. Chandler, and curiously, there is to me a better sense of nautical (and other) voyaging in the time-travel novels of the late Edward Llewellyn-Thomas (Edward Llewellyn). There is also another type of what is generally considered science fiction, the type called alternative history, which may be (but is not necessarily) a kind of time travel. There is even (a small subtype perhaps) a type that might be put somewhere on the spectrum running from imagined history to creative historical nonfiction, and which is science fiction principally in the sense that it is fiction based on science, but on the history of science. Charles Sheffield's stories about Erasmus Darwin would be a case in point here. These too have strong likeness to pageant.

In fact, the link between science fiction and pageant appears to me to be very strong, to the extent (as I said) that pageant might largely be considered the genre, and science fiction the subgenre. Science fiction in the Anglo-American tradition — in any tradition coming out of the English — would participate in the Englishness of English art, the use of detail to point to a moral as well as to adorn a tale, in an essentially didactic endeavor. But this does not mean that the pageant must be pastoral, nor that it must be in the fairy tale mode. Nor does it mean — though the intersection of pastoral and fairy-tale may mean — that a prologue is a necessary part of the tale. Yet in the classic Wellsian story, as in Lewis's, it is. And in those stories following the Wellsian model, such as (perhaps most recently) George Gaylord Simpson's *The Dechronization of Sam Magruder* (posthumously published 1996).

Prologue, Arcadia, and the Pattern of Pageant

We are not used to the prologue as an integral part of a literary —
or dramatic — work, though perhaps more used to it in drama than in
prose fiction. The classic case — where the prologue (as Chorus) appears
in the *dramatis personae* — is Shakespeare's *King Henry V.* "O! for a Muse
of fire that would ascend / The brightest heaven of invention, / — A kingdom for a stage, princes to act, / And monarchs to behold the swelling
scene ... O! pardon, since a crooked figure may / Attest in little place a
million; / And let us, ciphers to this great accompt, / On your imaginary
forces work. / Suppose within the girdle of these walls / Are now confined
two mighty monarchies, / Whose high unreared and abutting fronts /
The perilous narrow ocean parts asunder: / Piece-out our imperfections
with your thoughts; / Into a thousand parts divide one man / And make
imaginary puissance; / Think, when we talk of horses, that you see them
/ Printing their proud hooves i' th' receiving earth." That from the opening Prologue, and then again a prologue for each act of the play. Now,
it is arguably true that this prologue is required because these things cannot be seen on stage, but for our purposes here what is important is that
this is a pageant play, and the prologue is what links our flat quotidian
world, even with its playhouses, to the imagined world of the pageant,
making possible the "realizing" of the (apparently) unreal. For Arcady is
apparently unreal. Of course, as a realm of the spirit, it claims a different
kind of reality. Like Shakespeare's France. Like Lewis's Tellus. Or any
myth.

In Olivier's *Henry V*, there is a dissolve from the Chorus in the
Wooden O to the vasty fields of France: in a film, that is easily done. Of
course, we take those vasty fields as historical: within our history they
are, and designedly within Shakespeare's. But they are still the author's
imagining. And as each act in the play begins with Chorus setting the
scene, standing within our world and guiding us to the dissolve and the
round world's imagined corners, so each book in Lewis's trilogies or tetralogy begins in our world and guides us to the dissolve. But why do I say
that *our* vasty fields are Arcadian. The guide here is Sidney's (or the
Countess of Pembroke's) *Arcadia*. And for the guidance, we turn to Lewis
himself, in the *OHEL* volume (*English Literature in the Sixteenth Century,*

Excluding Drama, 1954, pp. 333–342). From this we learn what we might not have guessed, that the model for the book that effectively introduces Arcadia into English letters is in fact a Menippean satire. "The two great influences on Sidney's romance are the *Arcadia* (1501) of Sannazaro and the *Ethiopian History* (fourth century A.D.) of Heliodorus. There are of course others; Malory possibly, *Amadis* probably, and Montemayor's *Diana.* But Montemayor is himself largely a disciple of Sannazaro: it is from Sannazaro and Heliodorus that the two kinds of fiction which Sidney is fusing really descend" (p. 333).

"Sannazaro's work belongs formally to an extinct species, the Varronian *Satura Menippea* in alternating proses and metres.... The thread of narrative in the proses, though enriched with epic material ... and romantic ... is indeed very slight. But it has a momentous effect. It creates for the singing shepherds a landscape, a social structure, a whole world; a new image, only hinted by previous pastoralists, has come into existence—the image of Arcadia itself. That is why Sannazaro's work, though in one sense highly derivative—it is claimed that almost every phrase has a classical origin—is, in another, so new and so important" (pp. 333–334).

"Heliodorus, translated by Thomas Underdowne in 1569, ... had in Sidney's time an importance which the successive narrowings of our classical tradition have since obscured. In order to see that importance we must once more remind ourselves that the word 'poesie' could cover prose fiction. We must remember the taste for interlocked and endlessly varied narrative to which the medieval romances and Italian epics equally bear witness. These facts, taken together, explain why Scaliger cites the *Aithiopica* as a model of epic construction; why Sidney and Tasso both mention it among heroic poems.... From Sannazaro Sidney took over the Menippean form (though he made his proses so long that we hardly notice it) and the idea of Arcadia itself. From Heliodorus he took over the conception of the prose epic, filling his story with shipwreck, disguise, battle, and intrigue.... The first thing we need to know about the *Arcadia* is that it is a heroic poesy; not Arcadian idyll, not even Arcadian romance, but Arcadian epic. To call it a pastoral is misleading. The title seems to promise that, and the first few pages keep the promise. But almost at once Sidney leads us away from the 'shepherdish complaynts of Strephon' to a shipwreck, to the house of a country gentleman, to affairs of state, and to the royal family" (pp. 334–335).

The implication here is that the complaints of Strephon are in fact prologue, but almost accidentally so. Perhaps. But in the Arcadian (epic) science fiction we are discussing, the prologue is designedly Arcadian in the ordinary sense noted in our introduction. Also, of course, it is a prologue in the fairy-tale mode: we might say that it is not itself Arcadian, and that it is followed by the shift to Arcady. Or is it in fact Arcadian? At the very least, in some sense it introduces and foreshadows what is to come (as perhaps it did for Sidney), in much the way that Chorus (prologue) in *Henry V* introduces and foreshadows what is to come. In *Out of the Silent Planet*, there is a "down-to-earth" quality to Ransom's fantastic voyage from the beginning — and even before the voyage begins, there is the Pedestrian (*Out of the Silent Planet*, p. 7). "The last drops of the thundershower had hardly ceased falling when the Pedestrian stuffed his map into his pocket, settled his pack more comfortably on his tired shoulders, and stepped out from the shelter of a large chestnut tree into the middle of the road. A violent yellow sunset was pouring through a rift in the clouds to westward, but straight ahead over the hills the sky was the colour of dark slate. Every tree and blade of grass was dripping, and the road shone like a river."

In *An Exchange in Time* (that is, *The Dark Tower*), we begin at the academic beginning and particularly the "chronoscope" sections. It may well be argued that this is not Arcadian: there is obviously no countryside here. The participants are in fact gathered in a college study. But here (at the risk of the personal heresy) we may note that, in many respects, Lewis's own Arcady was in his college study, or at least his college. It was from here his companions in Arcady came. "There were four of us in Orfieu's study. Scudamour, the youngest of the party, was there because he was Orfieu's assistant. MacPhee had been asked down from Manchester because he was known to us all as an inveterate sceptic [one can almost hear the capital *S*], and Orfieu thought that if once he were convinced, the learned world in general would have no excuse for incredulity. Ransom, the pale man with the green shade over his grey distressed-looking eyes, was there for the opposite reason — because he had been the hero, or victim, of one of the strangest adventures that had ever befallen a mortal man. I had been mixed up with that affair — the story is told in another book — and it was to Ransom I owed my presence in Orfieu's party" (*The Dark Tower*, p. 17).

In *Perelandra*, throughout, we deal with the demarcation between the real and the unreal, but there is less of the "real" as we generally understand that word — no newsboys on Perelandra. But the framework, with which we begin, is as close to the "real" as the book comes, but not as close to what we usually think of as Arcady. Still, it is some ways rustic. Here is the opening (p. 9): "As I left the railway station at Worchester and set out on the three-mile walk to Ransom's cottage, I reflected that no one on that platform could possibly guess the truth about the man I was going to visit. The flat heath which spread out before me (for the village lies all behind and to the north of the station) looked like an ordinary heath. The gloomy five-o'clock sky was such as you might see on any autumn afternoon. The few houses and the clumps of red or yellowish trees were in no way remarkable. Who could imagine that a little further on in that quiet landscape I should meet and shake by the hand a man who had lived and eaten and drunk in a world forty million miles distant from London, who had seen this earth from where it looks like a mere point of green fire...."

The four passages (or matters crossing several passages) that I have selected for discussion for *That Hideous Strength* form a spectrum of successful moral imagination — imaginatively or artistically successful, that is. The college meeting, which is the beginning of the pageant, is reporting, and Lewis remains angry at Weldon in the person of Feverstone: this is not really imaginative writing, except perhaps in the wit of the "we're-not-out-of-the-wood" passage, which reminds me of Lewis's own wit. But the opening itself (before the college meeting), the real prologue, is something different (p. 13). "'Matrimony was ordained, thirdly,' said Jane Studdock to herself, 'for the mutual society, help, and comfort that the one ought to have for the other.' She had not been to church since her schooldays until she went there six months ago to be married, and the words of the service had stuck in her mind. Through the open door she could see the tiny kitchen of the flat, and hear the loud, ungentle tick tick of the clock. She had just left the kitchen and knew how tidy it was. The breakfast things were washed up, the tea towels were hanging above the stove, and the floor was mopped. The beds were made and the rooms done...."

Lewis found Gavin Douglas's Prologues in his *XIII Bukes of the Eneados* saved from the flatness of mere description by the presence of the author. Though Lewis is less directly and obviously present here in *That Hideous Strength* than in the other books, or than Douglas in his great book, he is nonetheless present (by implication and experience, as it were) in every description of the academic life.

We think of pageant as having its medieval origins in the pageant plays — sometimes called the morality plays or miracle plays. Except for conscious reconstruction (as in *Jesus Christ, Superstar*) and in the lingering attenuated form represented by circus parades, these are pretty much gone from the English-speaking world. The point to be emphasized here is that these plays represent a progress from the quotidian to the more-and-more miraculous, the more-and-more exciting, the more-and-more gilded and heraldic and wonderful (full of wonder), with comic relief along the way (Herod in the miracle plays, the clowns in the circus parade) — and, of course, a moral at the end. This fits well with the Arcadian pattern, as Sidney built it from Sannazaro's *Arcadia* and the *Aithiopica* of Heliodorus. Of course, the creaking carts of the morality play (or the circus parade) leave much to the imagination: the dissolve, the shift to the real Arcady (or in *Henry V* to the real vasty fields of France), is much easier for the writer of fiction, still more in Olivier's *Henry V*. But the progress is the same. And the real is, in both cases, a realm of the spirit. And in written fiction, there must be a kind of machine to bring about the shift.

Expeditions in Arcady

In *Out of the Silent Planet*, it is Ransom as philologist that begins our transition to the realms of the spirit. Here is the relevant passage (pp. 54–55). "There was no sound of pursuit. Ransom dropped down on his stomach and drank, cursing a world where *cold* water seemed to be unobtainable.... His eyes were upon the blue water. It was agitated. Circles shuddered and bubbles danced ten yards away from his face. Suddenly the water heaved and a round, shining, black thing like a cannon-ball heaved into sight. Then he saw eyes and mouth — a puffing mouth bearded with bubbles. More of the thing came up out of the water. It was gleaming black. Finally it splashed and wallowed to the shore.... It was something like a penguin, something like an otter, something like a seal; the slenderness and flexibility of the body suggested a giant stoat.... Then something happened which completely altered his state of mind. The creature, which was still steaming and shaking itself on the back and had obviously not seen him, opened its mouth and began to make noises. This in itself was not remarkable; but a lifetime of linguistic study assured Ransom almost at once that these were articulate noises. The creature was *talking*. It had a language."

This is a scene out of a philologist's dream, one might say. This is paradisal — indeed, in a later passage, Ransom remarks (p. 58), in connection with his sudden losses of confidence when with the *hrossa*, that they "arose when the rationality of the *hross* tempted you to think of it as a man. Then it became abominable — a man seven feet high, with a snaky body, covered, face and all, with thick black animal hair, and whiskered like a cat. But starting from the other end you had an animal with everything an animal ought to have — glossy coat, liquid eye, sweet breath and whitest teeth — and added to all these, as though Paradise had never been lost and earliest dreams were true, the charm of speech and reason." Here is a paradisal *animal rationale*, in the unspoiled countryside of an unfallen world, Arcady, as it were, transmuted into Paradise, but Arcady nonetheless. And the knowledge of the hross's speech is the key that turns the lock in the gates of Paradise.

In the fragment (*The Dark Tower*), the discussion of the nature of time is the transition. Orfieu argues (p. 21) that we directly experience past and future, to which Lewis responds that we must then most often experience our own past, which we take as memory. Orfieu says, *not so*. Ransom asks, Why? "Because the fragments of our own lives are the only fragments of the past which we recognize. When you get a mental picture of a little boy called Ransom in an English public school you at once label it 'memory' because you know you *are* Ransom and were at an English public school. When you get a picture of something that happened ages before your birth, you call it imagination; and in fact most of us at present have no test by which to distinguish real fragments of the past from mental fictions ... of the ... things going through your mind at any moment, while some are mere imagination, some are real perceptions of the past and others real perceptions of the future. You don't recognize most of the past ones and, of course, you recognize *none* of the future" (pp. 21–22).

Comprehending what may be the full force of this transition probably involves some knowledge of the connection between dream and Arcady in Lewis's formative years. The *textus receptus* here is Kenneth Grahame's *Dream Days*—and also his *Golden Age*. Looking at the function of dream in the shift to Arcady leads also to the dream-timelessness of Novalis and George MacDonald (those who are curious about this may look in my study of *The Rise of Tolkienian Fantasy*, coming out this fall). Suffice it to say here, Lewis's use of a J. W. Dunne schema for rationalizing timelessness marks this as science fiction; the timelessness marks it as taking place in a realm of the spirit. The pattern of the tetraology (if this is a tetralogy) is from Malacandra's red and pleasant land to the dark tower to Perelandra's green and pleasant land to the dark shadow of that hideous strength. On the one hand — on the other. On the one hand, unfallen worlds — Arcadian and more than Arcadian. On the other, the chronoscope and the Nazi industrialism (and unattractive sexualism) of Faerie, the pragmatometer and the Nazi sadism of Fairy Hardcastle.

In *Perelandra*, it is the pageant of what I call the Great Conversation, much of it Miltonic in inspiration, that is the closest thing to a link between our world and the perilous realms (but it must be remembered that *Perelandra* is not fully in the fairy-tale mode, nor the mode of science fiction, so there may be some differences here). Here is the beginning of the transition, the beginning of the expedition into Paradise, as I see it (p. 57): "At first he thought that the green Creature had, of herself, begun to turn bluish and to shine with a strange electric radiance. Then he noticed that the whole landscape was a blaze of blue and purple — and almost at the same time that the two islands were not so close together as they had been. He glanced at the sky. The many-coloured furnace of the short-lived evening was kindled all about him. In a few minutes it would be pitch black ... and the islands were drifting apart. Speaking slowly in that ancient language, he cried out to her, 'I am a stranger. I come in peace. Is it your will that I swim over to your land?' The Green Lady looked quickly at him with an expression of curiosity. 'What is "peace"?' she asked."

Just as the academic discipline of philology is the bridge in *Out of the Silent Planet*, and the academic discipline of time dimension study (in *Othertime*) is the bridge in the fragment (*The Dark Tower* or *An Exchange in Time*), so it is a conversation in theology that is the bridge in *Perelandra*. It is borne in on us that, for Lewis at least, the mind is the way to the realms of the spirit. It may be said that *Perelandra* is the full statement of which *Out of the Silent Planet* is the adumbration, and *That Hideous Strength* is the full *per-contra* statement of which *An Exchange in Time* (or *The Dark Tower*) is the adumbration. The bridge, the beginning of the expedition, in *That Hideous Strength* is likewise an academic bridge. Unexpectedly, as I have argued, it comes through the mention of Distributism, so the discipline is economics, or perhaps economic sociology (since Denniston, Mark's rival for his fellowship, may also be a sociologist), or even political economy.

Now the shift to Arcady in the projection of Distributism in *That Hideous Strength* involves both the right order of the soul and the right order of the commonwealth. But Lewis's disdain for the ordinary terms of economic discourse, his socialism in a Kelmscottian sense, and the same lack of interest in "the other culture" (of Sir Charles Snow's two) that fastens dubious science on the N.I.C.E., all make this (though good as far as it goes) an incomplete piece of work — which, given its general lack of importance in *That Hideous Strength*, is not unreasonable. The passage that introduces the idea is very brief. Mark Studdock is talking to the Subwarden of Bracton College, Curry, who has just told him that Devine (Lord Feverstone) is the one who got him his fellowship, over his (then friend) Arthur Denniston (pp. 18–19). The words might almost slip by, but they are significant (p. 19). "'Yes,' continued Curry, pursuing another train of thought. 'One sees now that Denniston would never have done. Most emphatically not. A brilliant man at that time, of course, but he seems to have gone quite off the rails since then with all his Distributivism and what not. They tell me he's likely to end up in a monastery.'"

We have already discussed Distributism and Chesterton's League for the Defense of Liberty by the Distribution of Property, and we called St. Anne's a Distributist idyll. The idyllic life is part of the traditional Arcady, though here, in *That Hideous Strength,* indeed in all four novels, we are in Arcadian epic, rather than Arcadian idyll (or even, I believe, Arcadian romance). The implicit suggestion of St. Anne's as monastery, and the monastery therefore as idyllic and Arcadian, is unusual — but I think the texts support it. In any case, once again, we enter the Arcadian world through the mind — though Lewis, as a scholar and in analyzing his own fiction, has staked out a claim to Sidney's position (in the *Poesie*) that poetry is a speaking picture (*English Literature in the Sixteenth Century,* p. 343). Yes, it all began with a picture, but here it begins with the mind.

It might be suggested that we have still not fully justified the word *Arcadian.* Why not, for example (it is not an irrelevant question), *Olympian?* After all, Olympus is where Mars and Venus are to be found, Ares and Aphrodite, and here we have, unquestionably, Ares (Malacandra) and Aphrodite (Perelandra). But Olympus is not for mortals, and Arcady is. And animals. Moreover, we discover in *That Hideous Strength,* that of old (p. 290) it was "Not the very Oyéresu, the true powers of Heaven, whom the greatest of our craft meet, but only their earthly wraiths, their shadows. Only the earth–Venus, the earth–Mercurius; not Perelandra herself, not Viritrilbia himself." Just as Sidney's *Arcadia* is theoretically pagan but with knowledge of the Redemption (as Lewis observes in *English Literature in the Sixteenth Century,* p. 342), so the gods in Lewis's Arcadian epic are Christian angels, and Merlin who had converse perhaps with their earthly wraiths, is a Christian magician. There is a passage worth quoting here at length, in which Lewis speaks of Sidney's *Arcadia* (*English Literature in the Sixteenth Century,* p. 336): its applicability should be evident.

"We can paint Arcadia all 'humble vallies comforted with refreshing of silver rivers,' all trees that 'Maintaine their flourishing olde age with the onely happinesse of their seat, being clothed with continual spring because no beautie here should euer fade.' We can people it with lovers who 'Stoppe their eares lest they grow mad with musicke' and who, on seeing their mistresse in an orchard, exclaim 'The apples, me thought, fell downe from the trees to do homage to the apples of her breast.' We can mention the war horse 'milk white but that vpon his shoulder and withers he was fretted with red staines as when a few strawberies are scattered into a dish of creame,' his mane and tail 'died in carnation' and his harness 'artificially made' like vine branches. Such is the *Arcadia* we know from popular tradition before we open the book. And all this is really there. But it is not there alone. Against these passages we can quote almost as many of a sterner and graver kind. 'Judgment,' says Euarchus (as if he had been reading Burke), 'must undoubtedly bee done, not by a free discourse of reason and skill of philosophy, but must be tyed to the laws of *Greece* and the municipall statutes of this kingdome.'" Lewis goes on (pp. 336–37) to give more examples, many in a style recognizable from the mighty conclusion to Ralegh's *Historie of the World*.

It is important to remember that Lewis's Ransom books are a continuing story. A trilogy or tetralogy, yes, but also the continuing story of Elwin Ransom in space and time. Some of the narrative (as in *That Hideous Strength*) is polyphonic, as is some of Sidney's *Arcadia*. If our reconstruction of the over-all progress of the tetralogy is correct (or even another reconstruction), the four books in fact make up a single story. It might even be said that its progress (like that of the *Aithiopica*) combines a "variety of adventure with an ultimate unity of action. This supplied the *delectare*; the *docere* was provided by … constancy, lawfulness, and (almost medieval) courtesy…" (Lewis on the *Aithiopica* in *English Literature in the Sixteenth Century*, p. 334). We might especially note Lewis's reference to Burke in the last paragraph, and recall how the eighteenth century saw the final working out of the classicism of the sixteenth. Much of what Lewis says of the *Aithiopica* could with considerable justice be said of *Tom Jones*, and of the Ransom stories. One reason I believe it would be worthwhile to have a knowledgeable student of Lewis finish the time fragment is to see the full epic in its intended order.

Has enough been said to suggest the applicability of the term *Arcadian*? There are, in fact, at least three reasons for using it. The first is the common meaning or significance of the word — what everyone knows about Arcady before reading about it: the pastoral, the countryside, the green and pleasant land with animals. The second is what one finds in Sidney's *Arcadia*: the Arcadian epic drawing from both Sannazaro's Menippean satire and the epic adventure story of Heliodorus. The third is the particular irony of the eighteenth century vision of Arcadia, most notable in Poussin but characteristic of the century — irony matching the irony of science fiction as Lewis's follower James Blish has defined it. Possibly the pageant detail of English pastoral, and specifically of Sidney's *Arcadia* provides a fourth reason. In this, Elwin Ransom is indeed God's good Englishman. The term at least seems useful, to distinguish this particular version of science fiction,— unless, of course, it distinguishes all science fiction, which seems doubtful, or else someone would have noticed it.

The Threat to Arcady

Very well, then, we have begun our expedition through Arcady. What next? What is next, in all the four books, is the threat to Arcady. In *Out of the Silent Planet*, there is the threat of madness. We might keep in mind, here, Lewis's own concern with madness, and what he wrote about his ravenous lust for interplanetary spaces (*Surprised by Joy*, 1955, pp. 35–36). "The idea of other planets exercised upon me then a peculiar heady attraction, which was quite different from any of my other literary interests. Most emphatically it was not the literary spell of *Das Ferne*. 'Joy' (in my technical sense) never darted from Mars or the Moon. This was something coarser and stronger. The interest, when the fit was upon me, was ravenous, like a lust. This particular coarse strength I have come to accept as a mark that the interest which has it is psychological, not spiritual; behind such a fierce tang there lurks, I suspect, a psychoanalytical explanation. I may perhaps add that my planetary romances have not been so much the gratification of that fierce curiosity as its exorcism. The exorcism worked by reconciling it with, or subjecting it to, the other, the more elusive, and genuinely imaginative, impulse."

That is, for Lewis, these books are an exorcism of a certain madness in himself. It is not accidental, therefore, that in the two most Arcadian of the four books, *Out of the Silent Planet* and *Perelandra*, the threat of madness is the clearest. In what I have called the *per-contra* books, the "on the other hand" books, the fragment (*The Dark Tower* or *An Exchange in Time*) and *That Hideous Strength*, the madness is in all the world (Othertime or Tellus). Chad Walsh has spoken of the Ransom stories as "the re-education of the fearful pilgrim," and, of course, it is when the fear subsides that the re-education takes place. In *Out of the Silent Planet*, the re-education — which is in the living on Malacandra and the journey to the Oyarsa — culminates in the scene where Ransom sees Weston and Devine and does not at first recognize them (p. 125). "After them came a number of others [that is, other *hrossa*] armed with harpoons and apparently guarding two creatures which he did not recognize. The light was behind them as they entered through the two farthest monoliths. They were much shorter than any animal he had yet seen on Malacandra, and he gathered that they were bipeds, though the lower limbs were so thick and sausage-like that he hesitated to call them legs. The bodies were a little narrower at the top than at the bottom so as to be very slightly pear-shaped, and the heads were neither round like those of the *hrossa*, nor long like those of the *sorns*, but almost square. They stumped along on narrow heavy-looking feet which they seemed to press into the ground with unnecessary violence. And now their faces were becoming visible as masses of lumped and puckered flesh of variegated colour fringed in some bristly, dark substance.... Suddenly, with an indescribable change of feeling, he realized that he was looking at men. The two prisoners were Weston and Devine and he, for one privileged moment, had seen the human form with almost Malacandrian eyes." That is a paradigm-shift with a vengeance.

There is no point in rehearsing here the entire story of the trip to the Oyarsa at Meldilorn. That would be to repeat much of the book. But it is clear that the threat to Arcady, while initially the threat of madness (or the fear of madness) in Ransom, is in general the threat of fear. Here is the Oyarsa speaking to Weston (p. 140), after Weston has said to him, "And see what come.... You are now very few — shut up in *handramits*— soon all die." The answer comes, "Yes ... but one thing we left behind us on the *harandra*: fear. And with fear, murder and rebellion. The weakest of my people does not fear death. It is the Bent One, the lord of your world, who wastes your lives and befouls them with flying from what you know will overtake you in the end." It is courage, as in Sidney's *Arcadia*, that preserves and frees. It is fear, fear of the Bent One, fear of the Dark Lord, that befouls the world and its races. First, specifically, here, it is the fear of madness, akin to nameless fears — and then, quite simply, it is Fear. In *Perelandra*, as we will see, it is Lewis who fears and Ransom who comforts him, though this fear plays an insignificant rôle in the book.

In *An Exchange in Time* (*The Dark Tower*), we may see Scudamour's visit to the place of the Stationary Smokehorses, as an excursion in the realms of the spirit. Perforce, I am looking at the visit to the place of the Stationary Smokehorses in part for the light it sheds on the difference between the real and the unreal, and we may here make use of a discussion of the *eldila* in *Out of the Silent Planet* in this connection (p. 95). "To us the *eldil* is a thin, half-real body that can go through walls and rocks: to himself he goes through them because he is solid and firm and they are like cloud. And what is true light to him and fills the heaven, so that he will plunge into the rays of the sun to refresh himself from it, is to us the black nothing in the sky at night." Note that when K (*The Dark Tower*, p. 90) has duplicated what he calls the Othertime (meaning our) building where the Stationary Smokehorses are kept, in the exact space occupied by the building in our world (our time), "Smokehorses and even Othertime [our time] human beings now became faintly, but continuously, visible even to untrained observers."

It was earlier suggested that this place of the Stationary Smokehorses (in the "Southwestern region"—that is, Cornwall, in our world), the smokehorses might be mine engines. That would not be necessary, of course, but this portion of the fragment may have been drafted after Lewis's trip to Cornwall in 1944–45, and whether they are mine engines or not, the trip was to visit his old Oxford friend, Kenneth Hamilton Jenkin (1900–1980), a great expert on Cornish mines. Sir Scudamour's visit to the mines in the *Faerie Queene* is surely relevant to our reconstruction. Note that the Smokehorses are creatures of fear (p. 80): "This led to his (K's) famous experiment with the Smokehorse. He selected this familiar horror of the nursery because it is almost unique among such images in having arisen in historical times—no evidence having been found of its existence before the last century." The operative word is *horror*. And the exchange (p. 91) was effected through fear and desire to escape from the source of the fear.

The extrapolated episode in the fragment, the threat to Scudamour's inner Arcady, can be suggested here. Scudamour, seeking a way to return to our world, approaches the round-house. He hears the sound of hammers and drills, working on (perhaps repairing, perhaps simply working on) the engines, steel on steel. He looks in and finds a team of workers (six in number on each engine on this shift), wearily and painfully hammering without ceasing. The workers are arguing, almost fighting, as they work. The foreman, wielding the largest hammer, keeps at them to work harder. The racket is like the ringing of infernal bells, the larger hammers making the deeper sounds, a hellish music. The heat is fierce, the hammering so violent it seems to Scudamour it could split a diamond. He stands watching, invisible or at least unnoticed to the weary crew. He sees their work and their weary pain, but though he speaks to them, they cannot or will not hear, nor will they stop working. The sounds rise to a crescendo. He feels the blood rushing to his head. I recall a passage in a mystery novel that I believe Lewis read (certainly Charles Williams did), describing climbing through the bell chamber of a church when the bells were being rung (Dorothy L. Sayers, *The Nine Tailors*, pp. 304–05). This will do for a substitute description of Scudamour in the Place of the Stationary Smokehorses.

"He was pierced through and buffeted by the clamour. Through the … clash and clatter there went one high note, shrill and sustained, that was like a sword in the brain. All the blood in his body seemed to rush to his head, swelling it to bursting point. He … tried to shut out the uproar with his fingers, but such a sick giddiness overcame him that he swayed…. It was not noise — it was brute pain, a grinding, bludgeoning, ran-dan, crazy, intolerable torment. He felt himself screaming, but could not hear his own cry. His eardrums were cracking; his senses swam away. It was infinitely worse than any roar of heavy artillery. That had beaten and deafened, but this unendurable shrill clangour was a raving madness, an assault of devils. He could move neither forward nor backwards, though his failing wits urged him, 'I must get out, I must get out of this.'" And this, I believe, would be enough to bring Scudamour back to our time, through the Othertime Principle of Exchange — though possibly somewhat the worse for wear.

In *Perelandra*, the threat comes clear in the travel through the realms of Perelandra (the planet), which are spiritual realms (obviously Arcadian in almost the traditional sense), and particularly the floating islands and the caves on the fixed land, after the Great Conversation has begun. Ransom is speaking to the Lady (p. 68). "It was suddenly borne in upon him that her purity and peace were not, as they had seemed, things settled and inevitable like the purity and peace of an animal — that they were alive and therefore breakable, a balance maintained by a *mind* [my emphasis] and therefore, at least in theory, able to be lost. There is no reason why a man on a smooth road should lose his balance on a bicycle; but he could. There was no reason why she should step out of her happiness into the *psychology* [again, my emphasis] of our own race; but neither was there any wall between to prevent her doing so. The sense of precariousness terrified him: but when she looked at him again he changed that word to Adventure, and then all words died out of his mind. Once more he could not look steadily at her. He knew now what the old painters were trying to represent when they invented the halo. Gaiety and gravity together, a splendour as of martyrdom yet with no pain in it at all, seemed to pour from her countenance. Yet when she spoke her words were a disappointment."

The spiritual realm of Perelandra is also a physical realm, as Arcady is a physical province of Greece. But it is the mental precariousness of the realm — the kingdom inside — that terrifies Ransom. I think here of the great passage in the *OHEL* volume, on the "sudden extinction of a poetical literature which, for its technical brilliance, its vigour and variety, its equal mastery over homely fact and high imagination, seemed 'So fair, so freshe, so liklie to endure'" (p. 113). "But however we explain the phenomenon, it forces on our minds a truth which the incurably evolutionary or developmental character of modern thought is always urging us to forget. What is vital and healthy does not necessarily survive. Higher organisms are often conquered by lower ones. Arts as well as men are subject to accident and violent death. The philosophy of history outlined by Keats's Oceanus is not true.... An art, a whole civilization, may at any time slip through men's fingers in a very few years and be gone beyond recovery." (Note that Keats's Oceanus speaks for the romantic age against the eighteenth century, against Johnson and against the Johnsonian Lewis.)

In *That Hideous Strength*, the threat — present in all the polyphonic narrative intertwining Jane's story and Mark's — comes to fruition in the coming of Merlin, and the "last dinner" is a fully-conceived, planned out, and very Ludovician exercise. Those who find the scenes unpalatable and the punishment disproportionate may be making any one of several statements, none of which (I think) detract from seeing this as an exercise in moral imagination, and few of which would have been understood by Heliodorus or Sidney or Swift or Dr. Johnson. First, they may not like bloody *carnival.* It is not, as it happens, much to my taste, but here at least *de gustibus non disputandum* holds, and it is perfectly reasonable to say it is good of its kind, well-done, consistent — and I do not much care for it. I am (relative to Lewis) a modern man, not one steeped in the medieval tradition of the morality play or *serio ludere* or the *Aithiopica* or the age of Johnson. Second, they may not "buy" the doctrine of damnation by the gentle downward road, with few signposts and turnings, so that an elderly *bon viveur* might well simultaneously be a damned soul: if this is the case, the abrupt spectacle of damnation might well make them uneasy — but that is no criticism of Lewis's achievement: those who do not search the country through which they travel for views and prospects may not even welcome them when they find them. Third, they may simply not like excess, may practice (or wish to practice) moderation in all things — except, presumably, in moderation. Damnation, *Grand Guignol,* Hieronymus Bosch, planetary angels, and pantomime animals may all be equally *anathemata* to them. The very mode of the fairy tale may revolt them. Likewise the gruesomeness of scenes in the Arcadian (or Heliodoran) epic. Likewise albatrosses and sea snakes — and Dr. Faustus and Wagner and Clown. But I have been speaking to another sort.

Let us see if we can isolate the passage that serves to introduce the reader to this threat to Arcady, remembering that here (as in the fragment) Arcady is a realm of the spirit placed in counterpoise to the realm of our daily life (whereas in the other two books it *is* the realm of daily life). Possibly, here, it is internal in Logres, but it is external to Britain. And remembering also that the threat has been there all along; what we are looking for is the point at which it is explicitly introduced in the book. Right after Jane learns that the Dimbles are being forced to move and lose their famous garden, there comes a passage where Dr. Dimble is describing the Arthurian world (p. 31). "'It's really wonderful ... how the whole thing hangs together, even in a late version like Malory's. You've noticed how there are two sets of characters? There's Guinevere and Launcelot and all those people in the centre: all very courtly and nothing particularly British about them. But then in the background — on the other side of Arthur, so to speak — there are all those *dark* people like Morgan and Morgawse, who are very British indeed and usually more or less hostile though they are his own relatives. Mixed up with magic. You remember that wonderful phrase, how Queen Morgause 'set all the country on fire with ladies that were enchantresses.' Merlin too, of course, is British, though not hostile. Doesn't it look very like a picture of Britain as it must have been on the eve of the invasion?"

On the eve of the invasion — the invasion that turned the dark side of Arcady (and of the royal family) against the bright side, against the Table Round. The invasion that brought down Arthur and sidestepped Merlin out of time. This is the threat to Arcady here — and of course Merlin returns when the threat returns in our days of *That Hideous Strength*. To put it briefly, here also the threat is to the spiritual Arcady (would that be Logres?) through the invasion of the physical. In the fallen world, Arcady, as we have defined it, is a counterpoise to daily life — though some, specially, do live it as a daily life, in St. Anne's or Camelot. In the unfallen, well, Arcady is Paradise, and that is where daily life takes place.

The Journey Homeward to Habitual Self

In *Out of the Silent Planet*, the scene with the Oyarsa at the end is the climax, followed by the literal journey homeward to habitual self and the "A pint of bitter, please!" as coda. The journey homeward here is literal. Here is the beginning, with its characteristic paradigm shift. "He was surprised to find that they were already thousands of feet up. The *handramit* was only a straight purple line across the rose-red surface of the *harandra*. They were above the junction of two *handramits*. One of them was doubtless that in which he had lived, the other that which contained Meldilorn.... Each minute more *handramits* came into view — long straight lines, some parallel, some intersecting, some building triangles ... he turned again to the landscape below — the landscape which became every moment less of a landscape and more of a diagram. By this time, to the east, a much larger and darker patch of discoloration than he had yet seen was pushing its way into the reddish ochre of the Malacandrian world — a curiously shaped patch with long arms or horns extended on each side and a sort of bay between them…. Suddenly he saw a bright point of light in the middle of this dark patch and realized it was not a patch on the surface of the planet at all, but the black sky showing behind her" (pp. 144–145). And then, after he eats and sleeps, he "woke, and saw the disk still hanging in the sky. It was smaller than the Moon now. Its colours were gone except for a faint uniform tinge of redness in its light…. It had ceased to be Malacandra; it was only Mars" (p. 146). And after a harrowing journey, nothing "was further from his mind than sleep. It must have been the exhausted atmosphere which made him drowsy. He slept. He awoke in almost complete darkness in the midst of a loud continuous noise he could not at first identify…. Suddenly his heart gave a great leap. 'Oh God,' he sobbed. 'Oh God! It's *rain!*'" (p. 150). After which he slithers to the ground, gets up, and, after a half hour's walk finds a pub and his habitual self.

In the time fragment, the journey homeward is literally the return to our time — not our time meaning the present day, as against past days, but our time meaning our whole scheme of time, as against Othertime. Of course, this is an extrapolation, and in fact my imagined reconstruction. It might run like this (if it were in verse). "Long was the road. The journey passed; / to Winchester he came at last, / his own belovéd city free; / but no man knew that it was he. / Beyond the town's end yet to fare, / lest men them knew, he did not dare; but in a beggar's narrow cot / a lowly lodging there he got / both for himself and for his wife / as a minstrel poor of wandering life /…. Next day, when hour of noon was near, / he bade his wife await him here; the beggar's rags he on him flung, / his harp upon his back he hung, / and went into the city's ways / for men to look on him and gaze / … 'Lo' then he cried, and up he stood, 'Steward, now to my words give ear! If thy king Orfeo were here, / and had in wilderness full long / suffered great hardship sore and strong, / had won his queen by his own hand / out of the depths of fairy land, / and led at last his lady dear / right hither to the town's end near, / and lodged her in a beggar's cot; / if I were he, whom you knew not, / thus come among you, poor and ill, / in secret to prove thy faith and will, / if then I thee had found so true, / thy loyalty never shouldst thou rue" (*Sir Orfeo*, ll. 477–486, 497–502, 556–570).

Doubtless this is, at most, a likely source for the unwritten scene. But, however it would have been modified, or used, or even if in the end rejected (though I doubt it), it provides a kind of model for the journey homeward to habitual self—even if, here, with the poem's emphasis on clothes, there may be a pun in *habitual*: would one, for example, call a nun's dress habitual? In any case, if this is a clue, Orfieu, after his journey to Othertime, in search of his Heurodis, would return unrecognized—and then the recognition would come. (Whether his assistant would succeed him, as Orfeo's Steward eventually succeeded him, we cannot say—though it seems likely.)

In *Perelandra*, there is the return after the Great Dance at the end. "'It is now his time to go,' said the tingling voice of an *eldil*. Ransom found no words to say as he laid himself down in the casket. The sides rose up high above him like walls; beyond them, as if framed in a coffin-shaped window, he saw the golden sky and the faces of Tor and Tinidril. 'You must cover my eyes,' he said presently: and the two human forms went out of sight for a moment and returned. Their arms were full of the rose-red lilies. Both bent down and kissed him. He saw the king's hand lifted in blessing and then never saw anything again in that world. They covered his face with the cool petals till he was blinded in a red sweet-smelling cloud. 'Is all ready?' said the King's voice. 'Farewell, Friend and Saviour, farewell,' said both voices. 'Farewell till we three pass out of the dimensions of time. Speak of us always to Maleldil as we speak always of you. The splendour, the love, and the strength be upon you.' Then came the great cumbrous noise of the lid being fastened on above him. Then, for a few seconds, noises without, in the world from which he was eternally divided. Then his consciousness was engulfed" (pp. 221–222).

If this is indeed the journey homeward to habitual self—and it is— then we should note two things especially. First, it is very like a description of dying, which may be taken as a commentary on the life of Thulcandra as against that of Perelandra, and is in fact this, and more. Second, the rhythms or patterns of the passage are, I think, Cranmer's rhythms, prayer book patterns, which were in turn the rhythms and patterns of the Greek New Testament. The king's hand lifted in blessing is Christ's and the priest's hand. "Speak of us always to Maleldil as we speak always of you" has a Dominical pattern, if not a Dominical rhythm (but remember what Lewis said about Biblical rhythms in *The Literary Impact of the Authorised Version*— does "At the regatta Madge avoided the river and the crowd" really and truly remind us of "In the beginning God created the heavens and the earth"?). And "The Splendour, the Love, and the Strength be upon you" calls to mind the tripartite blessing, or any of several of them, at the end of the service, while "the Cross comes before the Crown, and tomorrow is a Monday morning" (*The Weight of Glory*).

In *That Hideous Strength*, the end of the journey homeward to habitual self is seen in Jane's reaction to Mark's shirt hanging over the windowsill. The "salvation" of Curry — salvation by a taste for tripe and onions — shows perhaps the fullest this-worldly working out of the moral imagination, not only because Curry is saved while Feverstone (Weldon) is damned, but partly for that reason: Lewis has gotten away from "the flatness of mere description" into the realms of the illative sense. Note his description of Curry, on his hearing the news. But one might well believe that this is Lewis as artist *malgré lui*: I would not be surprised if he had been surprised at how Curry turned out.

"All this time, without the least hypocrisy, habit and instinct had given his shoulders just such a droop, his eyes such a solemn sternness, his brow such a noble gravity, as a man of good feeling might be expected to exhibit on hearing such news. The ticket-collector was greatly edified. 'You could see he felt it bad,' as he said afterwards, 'But he could take it. He's a fine old chap.' 'When is the next train to London?' asked Curry. 'I must be in town first thing tomorrow morning'" (p. 374). So Curry is off to London to pull strings and refound Bracton College, his journey back to his habitual self. And Mark leaves his shirt over the sill in the damp, and it's high time Jane went in, and that's their journey. Nothing has changed, you might say, but you might equally say that everything has changed, because they — Curry and Mark and Jane — have been changed. They have been judged, and not been found wanting.

The climax of *Out of the Silent Planet* is Meldilorn (which is classical), with the voyage home what Northrop Frye would call the *Penseroso* phase of the story, though I prefer to think of them as beginning and end of the same part of the story. The climax of *An Exchange in Time* would be the battle carnage and Orfieu's visit to the king (which is medieval or Renaissance). The *Penseroso* phase would be Orfieu's return and the discussion of the king as Ransom's double. In *Perelandra* the climax is the Great Dance, which fades into Ransom's return, with the briefest *Penseroso* at the end (because part of the afterword is in the foreword). The climax of *That Hideous Strength* is in the perilous realms, the Last Dinner and the destruction of Belbury, with a longer *Penseroso* before Ransom's leave-taking, but the journey homeward to habitual self involves Curry, and Mark and Jane — except that Mark and Jane are changed, which is not part of the fairy-tale mode. On Malacandra and Perelandra, the climax is solemn and joyful, in the Earth-bound romances more *Grand Guignol*, but less so perhaps in *An Exchange in Time* than in *That Hideous Strength*. At least, that is what makes sense to me.

There is, in the *Arcadia*, as in English pastoral generally, a kind of judgment after pastoral, which is linked with the fundamentally hierarchical, elegiac, and complex nature of pastoral. One may find examples not only in Sidney but in Milton's *Lycidas* and even *L'Allegro* —even *Comus*— and in Spenser's *Shepheardes Calender*. Even in Crashaw's great anthem, *In the Holy Nativity of Our Lord God: A Hymn Sung as by the Shepherds*. (There is, by the way, an interesting and relevant discussion of pastoral and masque in Bernadette Bosky's introduction to David Bratman's edition of Charles Williams, *The Masques of Amen House*, 2000, pp. 17–25, though it is overly harsh on George Wither.) This underlying combination of hierarchy, elegy, and complexity is revealed and realized in the trial and judgment in the *Arcadia*, and even in late exemplars of pastoral (as Empson has reminded us) like *The Beggar's Opera* (itself a descendant of masque) and *Alice in Wonderland* and *Through the Looking Glass*. Before leaving our discussion of pastoral, we can look at the judgment in these for exemplars of what I have called Arcadian science fiction. And after that we can look at Lewis the myth-maker, or rather at Lewis and the nature of *mythopoeia*.

In *Out of the Silent Planet*, the judgment is evident. "You are guilty of no evil, Ransom of Thulcandra, except a little fearfulness. For that, the journey you go on is your pain, and perhaps your cure: for you must be either mad or brave before it is ended. But I lay also a command on you; you must watch this Weston and this Devine in Thulcandra, if ever you arrive there" (p. 142). Here are Ransom's thoughts the day of his "trial" (p. 119): "He might, when the time came, be pleading his cause before thousands or before millions: rank behind rank about him, and rank above rank over his head, the creatures that had never yet seen man, and whom man could not see, were waiting for his trial to begin. He licked his lips, which were quite dry, and wondered if he would be able to speak when speech was demanded of him."

In *The Dark Tower*, we are somewhat constrained in our analysis by the fact that the book is incomplete, and one of the parts lacking is the trial scene. But the passage we have quoted from *Sir Orfeo* includes a trial scene, where the steward "tries" (tests) the ragged minstrel to see who he is, and the minstrel (Orfeo) "tries" (tests) the steward to see if he is true. It is very likely the trying and testing will take place on Orfieu's return from Othertime, though its exact mechanics are not yet fully evident to me.

In *Perelandra*, the trial, one might say, is the temptation of the Lady (and in that, perhaps, of Ransom); the judgment is then the Great Dance. There is a model in Chesterton's *The Man Who Was Thursday* (and for that, avowedly, in *The Book of Job*). (That *Perelandra* and *The Man Who Was Thursday* are pastorals is evident; of *Job* I cannot be so sure.) Here the trial is, in a way, the story, and almost the whole of the pastoral: *Perelandra* seems to push hard against whatever limits of form we assign to it, not only eighteenth-century novel but sixteenth-century pastoral. And yet, if hierarchy, elegy, and complexity, with judgment, in a country setting of classical reference, are the marks of pastoral, and thus of Arcady, this exemplar is nearly perfect.

In *That Hideous Strength*, one might almost capitalize *Judgment*, and one is tempted to add (in one's thoughts, at least) the word *Last*. Of course, it is not the Last Judgment, but it is God's judgment nonetheless: *qui Verbum Dei contempserunt, eis auferetur etiam verbum hominis* (p. 350). The beasts released, the loss of language, the destruction of Belbury and Bracton, the earthquake, the deaths of Wither and Frost and Devine, and Miss Hardcastle, and Straik, and Filostrato (among many others), the use of Merlinus Ambrosius for God's purposes despite (or rather, indeed, because of) his sins — these are part of the Judgment. And the revels behind the wainscoting, and Jack who finds his Jill — the setting of things right after Judgment.

To see our setting in Arcady I need not quote the descriptions of countryside in *That Hideous Strength* any more than in the others (though we may have to imagine some of them in the unfinished novel). Certainly, the descriptions in *That Hideous Strength* are many of them of countryside in chaos rather than in peace, but no more than in the flood scenes of George MacDonald's *Sir Gibbie* —and there may well be chaos in Arcady. Think of the hammering in Spenser's *Faerie Queene*. And certainly, whatever else one may say of it, *That Hideous Strength* as a whole rarely if ever falls into a flatness of mere description. Moreover, even Lewis as reporter faithfully reports not only the hum-drum at rest, but its frenzied ceremonial humming, wherein it becomes the war-drum, and the Word of God goes forth to war.

Perhaps that brings us further into the realms of myth. And perhaps we might now take a look in that direction.

VII

C. S. Lewis and the Myth in Mythopoeia

There is a society, called the Mythopoeic Society, whose view of mythopoeia makes a reasonable starting place for this final part of our inquiry. The society is devoted principally to the works of C. S. Lewis, Charles Williams, and J. R. R. Tolkien. That these are very different kinds of works from each other should be apparent, and has in fact been argued at our opening, and seriatim in this book as in my *Detective Fiction Reviews of Charles Williams* and *The Rise of Tolkienian Fantasy*. But it should also be apparent that the society, being devoted to these three, is thereby in part devoted to the study and re-enactment of what is called fantasy (even perhaps "science fantasy"), though its members (like other critics) cannot always agree on what is meant by that word. Nevertheless, even though Lewis, Williams, and Tolkien are different, and even though "fantasy" as a genre (unless "fantasy" simply means "romance") is largely a creation of Tolkien's *The Lord of the Rings*, and therefore partly irrelevant to Lewis (entirely so to Williams), we will start here. From this starting-place I hope to go on to find out something of what we mean when we speak of mythopoeia, and particularly, what is the myth in mythopoeia. But this is not a simple and single question.

In exploring this matter, I suggest we should ask, first, "Is there really something called mythopoeia?" Second, we should ask, "Who writes mythopoetically, and does this mythopoeia really link these three?" Third, we should ask, "What is the relation of this mythopoeia to 'fantasy'? and, what of atmosphere or 'taste' (meaning 'flavor')?" And fourth, we should ask, "What is the relation of this mythopoeia to language and the use and style of language?" I propose to deal with these questions in this order, though there may be some overlap.

Before going there, we may observe that there is a note in the front matter of *Out of the Silent Planet* that may be considered germane to our inquiry. "Certain slighting references to earlier stories of this type which will be found in the following pages have been put there for purely dramatic purposes. The author would be sorry if any reader supposed he was too stupid to have enjoyed Mr. H. G. Wells's fantasies or too ungrateful to acknowledge his debt to them." The indebtedness is well known and widely acknowledged. What I am calling attention to is the word *fantasies*. Not, to be sure, *fantasy*— and, of course, as we have noted, Lewis also used the word "scientifiction." But the point remains that Lewis is implying two things here. First, he is implying that (as with Cyrano in *The Comicall Historie*) science is simply the "machine" in science fiction. Second, he is implying, I believe, that Wells's work is in the nature of *jeux d'ésprit*, to which this is in fact an answer in kind, but in a very different spirit. And with very different mythology (or myth) in mind.

Is There Really Something Called Mythopoeia?

Lewis himself seems to be partly responsible for the currency of the word mythopoeia, and he chose two of his favorite authors as particularly having the "mythopoeic" gift, while not being particularly good writers by ordinary standards. These are George MacDonald and Rider Haggard (in whom the mythopoeic gift is "almost pure"). It is noteworthy that Lewis also praised pretty much the same gift in Walter Scott. These writers, and this particular analysis of mythopoeia as being distinct from ordinary canons of good writing, strikes me as suggesting not the best coign of vantage from which to view such stylists as Lewis and Tolkien, but it is the one Lewis gave us, and let us see. It is not always the most promising road that yields the best results.

MacDonald and Scott have both been defended against attacks on their style of the kind implicit in Lewis's remarks, MacDonald in the recent Oxford Classics edition of the Curdie books, Scott by John

Buchan. It might be thought that this is a matter of taste, and of course it is, but I would contend that it is not merely a matter of taste in the *de gustibus* sense. The same attacks have been leveled against Dickens and Fenimore Cooper. What Lewis seems to mean by "pure" mythopoeia is creation in which story is everything (and types rise to the dignity of archetypes) and in which style is nothing. The great sprawling novels of Dickens's England or Sir Walter's Scotland or Fenimore Cooper's Wilderness America are novels where story is great and style only intermittently so — but note that these are not the books that first occur to Lewis as examples of mythopoeia.

Nor would he say, nor can we say, that this is simply the nature of the novel at that time. That is not true of all the novels of the time from 1820 to 1870, nor even of all the novels in English: Thackeray's *Henry Esmond* is an almost perfectly controlled novel in an almost perfectly controlled style. But the preeminence of story over style (whatever may be the beauties of style at the great points of the story) is still highly characteristic of the novel/romance, before it split in two (using Ian Watt's critical schema), in the middle nineteenth century. Not all sprawling novels, certainly, are mythopoetic: that may be so obvious as not to require saying. Nor are types rising to the dignity of archetypes in themselves sufficient to produce mythopoeia, though they may characterize it.

But we should not, in fact, discuss mythopoeia without first discussing myth, nor should we define mythopoeia without defining myth, since mythopoeia is defined by formation as the making of myth, or of a *mythos*, as with Tolkien's mythology for England — to which definition H. P. Lovecraft and his ilk would conform. (But note that Northrop Frye would consider this an improper use of the word *mythos*.) Lord Dunsany would also conform in this Lovecraftian sense, certainly in *The Gods of Pegana*. So far, perhaps, so good. Yet we have not defined myth: we have not quite said what it is that the mythopoets are making. What is a myth?

To be sure, we know, and can demonstrate our knowledge, by example. I grew up on Bulfinch and *Heroes of Asgard*, Sidney Lanier's version of *Arthur*, and other Victorian redactions of the world's mythology. Later on, as a Christian, I read and reread Genesis, and since C. S. Lewis was my favorite writer, I confronted at a relatively early age, in the confines of an Episcopal prep school, the question of Christianity and myth. One learned to recognize the mythological. One also learned to recognize the mythic. Davy Crockett, Sherlock Holmes, Alfred the Great and the cakes, Robert Bruce and the spider, Daniel Boone, George Washington, Abraham Lincoln, Babe Ruth, Bobby Jones, Robinson Crusoe, Natty Bumppo, Ahab and Moby Dick (and even the Old Man and Moby Minnow), Hamlet, Henry V, a host of other Shakespearean characters, Faustus, Tamerlane: the figures of literature intermingled with the figures of history, and some, like Richard III, who were both (though it was not the same Richard III in both). Mythic — but not mythological. Types becoming archetypes, as I have said — yes, that was part of it, archetypes (as we might say) of mythic proportions.

Yet Conan Doyle did not set out to create a myth, with Sherlock Holmes, but to write an intellectual story, or at least a story about an intellectual, which was also a detective story and an adventure story. Melville did not set out originally to write mythic books — indeed, he set out to write histories: it was not until *Moby Dick* that the mythmaking bent obvious in "Bartleby" and (later) in *Billy Budd* was melded with his experiences at sea to produce a myth of the sea. About Fenimore Cooper there is more doubt, but in my reconstruction the forest landscape (which provides much of the mythic quality) is an add-on to Natty Bumppo, not there at the beginning (and an add-on from classical paganism). Yet it is perhaps the atmosphere — the *taste* of the story — that gives the status of mythology to a story centered on a being of mythic proportions — and here, forsooth! I seem to be suggesting that the atmosphere, the taste, is an add-on. But we shall return to this.

If story of the mythic and mythological is indeed what constitutes mythopoeia, much of Scott is indeed mythopoetic, and of Dickens, at least *Pickwick* and *A Christmas Carol*. Surtees with his grocer of Great Coram Street is mythopoetic; so is Melville with Ahab and Moby Dick; so is Doyle with his Sherlock Holmes and Haggard with his She. But here we must address another question. Is what Haggard did in *King Solomon's Mines* truly mythopoetic? It involves a *mythos* — not in the Northrop Frye sense — the *mythos* being Dark and Secret Africa, and a past alive in the present. So also with *She*. But She-Who-Must-Be-Obeyed is a mythic figure in a way that the far less important Gagool of *King Solomon's Mines* is not. Is *She* therefore mythopoetic while *King*

Solomon's Mines is not? Does true mythopoeisis require the great mythic figure — the god or goddess?

However we may answer that question, it seems we are confronted with difficulties. Myth is a form — generally considered a pure or pattern form — of story. That definition is at the root of Frye's four *mythoi*: comedy, romance, tragedy, satire. But I do not think it is at the root of what Lewis finds to praise in MacDonald or Haggard. What he is praising in both seems to be a sense of myth in their world creation. That is, when one reads MacDonald, one senses that "thought beyond their thoughts to those high bards were given" — there are unexplained depths within depths — and over all, the spirit of Novalis's "Life is not a dream but it must and should become one."

Here I would remind you (and myself) that Lewis is not the only mid-century critic to look at the problem of mythopoeia. There is the late Edmund Wilson, though his mythmakers are that very Dickensian odd couple, Mr. Marx and Mr. Engels, while Lewis's, as noted, are that perhaps odder coupling of the Reverend Mr. MacDonald (dispossessed) and the sometime secretary to the governor of Natal, Sir Henry Rider Haggard. But listen, and see if this suggests a particular mythopoetic writer to you, someone perhaps enshrined at Wheaton College among the Seven: "Luther vanquished servility based upon devotion, because he replaced it by servility based upon conviction. He shattered faith in authority because he restored the authority of faith. He transformed parsons into laymen, because he raised laymen into parsons. He liberated men from outward show of religion, because he made religion to be shown inwardly in the heart. He struck the shackles from the body, because it was the heart he shackled."

Professor Huttar thinks it sounds like Williams; I think it sounds like Chesterton; it is in fact Mr. Wilson's mythopoet, Mr. Marx, a true believer, if not in our true belief. Perhaps belief entails paradox. This discussion here may seem to verge on floundering in taxonomic swamps, but the question is not merely — indeed, it is not largely — one of taxonomy. We are naming various books and writers as mythopoetic, or mythopoeic. The central figure in the naming is C. S. Lewis. But there are other critics using the word, and there seems to be a problem. There is a common thread among writers we today consider as "mythopoeic"

but it is not the common thread Lewis found among writers he considered mythopoeic. Nor do we particularly find the common thread Lewis
found among his writers, and that the word mythopoeia (making of myth
or *mythos*) would suggest. Nor do critics from without the camp seem to
agree with our categorizations. It looks as though we must do more.

Perhaps we can look at the matter in better focus by looking at one
characteristic of Lewis's mythopoeic story: the story will retain its form
and its essential genius even if told in other words. Let us see what we
can do with this. Does it apply to *King Solomon's Mines*? to Sherlock
Holmes? to *Pickwick*? to *Moby Dick*? to *The Lord of the Rings*? to *Phantastes* or *Lilith*? We come now to a crux of the matter, a test case: if
George MacDonald is a mythopoeic writer, what is the myth in his
mythopoeia? It is all very well, doubtless, to say MacDonald's pattern is
the pattern of dream. That is quite true — but the pattern of dream
depends on the associations of the dreamer, which is to say there is an
over-all logic, but not an over-all pattern. I think we need something
further, if we are (with Lewis) to list MacDonald among our leading
mythopoeic writers. Here I suggest recourse not to Freud (Robert Wolff
has shown us the difficulties of using Freud to approach MacDonald),
but to Jung. For Jung stands along the line that begins with Herder and
Novalis, to whose preaching MacDonald listened so attentively as to
make it, with him, preaching to the choir.

What Jung says, and here I am particularly thinking of *Psychologie
und Alchemie* (1944, trans., R. C. Hull, *Individual Dream-Symbolism in
Relation to Alchemy*, 1967), is not only that individual dreams have col-
lective patterns (which he said many times), but also and especially that
they are patterns appearing time and again in the literature of alchemy —
to which endeavor, it will be remembered, C. S. Lewis traced the myth
of progress (*De Descriptione Temporum*). The principal alchemical story
pattern is the making of gold from baser metals, which is Lewis's *fons et
origo* of the myth of progress. And Marx, I think, takes up the same
myth.

It is not my intention here to retrace Jung's analysis of dream and
vision (hypnogogic visual impression) in alchemical terms and according to alchemical motifs. That would be to repeat his book. But I do
wish, first, to note that the dreams and visions he records in *Psychologie*

und Alchemie, all twenty-two of them, accord with alchemical motifs, and second, to suggest their grounding in mythological motifs (as the rainbow bridge, the Naiads, the veiled Isis) and resemblances to events and motifs in MacDonald and Tolkien (as the greenwood and the wizard, though his has a pointed hat rather than a pointed beard). This is all part of the same world. And out of this world comes the myth of progress, as well as much other modern mythology. (We may remark here that this is the Wellsian mythology.)

To put it another way, just as modern mathematics, and particularly chaos theory, has a putative resemblance to the patterns of the real physical world, in a way that Bertrand Russell could never have accepted, so dreams and visions have a putative resemblance to the real spiritual world, the world of the *anima*, of the psyche. To put it in Novalis's terms, dreams, like the *Märchen*, show the real patterns of human behavior, which we enshrine or embody in myth. So it is not an argument against MacDonald's mythopoetic nature to say that he writes with the associative logic of dream.

Does this kind of mythopoeia require both mythic figure and mythic pattern? If it does not, then we have removed one of the common meanings of the word myth from our consideration, and, moreover, we seem to be jettisoning the whole type-to-archetype argument. But perhaps it is not all mythic larger-than-life figures, but only the true archetypes — the Scout, the Trickster, the Father of his Country, the Wizard — that are required for the creation of myth, for mythopoeia. Perhaps the separation between mythic pattern and mythic figure is not a true separation: in Jung's terms, perhaps one is the dream and the other the hypnogogic visual appearance, and both are present in all mythopoeisis, not merely in alchemical mythopoeisis. I am not sure I will answer these questions, or that they can be answered, but let us see.

Who Writes Mythopoetically (with Attention to Inklings)?

Of *King Solomon's Mines*, we can surely say, this is mythopoeia, this is story: as Lewis says, Haggard (at least here and in *She*) had the mythopoetic gift pure and undiluted. But what is it we remember from

Sherlock Holmes? Anti-Mormon detours making up most of the action in *A Study in Scarlet*? Anti-Molly-Maguire detours making up most of the action in *The Valley of Fear*? The actually risible plot of "The Red-Headed League" or Holmes's defeat in "A Scandal in Bohemia" or the impossibilities of "Silver Blaze" or the more scandalous improbabilities of "The Musgrave Ritual"? Obviously not: yet these have been rated as four of the six best of all Sherlock Holmes short stories. Of the other two, one is noteworthy not for plot but for deductions from a hat, while the other is more a poison-unknown-to-western-man adventure story than a feat in pure detection.

I think it fair to say that what raises Holmes to archetypal or mythic stature is character, incidents of detection (revealing Holmes's mind), and the world of late Victorian London. When we say that Doyle created the myth of Sherlock Holmes, we mean that he raised a type to the dignity of an archetype, or (in Tom Shippey's words) that he calqued one of the gods on Victorian England. We do not mean that he told a story or stories of a classic pattern. But perhaps we should note here, for further use, the point made long ago by Novalis, that *Märchen* is close to myth. And perhaps we should note also that Conan Doyle is credited with having perfected the formula detective story, and thus the pattern, that Poe first developed. In an essay on Charles Williams, in the Huttar-Schackel collection, I have gone more fully into the matter of detective story as mythic or redemptive comedy: suffice it to say here that there is a mythic pattern to the detective story, though in Conan Doyle it is frequently reduced to the unmasking and setting things right in the span of a very few pages — almost incident rather than story. There is something of a *Märchen* quality about Sherlock Holmes.

Now, what about the mythopoeic quality of *Pickwick* or *Moby Dick*? We may begin by noting that both these could be taken as the name of a principal character or of the book itself. And we may begin by asking what myth we are talking about in each case: How are we using the word myth? And what is the myth a myth *of*? The answer is easier for *Moby Dick*, despite whatever difficulties we may have with a sacramental or symbolic text. The myth of *Moby Dick* is the myth of the hunt for the great sea creature that destroys the hunter, and frequently those close about the hunter. It is the myth of the sea serpent that destroyed ships in the Middle Ages. It is the myth of Leviathan. It is, of course, legitimate to ask whether using or garnishing or calquing this myth is in fact mythopoeisis?

And Pickwick? Is there a pattern to Pickwick? A story? Are its strengths not rather the strengths of Old England, of Sam Weller, that "angel in gaiters," of the pathos of "But after all, Samivel, she died," of the Fat Boy, of Picwicaresque adventures through the England of coaching days and coaching taverns — a "mythology for England" one might say, but not a *mythos*, not a story pattern. And yet, is that the whole truth? Don Quixote would not have taken a coaching journey through Spain, nor yet D'Artagnan through France. But a journey from pillar to post, Land's End to John o' Groat's, tavern to tavern, as the rolling English drunkard made the rolling English road — yes, that is a kind of pattern story. Moreover, it is the pattern story of a particular people, a peculiar people (one might say), sanctified to the open road. Perhaps it goes back to the wonderment of Angles and Saxons and Jutes at the Roman high roads.

But let us remember Mr. Wilson's candidates for mythopoeia. Here in part is what Mr. Wilson says about Marx and mythopoeia, given not merely for its relation to Marx but to the German romantics and to the myth of progress (and thereby perhaps to *Alchemie*). The abstractions of German philosophy, he says, which may seem unmeaning or clumsy in English or French, convey in German, through their capitalized solidity, almost the impression of primitive gods. They are substantial, yet a kind of pure being; they are abstract, yet nourishing. "They have the power to hallow, to console, to intoxicate, to render warlike, as perhaps only the songs and old epics of other people do" (*To the Finland Station*, p. 189).

Very well, for the farther (or more modern) realms of myth. Now if we look at Lewis, Williams, and Tolkien — these three — as defining the Mythopoeic Society's view of mythopoeia, what is it we find they have in common? We find (besides their being a kind of "literary support group" — according to some observers) that they both revere and use the past, that they are sacramentalists (and Christians), and that they are more or less English, or at least lived most of their lives in England.

None of this gets us much forrader. Their stories deal with what we call the supernatural, and particularly (but what of *The Lord of the Rings?*) with the Christian supernatural, but since they are believing Christians, they are not fantasists as that term is generally understood. That is, they are not dealing with Todorov's "the impossible" as they would understand "the impossible." Now we might define mythopoeia as the equivalent of "believing fantasy"—it would not necessarily be believing *Christian* fantasy, of course: Haggard was a kind of theosophist, leading Lewis to remark on occasion that "if Ayesha was Wisdom's daughter, she surely did not take after her parent," and Kenneth Morris clearly believes the religious doctrine of *The Chalciuhite Dragon*. The word mythopoeia might thus be defined by its use as "believing religious fantasy (not necessarily Christian)."

The mention of England in connection with Lewis, Tolkien, and Williams might be taken to provide another clue. (I am working also, in this connection, on Marx and Engels as Englished Germans—see my forthcoming lost chapter of *Edwin Drood*, "The Angular Man Meets Mr. Angles"). Tolkien created a mythology for England, based (at whatever remove) on "Old English" language and literature, but also Welsh, and to some extent on medieval England (as with Tom Bombadil). Charles Williams orchestrated a mythology for England, based on his own idiosyncratic—but perhaps brilliant—reading of Arthurian legend. Lewis, in *That Hideous Strength*, sought to combine the two, with what Tolkien regarded as something less than complete success. Lewis also created or adapted myth in *Out of the Silent Planet* and *Perelandra*, though not entirely the same myth. In this particular and restricted sense, the three are involved in mythopoeisis, though Lewis principally in the Ransom stories and Williams principally in his poetry. But MacDonald is not: what he creates is not myth but Novalis's Dream, unless of course the two are the same. And, I would argue, Haggard is only intermittently mythopoetic in this sense—no "Mythology for Africa": this is not what *King Solomon's Mines* is about, nor even most of *She*. They are adventure stories with a mythic element, but they are not pre-eminently mythopoetic in this sense. To be sure, Haggard creates a myth in the person of She-Who-Is-To-Be-Obeyed, but She has an adverse effect on story in the innumerable sequels. We had best seek another sense of the word.

Lewis's visionary moments in *That Hideous Strength*, in particular, are of past worlds realized — made real. Bunyan's Protestant world, the vision of Arthurian Britain, and Mother Dimble's Elizabethanry, all share this characteristic. Williams's peculiar visionary talent gives a strongly characteristic taste to his fiction. The taste of Tolkien's world of the Rings is best distilled in *The Lord of the Rings*, but it is evident all through the ten or twelve volumes of the History of Middle-Earth. There is alas! no precise and particular taste of Narnia, which is part of what Tolkien objected to in *The Lion, the Witch, and the Wardrobe*, and there is a different Tolkienian taste to *Farmer Giles, Mr. Bliss, The Hobbit*, and the opening chapters of *The Fellowship of the Ring*. All very well for "realization" — but there remains the matter of story, pure or pattern, and here's the rub.

Lewis had grave trouble in constructing story lines: his strength is in his poet's eye for detail, and, of course, he eventually turns to established myth for his story lines, as in *Till We Have Faces* (and this is not mythopoeisis). Williams's novels are wonderful in the interrelation of past and present, heaven and earth, and the conflict of powers and principalities and depraved hypersomatic beings at great heights, but action and story line, even incidents in the story, are at a steadily reducing minimum. MacDonald passes from dream to vision to the everyday world, but his plot lines follow the associative logic of dream rather than the logic of the "real" world, so much is he Novalis's pupil. Curdie is a miner because miners are Novalis's priests or spirits or familiars of the earth: we know what he is, but it is not always clear what is happening to him, or what he is doing, or even who or what the other characters are. Particularly, in MacDonald, it is not always clear what is happening.

On the other hand, Tolkien's books are stories, though the *Notion Club Papers* — and indeed a good amount of the History of Middle-Earth — suggest that the creation of story did not always come easily even to him. But it came. Perhaps the rolling English road is not derived from the wonderment of the Angles and Saxons and Jutes, when Octa, called Hengest, came over from the world of Finn and Beowulf. But it is still a very English pattern story, and if stories of the road are particularly English, we should not be surprised to find the story growing from Tolkien's "mythology for England" to be a story of the road, highway and byway. In a curious Pickwickian sense, this story combines two mythic patterns, that of the English road, and that of the quest (or task) to destroy, which is far less common than the quest to acquire. We should not be put off by Tolkien's serviceable prose: he has the mythopoeic gift that Haggard had, for all the steps into and through the realm of the comic or the humorous.

Tolkien strikes deep into the immemorial lode of myth, and the secret of his striking deep is in his belief, not only in Christian doctrine and the Christian myth, but in the truth of myth: he is the one who (with Hugo Dyson) convinced Lewis of this. For there is a truth to myth. Even if one does not — as I do — accept the historic truth of the Incarnation of myth into history, of the *Logos* as Jesus Messias, there remains such a thing as mythic truth. Even if one quarrels with Jung's particular selection of archetypes and *anima*, hypnogogic vision and dream pattern — and I do not — there are patterns and types (and "atmosphere") true to the human psyche.

There is a truth to myth, if not always a historical truth: one need not expect to meet a broad-hatted one-eyed old man on a pony to acknowledge truth to the myth of Odin All-father. I have mentioned Kenneth Morris and *The Chalciuhite Dragon*, whose myth is Quetzalcoatl in Theosophic guise. My friend John Rateliff has argued that Morris's belief harms the fantasy, and of course in a Todorovian sense he is right. But the example (being of a non–Christian writer) is of importance here, for it shows that belief (not here Christian belief) makes mythopoeisis possible. Lewis has spoken of the "double distinction of myth from fact and both from truth" as being false and a symptom of our estrangement from the natural order of the heavens, including Deep Heaven. That is just. The operative point here is that mythopoeia is the creation of myth which is true at least in a Jungian (or some other similar) sense, and never mind, for the moment, what exactly we mean by creation, and how secondary it is.

We have still to consider the question whether mythopoeia is in fact a form of— or, alternatively, necessarily connected to — fantasy (as we have now defined it). I suggested earlier that it was *believing* fantasy, and that the mythopoeic writers (as defined by this Society) wrote Christian believing fantasy. I perceive that I am hovering on the edge of a problem here, as a result of my own beliefs. These beliefs may not be peculiar (in the colloquial sense), but they are pretty much peculiar to me. First, I accept a good bit of Jung's analysis as portraying real archetypes, as really proceeding from the gates of horn. Second, I am a believing Christian. And third (most idiosyncratic of the three), I accept Lewis's conditional belief in the pagan gods as real emanations of the divine, and may even go further than he. I really do believe there is a divinity that hedges us around, even if not always appareled in celestial light. Now this all makes it very easy for me to link archetypes, Jungian *anima*, mythopoeia, and believing Christian fantasy (story of the non-normal supernatural) — and not only believing Christian fantasy, but virtually any believing fantasy.

It is true that these beliefs of mine come from reading largely chosen according to the interests of C. S. Lewis, and my interest in what interested Lewis, and this is a datum which itself may be of value in pursuing these matters. But the immediate question is whether there can by mythopoeia without belief. It would be easy to answer "yes" — and most criticism of Dunsany (for example) points in that direction, though I think the pointing is awry. The belief need not be orthodox any more than the creation, the *poeisis*, need be orthodox Still, at the very least, I do not think it possible to write ghost stories effectively unless one comes from a culture that has traditionally believed in the possibility of ghosts, and I suspect belief in ghosts would not be amiss in the author. Similarly, I do not think it possible to write effective supernatural horror stories unless one comes from a culture that has traditionally accepted the possibility of supernatural horror.

Flavor and the Link Between Fantasy and Mythopoeia

Thus far at least some progress (I hope) toward answering the question whether there is indeed such a thing as mythopoeia. Whether it links Tolkien, Williams, and Lewis, we have not yet entirely determined, nor what other authors are to be included. What we have said about the fiction of Tolkien, Williams, and Lewis, is that it is a kind of "believing fantasy" (in their cases, "believing Christian fantasy") — and we have suggested that this may be a possible definition of mythopoeic fiction. But this means we need to define "fantasy" and that brings us to the third question we asked at the beginning of this paper — what is the link between mythopoeia and "fantasy"?

Before we try defining "believing fantasy" we must try our hand at defining "fantasy" itself. Todorov's definition as the fiction of the impossible is well known: the fact that C. S. Lewis developed a similar definition (in *Experiment in Criticism*) is not so well known. But here we must face the problem squarely: what is the fiction of the impossible to a non-believer is the fiction of the possible to a believer, and thus not (in Todorov's sense or Lewis's) fantasy. The wind that mimics the Aeolian harp in MacDonald's *Donal Grant* is actually playing through a stone structure to produce the sound: that is, if you like, a "naturalistic" explanation — if you believe in MacDonald's science. The appearance of Wither in the path when Mark Studdock makes his break for freedom in *That Hideous Strength* is traced to the sensory impressions on a building made by a strong personality in the last stages of decay, and removable not by exorcism but by architectural alteration: that is, if you like, a "naturalistic" explanation — if you believe in the Christian doctrine of the soul. Neither is within the purview of fantasy if Todorov's definition holds — but then, by his definition, "believing fantasy" is an oxymoron. Moreover, if his definition holds, stories written by a believer may accidentally be taken as fantasy by a non-believer. I think we need to do better, despite Todorov (and Lewis). But if fantasy is not the literature of the impossible, what is it?

I came across a use of the word recently that may cast some light here: in the course of studying Shakespeare's history plays, I found a quadripartite division of genre into comedy, fantasy, tragedy, and satire. This almost reproduces Frye's four great *mythoi*, with the substitution of fantasy for romance, and it suggests an earlier meaning of fantasy, from the time before the split between novel and romance. We might therefore call *The Faerie Queene* or *Orlando Furioso* a fantasy, and of course that usage has lingered in such 1960s places as Lin Carter's adult fantasy series and in the present bookshelf genre of fantasy, between "romance" and "sf" and much closer to the first: Katherine Kurtz, for example, would be a writer of fantasy in this sense, though (in my view as well as Ursula LeGuin's) perhaps in no other. One could, I suppose, define fantasy as that variety of romance (including Frye's Romance) that involves the supernatural. This gets us rather neatly over the impossibility question, but at a certain cost. For if, as James Blish has taught us, science fiction is a form of irony or satire, it would thus be exactly contrapuntal to fantasy in this sense — not only a differing genre but an opposed genre. We may need to back off from Frye, though I would prefer not. Nonetheless, use of the word "supernatural" to replace the word "impossible" is a step forward.

True, this is no more, and no less, than a working definition — or, if one wishes to indulge in the language of the philosophy of science, a scientific research program. But I think it works: I think we are getting forrader. It is true that satisfactory definitions even of the "supernatural" are themselves hard to come by, not least by critics who disbelieve in its possibility, but in general we pretty much know what we mean by the word. It is also true that the very idea of the supernatural is a modern one, dating I suppose from whatever time it was that the gods (or God) ceased to be regarded as part of the natural order of things — an event connected, I suppose, with the separation of novel from romance.

Fantasy is a form of unusual supernatural romance (with commonsense meanings given to our terms here). Because of the patterns we discern in the history of thought and the history of literature, we cannot really date the origins of fantasy much before the early nineteenth century, though there are earlier works that would have been fantasy (adult fantasy?) if they had been written after the great divide. Whether this fantasy is a subgenre of Romance in Frye's sense, or at least connected to Romance in Frye's sense (I think it is), we will leave till another time.

So far so good, I hope, but I would go further. I would claim that Lovecraft's horror fiction is marred by his unbelief, for which reason some of his "revisions" have a more genuine *frisson* than his own stories. I would claim that Dunsany is not a myth-maker but a writer of satiric light fiction (see my "The Man Who Didn't Write Fantasy"). I would claim that books merely embodying a mythic pattern — like *Till We Have Faces* or the Narnia series (their myth being the Christian myth) — are not mythopoetic because there is no *poeisis*, no making of myth, though myth is there. This is the contrary case to Dunsany, where there is *poeisis* of something, but no myth at all.

Let me now return to the point that there is a particular kind of atmosphere or taste (flavor) in a mythopoetic story. Lewis makes this point in connection with *King Solomon's Mines*, the film version of which not only drags in an entirely extraneous young lady (Sharon Stone, I believe, in one current version), but ends with fire rather than the silent ages of the cave — quite the wrong atmosphere. And it occurs to me that Novalis may be of interest here, also, for his insistence that dream and *Märchen* have an associative logic of space rather than a causal logic of time. The more I think on this point, the more I am convinced it helps to explain why atmosphere seems to me an inherent part of mythopoeia, atmosphere functioning as a kind of (or in line with) associative logic. Granted that times as well as places have atmospheres, or at least that places have certain atmospheres at certain times, it remains the case that hypnogogic visual impressions have atmosphere, dreams have atmosphere, the *Märchen* that embody primary story patterns carry their atmosphere with them down through the ages — and there are recognizably different atmospheres to different mythologies (as Lewis himself observed long ago).

When one reads Haggard, one is conscious of ineluctable age, the past alive in the present, things handed down from generation to generation, a world (like MacDonald's) with a particular taste, not quite like any other taste (and certainly not like MacDonald's). And while Haggard fell so in love with his creation Ayesha that his power of story declined, nevertheless *King Solomon's Mines* is a great story of its kind and stands as a major achievement of what Lewis apparently meant by the mythopoetic gift, and so does *She*. Of other writers we have mentioned, Conan Doyle had some gift for story — *The Lost World* is a classic — but much more for incident, and a considerable gift for atmosphere. Remember Vincent Starrett's words: Sherlock Holmes and Dr. Watson will "live for all who love them well; in a romantic chamber of their heart; in a nostalgic country of the mind; where it is always 1895" (these are the concluding lines of *The Private Life of Sherlock Holmes*, 2nd ed., Chicago 1960).

This is not a matter of plot but of *milieu*, not of incident but of atmosphere or taste. Detection deals in incidents, and incident does not a novel make; most of Doyle's best work is in his short stories, and many of his plots are no more his (and no more plots) than Poe's in "The History of Marie Roget." His "Last of the Legions" story is inferior to Kipling's or Benet's, and his "Greek meets Jew" story of Odysseus and David is inferior to Edward Everett Hale's of Homer and David. But *The Lost World* is genuinely mythopoetic as Lewis defined mythopoeia with Haggard's example. Perhaps because it is essentially the same story as *King Solomon's Mines*.

There is a modern writer named Frank Peretti, hailed in certain Christian circles as the successor to C. S. Lewis. His novels have angels attacking the forces of darkness under protection of battalions of prayer circles. His works suggest a weakness in our definitions, and should be dealt with here. It is true they may not necessarily be particularly good novels, but they are intended as realistic novels, not romances, and therefore by extension not fantasy, not even believing fantasy. They do not stand in succession to C. S. Lewis. They are a little closer, perhaps, to Charles Williams's later novels. But they are intended, I believe, as realistic portrayals of present-day Christian life, informed by biblical inerrancy, as Christian believers stand against the World, the Flesh, and — particularly — the Devil. I find no taste or atmosphere of fantasy, or of myth, about them.

I am convinced that taste ("flavor" one might say) is part of the creation both of fantasy and of myth, and is in fact a part of the link between the two, if "link" is not too weak a word. There is perhaps a case analogous to Peretti's born-again Christian realism and its relation to fantasy, in the nineteenth-century realistic Irish three-deckers that incorporated elements of the supernatural because they realistically portrayed the life of Irish peasants to whom the supernatural was an everyday affair — one might say a "natural" affair. But Peretti is preaching the beliefs of his characters, which the O'Haras were not: still, the comparison suggests that myth and fantasy do not inhere in what is treated as an everyday affair, and certainly mythopoeisis does not. There must be something of the unusual about fantasy, one might say something of the unusual supernatural.

I have elsewhere suggested a relationship between fantasy and feigned history (in my *Rise of Tolkienian Fantasy*), and that feigned history cannot exist until there is such a thing as "scientific" history to set over against it. Similarly, I suggest there cannot be "fantasy" until there is something to set over against it: it is a creature of an age in which the supernatural is not usual, not a part of everyday life, an age which recognizes a great divide between nature and supernature. I suggested a moment ago that this great divide is very likely connected with the great divide between romance (or "fantasy") and novel. And I will go further, to say it is connected with a still greater divide.

For all his disclaimers (who can be proud of knowing his mother tongue or the way around his father's house?), C. S. Lewis justly exulted in his status as an "Old Western" man. That left him on the far side of the divide from us, as it left Tolkien and most of the other Inklings — the Great Divide between Jane Austen and the present day, the Great Divide of the machines and the idea of progress. If this is as important as I think it is, we may be on our way to some resolution of our problems, a path (so to speak) out of the taxonomic swamp. Let us see what we have.

What is the myth in mythopoeia? It is pattern — pattern story, pattern dream, pattern vision — and it may be based on a logic of place, an associative logic, as much as, or more than, a logic of time. It is perhaps the hero with a thousand faces taking yet another: but it is more than that, for the hero is a god not yet euhemerized, and what is made is a new story, a story adding to the pattern, not merely a new face for the old hero. The myth is a myth, a story pattern, a dream and a vision, of the divine, the unusual supernatural, and it is a myth made by a believer in the myth. Must it have a figure of mythic proportions? Yes, because the figure will be the figure of a god, even if it is a great white whale or a great fish. If there is mythopoeia to *Huckleberry Finn* (and I think there is), well, I too "do not know much about gods, but I think the river is a strong brown god." And the forest is a strong green god, with trees like men walking, or at least the sanctuary of the god. It has been noted that Fenimore Cooper's forests have classical pagan antecedents — and Ahab tries to draw out Leviathan with a fishhook, adding a new story (but it is very old) to the stories of men that go down to the sea in ships. And Pickwick's pilgrimage is a *pèlerinage de la vie humaine*, no less than Long Will's.

Mythopoeia and Language

We should now (at long last) look at the question of language, partly if not only because Lewis has suggested (in Haggard's case and to some degree in MacDonald's — and certainly in the case of David Lindsay of *Arcturus*) that the mythopoetic gift is separate from the gift of style in language, owing to the importance of pattern above style. I think this is a more difficult point than it appears at first, in part because it is Lewis's point, the same Lewis who wrote of "great syllables of words that sounded like castles" and of Barfield's ancient unities. And the same Lewis whose coadjutor Tolkien turned Max Muller on his head and suggested language might be called a disease of mythology. That is to say, words themselves have — language itself has — the power of myth. If myth is not inherent in language, then language is inherent in myth, a by-product if not a disease. Perhaps what we have then with Haggard and MacDonald is really akin to a problem in translation.

In the opening chapter of *Perelandra*, "Ransom" takes Lewis up rather sharply for saying what has happened to him is "too vague" for language: it is rather too definite. Any translation of mythic experience will be at some remove from the "definiteness" of the experience. The implication of this is that the myth must be in some sense true, the creation turns out to be subcreation, and the sub-creator, the mythopoet, must needs be a believer. In our time, since the Great Divide, mythopoeisis occurs in what we call fantasy, and mythopoetic literature has come to be considered a form of the literature of "fantasy" — all well and good, but it is not the only form.

Remember Edmund Wilson, the more valuable a witness for being from an opposing camp. With German nineteenth-century philosophy, it is, he suggests, as if the old tribal deities of the North had first been converted to Christianity, while still maintaining their self-assertive pagan nature, and as if, when Christian theology was displaced by eighteenth-century rationalism, they had put on the mask of pure reason. But they are not the less mythopoeic (his word) for becoming less anthropomorphic. "The *Ewig-Weibliche* of Goethe, the *kategorische Imperativ* of Kant, the *Weltgeist* with the *Idee* of Hegel — these have dominated the minds of the Germans and haunted European thought in general like great hovering legendary divinities" (*To the Finland Station*, p. 190).

The Scientifiction Novels of C. S. Lewis

As Lewis suggests that Wagner's Ring embodies the alchemical myth of progress (*De Descriptione Temporum*, p. 8), so Edmund Wilson suggests that the Nibelungen cycle is a music-drama on the dialectic, implied in the relations between Wotan, Brunhilde, and Siegfried (p. 190). Now Wilson's view, throughout this argument, seems perilously close to Max Muller's, that mythology is a disease of language, rather than Tolkien's contrary, that language is a disease of mythology. My own view is Tolkien's, but like his, rather in the sense that pearls are an irritation of oysters. Mythology is, after all, in some sense about the gods. Our contact with (and benefit from) the oyster — unless we are eating it — is the pearl. Our contact with (and benefit from) the gods — should I venture to say, unless we are eating our God — is the language. But what kind of language? Lewis suggests a characteristic of mythopoeia that the strength of the myth, by which he means the story, is independent of the language.

Tom Shippey's use of the word *calque* presents us with a clue we have not yet used, for calquing is a process of translation, as from English *loud-speaker* to French *haut-parleur*. I have elsewhere written of the calquing of archetypes and the shire on England, which could also be called the development of the *mythos* inherent in the language of England. The point I am making here is that mythopoeisis is a kind of calquing, a kind of translation from the definiteness of myth to the vagueness of language — any language but that in which the meaning is truly inherent, as when language first sprang from the molten quicksilver of that orb called Mercury on Earth but Viritrilbia in Deep Heaven. And perhaps that, in the end, is why mythopoeic gifts can apparently coincide with infelicities of style. On this showing, in mythopoeia, all style is less than perfectly felicitous, and it is only non-believers like Oscar Wilde who can afford to be fully conscious of style — and I find that in *The Picture of Dorian Gray*, Wilde's chief mythopoeic work, the quirks of style are not omnipresent, not so obtrusive, as in most of Wilde.

Coleridge, by a just instinct, chose the ballad form for his great mythopoeic work. Irving's "Rip Van Winkle" (except in its playing for humor in the ordinary sense) is virtually *Märchen*. In both cases, the language has a traditional form, based in the common experience of humankind. But the more uncommon the myth (and Haggard's Ayesha was uncommon in her day), the more difficult it is to find language to express it. And we should find that particularly true if we are speaking of any modern myth having its origins (if any does) in the abstractions of German philosophy. Haggard and MacDonald could write good serviceable prose: but they tried to express the atmosphere, the taste, the flavor, they sensed in their myths, and for that their prose was inadequate, if not perhaps always quite so inadequate as Lewis found it.

Charles Williams could write a spare and serviceable prose — but he too found it difficult to convey the atmosphere he sensed in his own creation (besides falling, from time to time, as with Rochester, into a parody of himself): the classic example is his short story, "Et in Sempiternum Pereat," in which manages to convey the atmosphere at the expense of telling any but the most devoted reader what is happening. Lewis, perhaps wisely, had recourse to the objective correlatives of our literary tradition — even the bubble-trees of the Third Heaven are found in the *Book of the Secrets of Enoch*— rather than even trying to convey atmosphere or flavor *de novo*.

Lewis remarked on the absence of weather in *The Three Musketeers*, and found it a grave flaw in the book: what is weather here but a particular case of atmosphere or flavor? The rosy-fingered (*rhododactylos*) dawn and the wine-dark sea are epithets that with repetition bring atmosphere or flavor, and mythologies, as Tolkien and Lewis have both reminded us, each has its own flavor, its own atmosphere, somehow cognate with its language. There is a hard sun shining on Grecian heights, and the myths of the North are wrapped in mist and fog: the very bridge of the Gods rises out of clouds. *Naus* does not "mean" *ship*— behind both words is a picture, similar, but not the same. But note that the flavor is the flavor of the myth world, not of the myth — of the Mythos in one sense (Lovecraft's) but not the *mythos* (Frye's sense). In a way, what the myth-maker makes is not the *mythos* in either sense, but a new character in the story (Treebeard or Ayesha or Lord Arglay or Scrooge or *Proletariere alle Länder* or the Ancient Mariner or Bilbo or Malacandra or Sherlock Holmes or Allan Quatermain or Uncas or Curdie). Whether his language is sufficient for the task depends on us, the readers — that is part of the point of the objective correlative. But that a writer can create a great mythic character without being a great writer I am not entirely sure — though that question will get us into the discussion of Lewis's *Experiment in Criticism*, if we don't watch out.

What is the myth in mythopoeia? It is an addition to the story pattern of the divine, made by a believer in the myth — usually the addition of story involving at least one new mythic character. It takes form most often in believing fantasy (romance involving the unusual supernatural), and frequently in believing Christian fantasy. It has room for Haggard and MacDonald, Kenneth Morris, Williams and Tolkien and Lewis, Dickens and Scott, Melville and Cooper, Hegel and Kant and Marx, Richard Wagner. What is its relation to language? What of Lewis's view of the separateness of mythopoeia and style? No language is entirely adequate for it, for if it does not itself plant the seed of language, then it grows from it and bursts its seed. And where mythopoeia is the work of the house, in that house are many mansions. If it were not so, He would have told us, Who made us in His myth: *En arche en ho Logos, kai ho Logos pros ton Theon, kai Theos en ho Logos.*

Bibliography

Adams, Percy. *Travel Literature and the Evolution of the Novel*. Lexington: University of Kentucky Press, 1983.

Alexander, Samuel. *Space, Time, and Deity*. London: Macmillan, 1920.

Barfield, Owen. *History in English Words*. London: Faber, 1926.

_____. *Poetic Diction*. London: Faber, 1928; 3rd ed., Middletown CT: Wesleyan University Press, 1973.

_____. *What Coleridge Thought*. Middletown CT: Wesleyan University Press, 1971.

_____, trans. *Rudolf Steiner on Economics*. New York: Anthroposophical Press, 1934.

Beckford, William. *Vathek, An Arabian Tale*. London and Paris: 1786.

Benda, Julien. *The Treason of the Intellectuals* [*Trahison des Clercs*]. London: Routledge, 1928.

Benét, Stephen Vincent. "The Last of the Legions." In *Selected Prose Works*. New York: Farrar & Rinehart, 1942.

Blackwood, Algernon. "The Glamour of the Snow." In *Strange Stories*. London: Heinemann, 1929.

_____. "The Willows." In *Strange Stories*. London: Heinemann, 1929.

Blake, William. *The Marriage of Heaven and Hell*. London: 1790.

Blish, James. *A Case of Conscience*. New York: Ballantine, 1958.

_____ [William Atheling, Jr.]. "Cathedrals in Space." In *The Issue at Hand*. Chicago: Advent, 1964.

_____ [William Atheling, Jr.]. "Probapossible Prolegomena to Ideareal History." In *The Best of James Blish*. New York: Ballantine, 1979, pp. 349–358.

Bosky, Bernadette. Introduction to Charles Williams. *The Masques of Amen House*, ed. David Bratman. Altadena CA: Mythopoeic Press, 2000.

Boswell, James. *Life of Samuel Johnson*. London: 1791; Oxford: Oxford University Press, 1907.

Bradbury, Ray. *The Martian Chronicles*. New York: Doubleday, 1950.

Brewer, Derek. "The Tutor: A Portrait." In James Como, ed. *C. S. Lewis at the Breakfast Table*. New York: 1979. Pp. 41–67.

Buchan, John. *Greenmantle*. London: Nelson, 1918.

_____. *Prester John*. London: Nelson 1910; New York: Popular Library, n.d.

_____. *Salute to Adventurers*. London: Nelson, 1915.

_____. "Some Notes on Sir Walter Scott." *The English Association Pamphlet no. 58*. London: The English Association, 1924.

Bibliography

Bulfinch, Thomas. *The Age of Fable [Mythology of Greece and Rome]*. Boston: 1848.

Bunyan, John. *Pilgrim's Progress*. London: 1678.

Carpenter, Humphrey. *The Inklings*. London: Allen & Unwin, 1978.

Carroll, Lewis. *Alice in Wonderland*. London: 1867.

Chandler, A. Bertram. *Lieutenant John Grimes*. New York: Science Fiction Book Club, 2001.

_____. *John Grimes: Survey Captain*. New York: Science Fiction Book Club, 2002.

Chaucer, Geoffrey. *The Canterbury Tales*, ed. W. W. Skeat. 7 vols. Oxford: 1894.

Chesterton, G[ilbert] K[eith]. *The Father Brown Omnibus*. New York: Dodd, Mead, 1951.

_____. *The Man Who Was Thursday*. London: Simpkin Marshall, 1908.

_____. *The Outline of Sanity*. London: Methuen, 1926.

de Laclos, Pierre Choderlos. *Les Liaisons Dangereuses*. Paris: 1782.

Coleridge, Samuel Taylor. *Biographia Literaria*. London: 1817, 1821; Oxford: Oxford University Press, 1907.

Conan Doyle, [Sir] Arthur. *Best Stories* (pb.n.p., n.d.), including "The Red-Headed League," "A Scandal in Bohemia," "Silver Blaze," "The Musgrave Ritual," "The Blue Carbuncle," "The Speckled Band."

_____. *The Lost World*. London: Hodder & Stoughton, 1906.

_____. *A Study in Scarlet*. London: 1887.

_____, *The Valley of Fear*. London: Smith Elder, 1915.

Crashaw, Richard. "In the Holy Nativity of Our Lord God: A Hymn Sung as by the Shepherds." In Richard Crashaw, *The Poems, English, Latin and Greek, of Richard Crashaw*, ed. L. C. Martin. Oxford: Oxford University Press, 1927.

Crockett, S[amuel] R[utherford]. *The Black Douglas*. London: 1899.

_____. *Kit Kennedy, Country Boy*. London: 1899.

de Bergerac, Savinien-Hercule de Cyrano. *Comicall Historie of the States and Empires of the Sunne and the Moone*. London: 1651.

Defoe, Daniel. *The Life and Adventures of Robinson Crusoe*. London: 1719.

Dickens, Charles. *A Christmas Carol*. London: 1843.

_____. *The Mystery of Edwin Drood*. London: 1870.

_____. *The Posthumous Papers of the Pickwick Club*. London: 1837.

Donne, John. Devotion XVII, "Now, This Bell Tolling Softly for Another, Says to Me: Thou Must Die." In *Devotions Upon Emergent Occasions*. London: 1624.

Douglas, Gavin. *XIII Bukes of Eneados*. In Gavin Douglas, *The Poetical Works of Gavin Douglas*, ed. J. Small. 4 vols. London: 1874.

Dunne, J. W. *An Experiment with Time*. 3rd ed. London: Faber, 1934.

Eddison, E[ric] R[ucker]. *The Worm Ouroboros*. London: Jonathan Cape, 1922.

[Edward Moreton Punkett] Lord Dunsany. *The Gods of Pegana*. London: Elkin Matthews, 1905.

Empson, William. *Some Versions of Pastoral*. London: Chatto & Windus, 1935.

Fielding, Henry. *The History of Tom Jones, A Foundling*. London: 1749.

Fry, Christopher. *The Lady's Not for Burning*. London and Oxford: Oxford University Press, 1951.

Frye, Northrop. *The Anatomy of Criticism*. Princeton: Princeton University Press, 1957.

Gay, John. *The Beggar's Opera*. London: 1728.

Bibliography

Gibb, [Sir] Jocelyn, ed. *Light on C. S. Lewis*. London: Geoffrey Bles, 1965.

Glover, Donald. *C. S. Lewis: The Art of Enchantment*. London and Columbus: Ohio State University Press, 1981.

Grahame, Kenneth. *The Penguin Kenneth Grahame*. Harmondsworth: Penguin, 1983.

_____. *The Wind in the Willows*. London: Methuen, 1908.

Haggard, Rider. *King Solomon's Mines*. London: 1885.

_____. *She*. London: 1887.

Hale, Edward Everett. "A Piece of Possible History." In Edward Everett Hale, *The Man Without a Country and Other Stories*, ed. D. R. Angus. London: Wordsworth, 1995.

Heliodorus. *Ethiopian History*. Trans. Thomas Underdowne (1569), ed. Charles Whibley. London: 1895.

Herder, Johann Gottfried. *Sammtliche Werke*. Ed. J. G. Mueller. 45 vols. Tübingen: 1805–1820.

Hillegas, Mark. "Out of the Silent Planet as Cosmic Voyage." In Mark Hillegas, *Shadows of Imagination: The Fantasies of C. S. Lewis, J. R. R. Tolkien, and Charles Williams*. Carbondale: Southern Illinois University Press, 1969. Pp. 41–58.

Huxley, Aldous. *Brave New World*. London: Chatto & Windus, 1933.

Johnson, Samuel. *History of Rasselas, Prince of Abyssinia*. London: 1759.

Jenkin, A. K. Hamilton. *The Story of Cornwall*. London: Nelson, 1934.

Jung, Carl. *Psychologie und Alchemie*. 1944. Trans., R. C. Hull, *Individual Dream-Symbolism in Relation to Alchemy*. Princeton: Princeton University Press, 1967.

Keary, Annie. *Heroes of Asgard*. London: 1871.

Kepler, Johannes. *Somnium seu Astronomia Lunari*. 1634. Trans. Edward Rosen, *The Dream, or Posthumous Work on Lunar Astronomy*. Madison: University of Wisconsin Press, 1967.

Kilby, C. S., ed. *A Mind Awake*. New York: Harcourt Brace, 1969.

Kipling, Rudyard. "The Conversion of St. Wilfrid." In *Rewards and Fairies*. London: Macmillan, 1910.

_____. *Stalky & Co.* London: 1899.

Kirk, Russell. *Eliot and His Age*. LaSalle IL: Sherwood Sugden, 1988.

Kott, Jan. *The Bottom Translation*. London and Evanston IL: Northwestern University Press, 1987.

Lanier, Sidney. *The Boy's King Arthur*. New York: 1878.

Langland, William. *The Vision of William Concerning Piers Plowman*. Ed. W. W. Skeat. 2 vols. Oxford: 1886.

LeGuin, Ursula. *A Wizard of Earthsea*. Harmondsworth Penguin: 1971.

Lewis, C. S. *The Abolition of Man*. London: Oxford University Press, 1943.

_____. "After Ten Years." In C. S. Lewis, *Of Other Worlds*, ed. Walter Hooper. New York: Harcourt, 1967.

_____. *All My Road Before Me*. Ed. Walter Hooper. New York: Harcourt, 1991.

_____. *The Allegory of Love*. Oxford: Oxford University Press, 1936.

_____. "Awake My Lute!" Quoted in full in Chad Walsh, *C. S. Lewis: Apostle to the Skeptics*. New York: Macmillan, 1949. Pp. 62–63.

_____. *Boxen: Or, Scenes from Boxonian City Life, or The Life of John, Lord Big of*

Bibliography

Bigham, in 3 Volumes [title of original MS]. Printed in C. S. Lewis, *Boxen*, ed. Walter Hooper. New York: Harcourt Brace, 1984.

_____. "The Dark Tower." in C. S. Lewis, *The Dark Tower and Other Stories*, ed. Walter Hooper. New York: Harcourt, 1977.

_____. *De Descriptione Temporum*. Cambridge: Cambridge University Press, 1955.

_____. *English Literature in the Sixteenth Century, Excluding Drama*. Oxford: Oxford University Press, 1954.

_____. *An Experiment in Criticism*. Cambridge: Cambridge University Press, 1961.

_____. "Forms of Things Unknown." In C. S. Lewis, *Of Other Worlds*, ed. Walter Hooper. New York: Harcourt, 1967.

_____. *The Great Divorce*. London: Geoffrey Bles, 1945.

_____. *The Horse and His Boy*. London: Geoffrey Bles, 1954.

_____. "The Inner Ring." In C. S. Lewis, *Transposition and Other Addresses*. London: Bles, 1949.

_____. *The Last Battle*. London: Geoffrey Bles, 1956.

_____. *The Lion, the Witch, and the Wardrobe*. London: Geoffrey Bles, 1950.

_____. *The Literary Impact of the Authorised Version*. London: Athlone Press, 1950.

_____. *Mere Christianity*. New York: Macmillan, 1952.

_____. "On Science Fiction." In C. S. Lewis, *Of Other Worlds*, ed. Walter Hooper. New York: Harcourt, 1967.

_____. *On Stories*. Ed. Walter Hooper. New York: Harcourt, 1982.

_____. *Out of the Silent Planet*. London: Geoffrey Bles, 1938.

_____. *Perelandra*. London: Geoffrey Bles, 1943.

_____. *The Pilgrim's Regress*. London: Dent, 1933.

_____. *A Preface to Paradise Lost*. Oxford: Oxford University Press, 1942.

_____. *Rehabilitations and Other Essays*. London: Oxford University Press, 1939.

_____. *The Screwtape Letters*. London: Geoffrey Bles, 1942.

_____. *Spenser's Images of Life*. Ed. Alastair Fowler. Cambridge: Cambridge University Press, 1967.

_____. *Studies in Words*. Cambridge: Cambridge University Press, 1960.

_____. *Surprised by Joy*. New York: Macmillan, 1955.

_____. *That Hideous Strength*. New York: Macmillan, 1946.

_____. *Till We Have Faces*. New York: Macmillan, 1956.

_____. "The Weight of Glory." In C. S. Lewis, *Transposition and Other Addresses*. London: Geoffrey Bles, 1949.

_____ (and W. H. Lewis). *Pudaita Pie*. MS in Wade Collection, Wheaton College.

_____ (and E. M. W. Tillyard). *The Personal Heresy*. Oxford: Oxford University Press, 1939.

Lewis, W. H. *Brothers and Friends*. New York: Harcourt, 1984.

_____, ed. *Letters of C. S. Lewis*. Revised ed., ed. Walter Hooper. New York: Harcourt, 1993.

Lindsay, David. *A Voyage to Arcturus*. London: Methuen, 1920.

Llewellyn-Thomas, Edward [Edward Llewellyn]. *The Bright Companion*. New York: DAW, 1980.

_____. *The Douglas Convolution*. New York: DAW, 1979.

Lobdell, Jared C. "C. S. Lewis and the Myth in Mythopoeia." *Extrapolation* **39**, no. 1 (Spring 1998), pp. 68–84.

_____. "Caroline Vision and Detective Fiction Rhetoric." In C. A. Huttar and Peter Schakel, eds., *The Rhetoric of Vision: Essays on Charles Williams.* Lewisburg: Bucknell University Press, 1996. Pp. 290–308.

_____. *England and Always.* Grand Rapids: Erdmans, 1981; Rev. ed. as *The World of the Rings,* Chicago and LaSalle IL: Open Court, 2004.

_____. "An Irish Friendship in English Lit." In *Proceedings of the Frances Taylor Ewbank Colloquium on C. S. Lewis and Friends.* Upland IN: Taylor University, 2001.

_____. "The Man Who Didn't Write Fantasy." In *Extrapolation* **35**, no. 1 (1994), pp. 33–42.

_____. "Prolegomena to a Study of C. S. Lewis's Arcadian Science Fiction: How Would *The Dark Tower* Have Come Out?" *Extrapolation* **41**, no. 2 (2000), pp. 175–196.

_____. "The Ransom Novels and Their Eighteenth-Century Ancestry." In Charles Huttar and Peter Schakel, eds., *Word and Story in C. S. Lewis.* Columbia: University of Missouri Press, 1991. Pp. 213–231.

_____. *The Rise of Tolkienian Fantasy.* Chicago and LaSalle IL: Open Court, 2004.

_____, ed. *The Detective Fiction Reviews of Charles Williams 1930–1935.* Jefferson, NC: McFarland, 2003.

[Lord] Macaulay, Thomas. "The Poems of Mr. Robert Montgomery." In Thomas [Lord] Macaulay, *Critical and Historical Essays.* 2 vols. London: Dent, 1930–31.

MacDonald, George. *Donal Grant.* London: 1883.

_____. *Lilith.* London: 1895.

_____. *Phantastes.* London: 1858.

_____. *The Princess and Curdie.* Ed. Roderick McGillis. Oxford: Oxford University Press, 1990.

_____. *The Princess and the Goblin* (1872). Ed. Roderick McGillis. Oxford: Oxford University Press, 1990.

_____. *Sir Gibbie.* London: 1879.

Marlowe, Christopher. *The Tragicall History of Dr. Faustus.* 1591; published London: 1604 and 1616.

Melville, Herman. "Bartleby the Scrivener." In Herman Melville, *Piazza Tales.* New York: 1856.

_____. *Billy Budd, Foretopman.* 1881; published New York: 1924.

_____. *Moby Dick.* New York: 1851.

Milton, John. *L'Allegro.* In John Milton, *Poetical Works.* London: 1645.

_____. *Comus, A Masque.* 1634; published London: 1637.

_____. *Lycidas.* 1637; published in John Milton, *Justa Edwardi King Naufrago,* Cambridge: 1638.

Moberley, Charlotte Anne Elizabeth, and Eleanor Frances Jourdain. *An Adventure.* London: Macmillan, 1911.

Morfill, W. A. trans. *The Book of the Secrets of Enoch.* Oxford: 1896.

Morris, Kenneth. *The Chalciuhite Dragon.* New York: T. Doherty, 1992.

Morris, William. *The Dream of John Ball, and A King's Lesson.* London: 1896.

Bibliography

[Murray, James]. *Oxford English Dictionary [i.e., A New English Dictionary on Historical Principles]*. Oxford: Oxford University Press, 1921–1933.

Nesbit, E. *The Amulet*. London: Unwin, 1906.

_____. *The Five Children and It*. London: Unwin, 1902.

_____. *The Phoenix and the Carpet*. London: Unwin, 1904.

Nevius, Blake. *Cooper's Landscapes*. Berkeley: University of California Press, 1976.

Nicolson, Marjorie Hope. *Voyages to the Moon*. London: Macmillan, 1948.

Novalis [Friedrich von Hardenberg]. *Heinrich von Ofterdingen*. Weimar: 1802.

Orwell, George. *1984*. London: Secker & Warburg, 1949.

Ossian [James Macpherson]. *Fragments of Ancient Poetry Collected in the Highlands of Scotland*. Edinburgh: 1760. Also published as *The Poems of Ossian*. London: 1796.

Percy, Thomas. *Reliques of Antient English Poetry*. London: 1765.

[Perrault, Charles]. *Les Contes de ma Mère l'Oye*. Paris: 1697; trans. Salisbury: 1729.

Pevsner, Nikolaus. *The Englishness of English Art*. London: Praeger, 1954).

Poe, Edgar Allan. "The History of Marie Roget." In Edgar Allan Poe, *Complete Tales and Poems*. (Repr., New York: Barnes & Noble, 1992.

Pope, Alexander. *Essay on Man*. London: 1733–34.

_____. *The Rape of the Lock*. London: 1712; rev. ed., 1714.

Potter, Stephen. *Sense of Humour*. London: Reinhardt, 1954.

Pratt, Fletcher, and L. Sprague DeCamp *The Incompleat Enchanter*. New York: Doubleday, 1960.

Radcliffe, Anne. *The Mysteries of Udolpho*. London, 1794.

Russell, A. J. *God Calling, by Two Listeners*. London: R. J. James, 1938.

Sannazaro, *Arcadia*. 1501. In Sannazaro, *Poems*, ed. G. Castello. Milan: 1928.

Sayers, Dorothy L. *The Man Born to Be King*. London: Gollancz, 1943.

_____. *The Nine Tailors*. London: Gollancz, 1933.

Scott, Walter. *Ivanhoe*. Edinburgh: 1791.

Shakespeare, William. *The Life of King Henry the Fifth*. 1599; 1st folio ed. London: 1623.

Sheffield, Charles. *The Amazing Dr. Darwin*. New York: Baen, 2002.

Shute [Norway], Nevil. *An Old Captivity*. London: Heinemann, 1940.

_____. *Pastoral*. London: Heinemann, 1944.

Sidney, [Sir] Philip. *The Countess of Pembroke's Arcadia*. London: 1590; rev. ed., London: 1593.

Simpson, George Gaylord. *The Dechronization of Sam Magruder*. New York: St. Martin's, 1996.

Spenser, Edmund. *The Faerie Queene*. London: 1590; rev. ed., 1596; with the Mutability cantos, 1609.

_____. *The Shepheardes Calender*. London: 1579; rev. 1581, 1586, 1591, 1597.

Stapledon, Olaf. *Last and First Men*. London: Methuen, 1930.

Starrett, Vincent. *The Private Life of Sherlock Holmes*. 2nd ed. Chicago: University of Chicago Press, 1960.

Surtees, Robert Smith. *Handley Cross*. 1st illus ed. London: 1854.

Suvin, Darko. *Metamorphoses of Science Fiction*. New Haven: Yale University Press, 1979.

Swift, Jonathan. *Gulliver's Travels*. London: 1726.

Thackeray, William Makepeace. *Henry Esmond*. London: 1852.

Tolkien, Christopher, ed. *The Letters of J. R. R. Tolkien*. Boston: Houghton Mifflin, 1981.

Tolkien, J. R. R. *Glossary* to Kenneth Sisam, *Fourteenth Century Verse and Prose*. Oxford: Oxford University Press, 1922.

_____. *The Lord of the Rings*. 3 vols. Boston: Houghton Mifflin 1954–1955.

_____. *The Notion Club Papers*. In Christopher Tolkien, ed., *The History of Middle-Earth*, Vol. IX. Boston: Houghton Mifflin, 1992. Pp. 145–330.

_____. "On Fairy Stories." In J. R. R. Tolkien, *The Monsters and the Critics*. Boston: Houghton Mifflin, 1982.

_____, trans. *Sir Gawain and the Green Knight; Pearl; Sir Orfeo*. London: Allen & Unwin, 1975; repr., New York: 1980.

Twain, Mark. *The Adventures of Huckleberry Finn*. Hartford, CT: 1886.

Walpole, Horace. *The Castle of Otranto*. London: 1794.

Walsh, Chad. *C. S. Lewis: Apostle to the Skeptics*. New York: Macmillan, 1949.

Warren, Robert Penn. *New and Selected Essays*. New York: Random House, 1989.

Wells, H. G. *The First Men in the Moon*. London: Newnes, 1901.

_____. *The Time Machine*. London: 1895.

Wilde, Oscar. *The Picture of Dorian Gray*. London: 1890.

Williams, Charles. *The Figure of Beatrice*. London: Faber, 1943.

Wilson, Edmund. *To the Finland Station*. New York: Harcourt, 1940.

Wordsworth, William, and Samuel Taylor Coleridge. *Lyrical Ballads*. London: 1798.

Index

Index

Index

Index

Ruth, George Herman (Babe) 164

sacramentalism 18
Saemundsson, Sjéra Tomas 45
Sannazaro 139, 147
satire 1, 2, 4, 24, 35, 36, 95, 97, 103
Sayers, Dorothy L. 96, 133, 151
Scaliger 139
science fiction 1–3, 32, 35, 36, 39, 135–137
scientifiction 1, 4, 59–61
"scientifictitious bunkum" 36
Scott, (Sir) Walter 102, 162–164, 182
serio/buffo 125–126, 142, 153
Shakespeare, William 9, 12, 19, 93, 138, 140, 164
Sheffield, Charles 137
Shippey, Thomas 168, 180
Shute, Nevil 10, 50–51
Sidney, Philip 2, 9, 10, 139, 140
Simpson, George Gaylord 65, 137
Sinclair, Upton 7
Sir Orfeo 66–67, 78, 80, 81, 155–156, 159
Smart, Christopher 6, 8, 13, 22, 23
Spender, Stephen 7
Spenser, Edmund 9, 10, 23, 38, 66, 74–77, 150, 151, 160, 174
Stalin, Joseph Vissarionovich 70
Stapledon, Olaf 37
Stephenson, George 74
Sullivan, (Sir) Arthur 107
Surtees, Robert Smith 10, 11, 164
Suvin, Darko 123
Swift, Jonathan 7, 8, 22, 37, 41, 53, 55, 87, 88, 99, 112, 153
symbol 18, 127, 136

Tasso, Torquato 139
Thackeray, William Makepeace 163
Thomas of Ercildoun 66
Tillyard, E. M. W. 58
Tito, Josip Broz 70, 71

Todorov, Tzvetan 172, 174
Tolkien, Christopher Reuel 59, 64
Tolkien, John Ronald Reuel 1–4, 6, 7, 10, 13, 14, 24, 25, 27–29, 34, 39, 43–48, 57–59, 63, 64, 66, 67, 72, 73, 82, 86, 89, 99, 111, 161, 163, 166, 169–173, 178, 180–182
trahison des clercs 122, 130–131, 133
Trevithick, Richard 74
trilogy 3, 4, 25, 63, 87, 147
Tristram Shandy 41
Twain, Mark 178

Underdowne, Thomas 139

Vaughan Williams, Ralph 108

Wagner, Richard (*Ring Cycle*) 108, 180, 182
Wain, John 55
Walpole, Horace 7, 99
Walsh, Chad 42, 148–149
Warren, Robert Penn 18, 21, 25
Washington, George 164
Watt, Ian 163
Weldon, T. D. (Harry) 114, 116, 141
Wells, Herbert George 22, 35, 41, 65, 67, 88, 137, 162, 167
Wiblin, Vida Mary 108
Wilde, Oscar 180
Wilder, Thornton 7
Williams, Charles 1–3, 16, 28, 29, 31–32, 57, 58, 62, 64, 71, 76, 95, 96, 99, 103, 151, 158, 161, 168–170, 173, 177, 181, 182
Wilson, Edmund 165, 169, 179
Wind, Edgar 103, 137
The Wind in the Willows 32
Wither, George 158
Wolff, Robert 166
Woolf, Virginia 7
Wooster School (Danbury CT) 103
Wordsworth, William 7, 8

7516

HAY LIBRARY
WESTERN WYOMING COMMUNITY COLLEGE